The Media Machine

John Downing

The Media Machine

Pluto  Press

First published 1980 by Pluto Press Limited,
Unit 10 Spencer Court, 7 Chalcot Road, London NW1 8LH

Copyright © John Downing 1980

ISBN 0 86104 318 9 paperback

Photoset and printed in Great Britain
by Photobooks (Bristol) Limited,
28 Midland Road, St Philips, Bristol

Cover illustration by Peter Kennard
Cover design by Marsha Austin

Contents

Foreword

A large number of people have made this book possible in different ways, and I am sure that I will have forgotten some of them. The ones I remember and I want to be sure to mention, are those who opened my mind in important ways to the issues in the book, and/or encouraged me to keep writing when I was set to give up. They are Wilfred Wood, Robby Guttmann, Philip Schlesinger, Charlie Husband, Bettina Berch, Doug Holly, Mari Kuttna, Nira Yuval Davis, Bill and Marie Rolston, Yiannis Kitromilides, Patrick Duffy, Joan Lawton, Jim MacDonald, Johnny Merrington, Vito Conteduca, Livio Sansone, Floya Anthias, Firoz Haji and Richard Kuper of Pluto Press. There is one person beyond all who has kept me critical, self-critical, politically alive, sane (well fairly) and very-happy: Ash Corea. This book is dedicated both to her, and to the struggle against oppression.

John Downing

Introduction

I have written this book out of several convictions. First, that the inter-relation between class, racism and sexism is crucial to our present era. Second, that while the media are increasingly written about, somehow their influence for oppression or liberation is rarely accurately stated. Third, that there hardly exists a short, clear marxist overview of these issues. Lastly, as a spur to the socialist movement to take the possibilities of media communication away from their control by capital and the state.

I have not written the book, therefore, for defensive professional journalists, or for dedicated, footnote-conscious 'mass communication-ists'. (I have avoided footnotes, though anyone who wants to read more deeply can follow the writing which has influenced my understanding, set out at the end of the book.) I have written this as both analysis and handbook for media 'consumers'. I hope it stimulates further and more penetrating study and action.

The book's plan is to state as plainly as possible the nature of class exploitation in work, racism and sexism (chapters 1,3,5). Next to each of these is placed a chapter (2,4,6) summarising how capitalist media present each form of oppression. The data are mostly drawn from my own and others' studies in Britain. The strength of this second group of chapters will depend to a great extent on their power to awaken readers' own recognition that the media do indeed present these issues in these ways, and so to help develop in them a systematically critical perspective on the media.

The contrasts in the first six chapters taken together, between media definitions and oppressive realities, demand an answer to the question: what is the nature of capitalist media? This is the subject of chapter 7, which is followed in turn by two further chapters on their alternative, namely socialist media. Chapter 8 takes a critical look at examples of the British socialist press, and the final chapter examines one of the most advanced experiments in socialist mass communication within capitalism, revolutionary radio stations in Italy. Thus the book nowhere assumes that 'the media' belong exclusively to capital and the state, powerfully though these dominate them.

The division of the book into chapters on specific subjects means that I must state at once how I understand the basic connections between class exploitation and oppression by race or sex. It is only too common for them to be defined as separate. So, white male workers see themselves as bearing the brunt; black people, in the Third World or inside the imperialist countries, add up their tally and know they are bearing the brunt; women have been oppressed for millennia.

Sometimes there even emerges an absurd competition for Most Oppressed Group, almost as though winning that prize will help the oppression be lifted. Monstrous conclusions are drawn, that blacks and women are shouting about next to nothing; or that black women should not assert themselves but support their oppressed black menfolk; or that a girl should be taught to hate her own brother as her sexual foe; or that white/male workers are all the enemy. Fatuous games are played, such as obsessively arguing about whether wealthy black women are or are not to be counted as oppressed.

The position I take is different. Without any romanticism about the reality of racist and sexist prejudice among white workers, or the strong reactive hostility against whites or men from blacks or women, it is unavoidable that we recognise our interdependence. This interdependence arises, not from the fact that there is strength in numbers, but from the links between these oppressions. A crucial element in the total oppression of women, for instance, is their exploitation in the labour-process. The same is true for a gigantic number of black people across the planet. And no black woman will ever be liberated till all three oppressions are lifted.

4

The powerhouse of economic and social change in the last three centuries has been neither racism nor sexism, but capitalist relations. Yet these relations have not operated in a vacuum. They have relied on racism and sexism for their success, and have entrenched them in new ways. The simplest instance is the use of blacks' labour and women's labour at cheaper rates, but the linkages extend far further than this.

This is not meant to imply that under present conditions the movements against capital, racism and sexism should instantly unite by some magic decree. Capitalist society's achievement has been to push us into our separate boxes to the point where a joint resistance can only emerge from our organising independently in the first place, and then, painfully and painstakingly, splicing our attacks into a larger onslaught. What might clumsily be labelled as capitalism-imperialism-racism-sexism is now a global system. Its size is not an excuse for surrender, but the index of the necessary levels of our struggle.

The communicative power of the mass media must not be left out of this equation either. That is why this book is not only about direct oppression, but about the media definitions of it. These definitions are the hinge, in the final analysis, of oppression's stability or instability. I have written this book to try to increase its instability, by pinning down what capitalist media are, and what socialist media can be.

Readers will find that in the chapters on the media I have focused entirely on the general run of media output. The result is depressing, so much so that socialists and liberals inside established media may complain that I do not credit their achievements sufficiently. Others may complain that I do not provide enough detail to explain how capital and the state dominate and penetrate media organisations (though I try to set out the basic relation in chapter 7). There is a limit to what can be achieved in one book, and possibly this book is already an over-achiever. I have set myself the task of explaining the general run, not the impressive exceptions (or the finer interconnections), for it is the general run which generally shapes our consciousness.

5

1. Class Struggle in Work:
From the Wage to the Keynesian State

> You come in here sometimes and you think, 'I'd do anything to get
> out of this.' On the sealer you get all sleepy and then on the railhead
> you get a sore shoulder. You think, 'God, what am I doing this for?'
> But next day you're back. I think all of us are mad.

Another worker, complaining about lay-offs in the motor industry:

> It's always us. We *make* the fucking cars, we chase around here all
> day like fucking morons, and as soon as anything goes wrong it's us
> who get the shit. They'll be alright up there in the office. They'll get
> their wages. It's always the same, we take the knocks for their
> stupidities. We've got kids and mortgages as well. They don't seem
> to consider that.

Dependence on a wage: whatever the media may say about
job enrichment, affluent workers, the welfare state, this is the core
of workers' and their dependants' dilemma under capitalism. Mad
though the first worker may feel it to be, mad though it may be, the
iron necessity of providing for yourself drives you to work daily.
Of course there is variation in work, some people are better paid or
have jobs with some interest in them. Of course there has been a
switch from the family to the welfare state as the shock absorber if
you are sacked or permanently jobless. Of course people with jobs
are reassured they are useful members of society, and this can give
them a sense of identity and purpose in life. Of course they may
enjoy the company of their fellow-workers. *But*, slicing through all
these secondary realities about work you then hit bedrock:
dependence on a wage.

'Next day you're back.' 'It's always the same, we take the
knocks . . .'

Why would people subject themselves to their experiences in

work if this dependence was not a prime fact of their existence? To take an obvious example, though one rarely mentioned in the media, why else would people expose themselves to the physical hazards of work, such as deafness through noisy machinery, industrial accidents, chemically transmitted diseases, and even death? Kinnersly argues that the usual official figure for Britain (600 dead a year at work, 300,000 injured) would more realistically be 3,000 and nearly a million. (If first-aid injuries are included as well, then ten million a year.) And there are less measurable but real costs in things like the disruptions of shiftwork, and not least the wrecked physical condition of many retired workers. What old age means in our society is directly dependent on what work has meant. But work also means a wage . . .

Until recently, the wage-relation in its purest form could be found in the British docks. Up till 1967, dockers were hired on a Monday morning, sacked at the end of the morning or before if the particular job finished and there was no other work, rehired Monday afternoon, sacked again at or before the end of the afternoon, and so on through each and every working day, year by year. It was the fortunate ones who were rehired regularly, for everyone had to assemble and wait at the dock gate to be picked out. At times of high unemployment men would elbow and shove each other, climb over each other, even fight each other, to get the attention of the foreman. The insecurity and degradation of this situation are hard to convey or visualise. It was, nonetheless, the pure form of the wage-relation of capitalist and worker. Dependence and insecurity.

The docks might seem like a strange survival. But there are other ways that workers experience this dependence and insecurity. Lay-offs in the motor industry, the very image of modern assembly-line production, are a case in point. If one group of workers at Ford's strike, thousands of others may also be laid off and lose their wages. For the employers it is a way of making all their workers pay for the costs of a strike, and also of stirring up hostility within the workforce against the strikers. For the workers it is usually sudden, without notice. The night shift can come in by bus to find there is no work, and that there are no buses till next morning. At least till 1980, they were not entitled to lay-off pay, because the dispute is inside the company. Only small welfare payments are available in situation. Dependence and insecurity again. It always used to be the big selling point in favour of clerical work: the wage was rubbish, but it was secure.

If we are going to understand class struggle in work, as distinct from its many other forms, then the first item on our agenda has to be the wage. It is not the only item (or as straightforward as it may seem). We shall also examine forms of workers' resistance against this dependence, both as individuals and in solidarity with each other. And we will then look at two forms of the employers' offensive against this resistance: their introduction of new technology, and their development of state interventionism.

The wage: dependence, control and surplus-value

The basic issue in wages is the pressure to reduce their size as a section of all the costs capitalists have to meet. This pressure is not due to capitalists being greedy or vindictive, but because they compete with each other. Even the price-fixing agreements between giant monopoly firms are often unstable and break down because one firm has discovered and cornered a decisive competitive advantage over the others. The logic of this carve-up is that if you do not stay ahead, you are very liable to fall behind.

Now anyone can understand the pressures to reduce costs in order to make a larger profit and to stay ahead in the race. Out of that profit comes reinvestment in new, more efficient machinery. What is not so obvious at all is that reducing wage-costs does not just involve lowering wages, or holding them at the same level while profits rise, or cutting the wages bill through redundancies. All these are methods that are used, but they are still subsidiary to the main point. This point is highly specific, and is central to understanding the wage. It is this: the wage only represents one part of the workers' effort, only pays them for a fraction of what

8

they make in a working day. It is that *unpaid* slice of the workers' effort that provides the inner dynamic of production and expanding productivity under capitalism.

The tantalising side of this is that as well as being unpaid effort, the unpaid part is invisible! But what mystical mumbo-jumbo *is* all this: invisible, unpaid effort? In plain terms, a wage is reckoned to be a fair day's pay for a fair day's work. If someone gets much less than that, they're being exploited; if much more, then they're lucky. So where does this unpaid labour come in, especially if it's already said to be invisible?

The easiest way of answering this question, which is central to understanding this chapter (and capitalism as well), is to delve back into history for a moment. Under feudalism, a standard organisation of labour was to get serfs to work the land three days a week to keep themselves alive (which was necessary if only to keep them working), and then to get them to work three days a week free for the lord of the manor. This second period of work was surplus to their own necessities, but not to his demands. We will call it 'surplus-labour'.

Exploitation in this form is highly visible. This unpaid effort could be seen any day from Thursday to Saturday (or whenever it was). But, wait. There must also be a surplus in capitalism, for it is the most productive, fastest growing economic system ever known. The surplus must be ever-increasing in size. But where is the surplus-labour that creates it? Now we are back with our problem of invisibility, for unlike in slavery, feudalism and so on, there is no point in the working day or week when you can say: there it is! There's the unpaid surplus-labour! Look, that's what was made with it! All that seems to be there at the end of the week, all that's visible, is a fair five days' pay for a fair five days' work: a straight swap-over. Talking about surplus-labour seems like a fantasy until you remember that if wages *do* fully match the work done then there is no surplus created in work. No surplus-product means economic stagnation, that we are producing only what we directly consume, that we are back in the Stone Age.

So the surplus is in there somewhere, it has to be. Its peculiar feature in capitalist production is that it cannot be spotted by the naked eye. Every second of labour, every split second, is itself split into one fraction of paid work to keep people in necessities, and the other fraction of unpaid work which creates the surplus. Necessary labour and surplus-labour Marx called them. The less the proportion of necessary labour, and the more surplus-labour in the working day, the greater the surplus-value created. In capitalist production relations, the division between the two is 'invisible'. In other forms of production the time spent in necessary labour and surplus-labour is obvious to commonsense.

Now it has been necessary for us to penetrate through to this invisible reality, to make understandable the central place of the wage in the struggle between capitalists and workers. The size of the surplus-value created by unpaid surplus-labour, is the basis of every firm's expansion or contraction. If there is no surplus-value, and neither the banks nor the state will help out, the firm goes bust. If the surplus-value is smaller over time than it is for the firm's competitors, then it will be hard for the firm to survive. If its surplus-value comes to be larger than theirs, the others will find it hard to compete against it.

So if workers win higher wages *with no other changes in their work*, they are eating into surplus-value and the firm's capacity to compete. Vice-versa, if the firm can pull off a cut in the wage-bill (with no other changes in production), its surplus-value and its capacity to compete increase immediately. Spread this process across every firm and the entire working class, and you can see the capitalists' struggle to protect and raise the rate of surplus-value as the core of economic class struggle. (This rule also governs the growing body of wage-workers who do not create surplus-value.)

The capitalists' methods of struggling for an increase in surplus-value have varied historically. The classic one has been to make workers work longer for the same wage. It is a method which Marx termed 'absolute' surplus-value because it has an absolute limit, the 24-hour day. But faced with workers' resistance against long hours of work, and with the growth of laws limiting the length of the working day, a variety of alternative methods were worked

10

out to increase surplus-value. Examples are the shift-system, an ever more minute division of labour, different rates of pay for different tasks and workers. Above all, the capitalists turned to the introduction of more and more productive machinery, needing fewer and fewer workers to run it. These varying methods of increasing surplus-value which had no set limit on how far they could be refined, Marx defined collectively as 'relative' surplus-value.

To sum up so far then: the wage is the battleground, with the capitalist class constantly struggling to keep it low, not necessarily in itself but as a proportion of surplus-value. This enables more surplus-labour and so more surplus-value. The working class however is dependent on that wage, and so fights back against the constant inroads into the wage that the employers attempt to make. The more successful the workers are, the more risk the firm faces of not being able to compete against other firms, and of going bust.

Now though this is the essence of the matter, the form the wage takes does vary. In the history of capitalist production there has been a whole variety of forms in which the wage is paid. As a worker, you could be paid by each hour you worked (never *for* each hour!). Or by (never for) how many pieces you produced (piecework). Or by a flat time-rate (the basic wage), on top of which you were paid piecework rates. Or by extra payment through producing more than the scheduled amount (the bonus). Or by a time-rate on assembly-line work, where the speed of the line and an army of supervisors govern how much you produce (measured-day-work). Or by various combinations of these.

Let us look a little more closely at some of these forms in order to understand the wage better, how effective it is in controlling workers. To do so, first let us review an episode in US labour history that sheds a great deal of light on some of the fundamental principles involved.

A clear illustration of the common purpose behind the varied forms in which the wage is paid, comes from Katherine Stone's account of the changes in wage systems in the US steel

11

industry. Back in the 1880s, steelworkers were in a surprisingly independent position – for workers that is. To be sure, employers as usual owned the machinery and the raw materials. But they had to contract anew for each batch of production with the skilled steelworkers, and to do so within a fixed agreement that set a minimum rate for any job, and had moreover a sliding scale to match the fluctuations in the market price of steel. This was an amazing degree of control, for in most cases it was also the skilled steelworkers who paid the labourers out of their own wages. The Amalgamated Association of Iron, Steel and Tin Workers was the workers' union. A US Steel Corporation historian described the union's sway in these terms:

> The method of apportioning the work, of regulating the turns, of altering the machinery, in short, every detail of working the great plant, was subject to the interference of some busybody representing the Amalgamated Association.

This was then a form of industrial labour in which the wage had very little capacity to be used as a method of control. Once though the demand for steel began to soar in the 1880s, the stage was set for a sharp struggle by steel capitalists to wrest back full control over production. The confrontation came in the infamous Homestead lockout of 1892. The Carnegie Corporation (later to be the US Steel Corporation and the world's first billion dollar monopoly firm) built a barbed-wire fence three miles round the plant, barracks inside for strike-breakers and brought in three hundred armed guards. Then it dismissed its workforce and announced it would employ non-union labour only.

After four months, many workers killed, and massive assistance from federal and state governments, the Corporation won. The union's stronghold was smashed, and in the decade that followed in the US steel industry there was the most intensive mechanisation imaginable. Skilled work almost vanished. This flattening out of the workforce led naturally enough to very similar rates of pay for all work. But then the destruction of skill and control created a new contradiction, for once the workforce

12

found itself to be a single mass, there was every pressure to act for itself as a unified mass. Management found this out the hard way. As one said:

> When all are paid one rate, it is the simplest and almost inevitable thing for all to unite in the support of a common demand . . . There are not likely to be union strikes where there is no union of interest.

Hence, not out of a technical necessity but rather out of a political necessity, the steel capitalists created a whole new structure of wage differentials based around marginally different actions in the labour-process they had instituted in the first place. Different rates for slightly different jobs, the arbitrary definition of certain actions as needing training and experience, artificial job-ladders: these were all created precisely in order to disrupt any unification of the mass of workers, to foster competition amongst them.

This example shows how the form of the wage and its link to a definition of skill are often governed, not by technical necessity but by the battle for control.

A second illustration of how particular wage-forms can be manipulated by employers in their own interests comes from Britain, from the pivotal national docks strike of 1970. (The history of dock labour provides so many clear examples of basic elements in the struggle between capital and labour that we shall repeatedly draw upon it.) In that strike, the employers made great play with their offer of a £20 *guaranteed* weekly wage. The dockers refused it, and stuck out for £20 *basic* weekly wage. It was easy to present the dockers as hair-splitting, as turning down a generous offer of secure pay, guaranteed to them even if they were never called upon to lift a finger all week.

For the dockers, however, insistence on a £20 basic was crucial. The basic rate was the rate on which all other rates were calculated for shifting particular cargoes, working in the rain, and so on. A rise in the basic rate meant a percentage rise overall, whereas the guaranteed wage had no such escalator effect. There were more reasons still why the dockers held out for the £20 basic, but it is clear already why the *detail* of the wage-form must be

13

grasped in order to understand the issues at stake in many industrial struggles.

The wage, then, which at first sight seems such a straightforward thing, a simple payment for services rendered, is actually like a giant octopus facing the worker. Its control reaches into the heart of the working class's existence, maintaining workers in dependence on it while extracting their surplus-labour. Attack one tentacle and others come snaking round to grip the attacker. As I said at the outset of this chapter, in the days of the welfare state such imagery can seem overblown and melodramatic. But how else do you summarise the wage as an instrument of control/dependence? As a target for reduction in order to increase surplus-value? As well as being highly manoeuvrable in its forms?

The wage is neither harmless nor obvious: it is a centrepiece of capitalist control.

Workers' resistance: movement and organisation

Usually when people talk about the struggle for power in industry they have in mind formally organised resistance such as trade unions, or at least strikes. *The* evidence of working-class combativity is often taken to be the painful, and in some countries bloody growth of union organisation. There is a major problem with this view of unions, which will become crystal clear when we come to look at their role in the interventionist state at the end of this chapter. Straightaway though we can identify a vital flaw in this perspective on working-class resistance: you cannot have trade unions emerge at all without there first being a long period of ferment in the workers' *movement*. And that movement does not vanish into thin air once trade unions are formed.

In every phase of the expansion of trade unionism, from craft unions, through general industrial unions, to 'white-collar' unions, there has first been a long period of struggle, of victories and defeats, of seeming victories which turned out to be defeats. Much of the resistance that takes place afterwards, does so without official union backing. The figure often quoted for Britain in the

14

1960s, that 95 per cent of strikes were unofficial, is only one pointer to this.

Once too you stop thinking purely in terms of strike action, the significance of other forms of resistance becomes much clearer. After all, the strike is an action which in the short term at least means a lot of hardship for workers and their dependants. No wage! Strike pay (*if* available) and welfare payments (tightly controlled) together only come up to a part of normal pay. Workers with rents or mortgages and hire-purchase commitments, are immediately faced with acute problems. Management may victimise individuals at any moment for a long time afterwards. So strikes are not undertaken lightly. A majority of workers has never actually been on strike.

There are many writers on industrial conflict who point to this fact triumphantly to prove the acceptability in general of the capitalist labour-process. They conveniently forget the many, many other forms of resistance that workers engage in apart from trade unionism and strikes. These may be less dramatic, but they are very familiar in industrial work: absenteeism, lateness, theft, overmanning, deliberate inefficiency, sabotage, go-slows, working to rule, using work-tools to make things for themselves. They are worth investigating a little further in order to establish their importance.

Absenteeism is a major problem in industrial production, especially in mining and the motor industry. The importance of lateness can be judged from the prevalence of clocking-in and clocking-out. Theft varies between industries; in the docks it used to be an industry in itself. There is a whole folklore about the tricks used to get stuff out under the noses of the dock security guards. The tons of spirits that used to vanish are probably available to some researcher from insurance companies' files, but they can safely be estimated as sizeable in number.

Overmanning is of course a matter of definition. Most employers would be happy to get one worker to cover the work of two or three if they could. But there is no question about there being worker-organised overmanning in some industries and

15

firms. Once again, the docks provide an example. In Liverpool overmanning went by the name of 'welting'. This meant that once a work-gang was hired at the dock gate, only half of it was actually working at any one time. Officially this was an hour on, an hour off. In fact, sometimes by arrangement with their workmates, dockers would just not be there. But they would still get paid. This practice is known elsewhere, as far afield as Australia, where the inactive dockers are called judges (because they sit on a case) and California, where they are called witnesses!

Deliberate inefficiency is a form of resistance with a very long history. African slaves in the USA used to leave iron implements out overnight to rust – by accident! The importance of quality-control inspectors in modern industry is only partly to cover purely technical machine faults, a major part of their activity being to identify workers who are producing under-quality items. In the Soviet Union, where most sections of the working class are heavily repressed, faulty production is one of the few irreducible forms of resistance. The line between this and sabotage is a very thin one on occasion. A standard form of sabotage in Ford's is to accidentally let a car pass without one crucial and awkward bolt secured in it. This makes a bottleneck at the other end, slows down the assembly line, and creates more overtime. The prize for the most imaginative sabotage must go to the now famous worker at a Blackpool sweet rock factory who changed the letters inside the rock from 'Blackpool' to 'Fuck Off'. Half a mile of sweet rock had to be junked.

Go-slows and working to rule are quite finely judged forms of resistance. They force employers to continue to pay workers, but threaten the production of surplus-value. The practice of working to rule represents the use against employers of their own rule-book, their own attempt to legislate control of workers' shopfloor activities.

Using tools at work to make objects for your own use is obviously limited to certain types of production. Nonetheless it is widespread there. In one British factory these products were called 'foreigners', in a Hungarian factory they were called 'homers'!

16

They are significant actions, for in them workers are reclaiming some surplus-value, and consciously expressing their own skills against their use by their employers.

All these forms of workers' resistance against the tyranny of the wage are less organised than trade unionism or than any large-scale strike. They tend to be viable only in particular plants or workgroups, or in some cases individually. They cannot be nationally organised. Nonetheless, they are part of the self-activity of the working class, not channelled or sponsored by official bodies such as trade unions. It is *crucial* to recognise the actual priority of labour movement over its particular organisations. This *self-activity*, never collected together in official statistics by state or unions, is the movement of the class without which trade unions would be an empty shell.

This is not to dismiss trade unions, let alone major strikes, but merely to redress the balance which is often absent in analyses of class struggle in work. The more formalised the trade-union structure, the more 'keynesian' as we shall see shortly, the more important it is to maintain this balance. However, in some industries and in some firms, workers' organisation does become built up to a very advanced level by comparison with unorganised sectors.

The classical occupational sector of this unionisation was in craft skills, with the printers being perhaps pre-eminent. Their craft unionism has its roots in medieval trade guilds. The steelworkers in the first phase of Katherine Stone's study, cited above, were another example. Shipbuilding, another old occupation, furnished several examples: shipwrights, platers, riveters, caulkers, smiths, pattern-makers and others. The list is capable of being stretched a long way. Some of these skilled jobs are still with us, some have been driven out by new technology. But in every case, the mechanism for their industrial strength was always the apprenticeship and a well-organised union which excluded non-apprentices from entry to the occupation. In these trades, a degree of control was wrested from the employers both over the wage level and the hiring and firing process.

17

Outside craft trades the strongest organisation grew in certain strategic industries. In coalmining and railways, in the docks and the motor industry, there developed forms of struggle with equal effectiveness. These struggles were often typified much more by the 'wildcat' strike, developed by the workers themselves without official union assistance (or often support). This strike has the virtue of being unexpected, unless it is deliberately provoked by management during a period of slack order-books. Being unexpected, it throws employers' production schedules awry much more than a slowly developing strike.

In the docks, too there grew up a kind of substitute for craft trade controls over entry. Entry to work in the docks was largely restricted to relations of dockers. This solidarity of community and kinship developed as a defensive strategy against the insecurity and degradation of casual labour. Also, dockers usually clubbed together in work-gangs with a recognised leader, and so were hired together, gaining a little more security this way. The groups the foremen favoured at the gates were called the 'blue-eyes'.

Looking at the whole range of workers' resistance against the rule of the wage, we can see how this resistance is almost always present, though expressed in varying forms to meet different types of attack. Any knowledge of industrial work reveals the incessant grinding away of employers against workers *and* workers against employers. The class struggle is never absent, right down to an argument over whether a worker has spent too long in the lavatory, or whether they have the right to go to the lavatory when they wish.

Technology and the de-composition of the working class

Technology and progress: these are usually coupled together in people's minds. Technology and attack: to most people this means electronic warfare, guided missiles, satellite reconnaissance. But historically and up to the present, a major use of technology has been in a war against the organisation of workers' resistance. Let us illustrate this point in the first place by returning once more to the docks industry.

18

In the case of the docks, from the 1950s onwards British capital in general was faced with an enormous strategic problem. It was not just the dock employers or the ship-owners who had this problem, but all capitalists who were dependent on imports or exports. In Britain, that means almost all capitalists. The dockers' organised resistance that has already been mentioned that in family recruitment, overmanning, the gang-system, manipulation of piece-rates, theft and strikes, presented continual headaches for any firm trying to keep to its schedules. Turnover time of invested capital could be stretched out unbearably. So what was their counter-offensive?

First, the state stepped in, in the shape of the 1965 government report on the industry (the Devlin Report). This report promised a final stop to the insecurity of casual labour ('decasualisation'). This looked good: dockers would be put on a register and guaranteed a wage even when there was no work. No unregistered dockers would be allowed to work in the docks, so the use of other labour to undercut wages would be protected against . . .

But, second, this only happened in conjunction with certain other developments. The crucial development was the introduction of container-ships, very large ships which packed the cargoes in standard-sized containers which could be lifted out by crane in a fast, repeated operation. They could then be placed on lorries in the same operation, driven away, and unpacked anywhere that suited their owners. Containerisation had already begun at some European ports such as Rotterdam.

The media consistently described containerisation as 'modernisation', and indeed it could seem to be just that. It did away with the heavy and often dangerous loading and unloading of different cargoes in ships' holds. It meant the container could be unpacked where it was needed. It meant that much bigger ships could be used, bringing more goods at one time, and to deepwater ports outside big cities. It meant that British Tilbury could avoid losing the race with Dutch Rotterdam for European cargoes.

For the dockers, however, this 'modernisation' brought with

19

it the destruction of their organised strength, the defeat of a strategic focus in the class struggle in Britain since most goods must be imported or exported by sea. This defeat took several forms, the chief one being that cheaper unorganised labour could be used to unpack the containers many miles from the docks. Cranes and containers further reduced the demand for dockers even to unload or load cargoes. At a stroke, their accumulated skill in handling varied cargoes, and the availability of their labour close to existing docks, became irrelevant. Indeed, London and Liverpool docks, once the biggest, most cohesive and most truculent of the centres of dock labour in Britain, became ghosts of their former selves. The dockers were left holding their hollow prize of being 'registered dockers', but increasingly without work, and so with only their minimal guaranteed weekly wage.

This introduction of new technology, and the far higher rate of surplus-value it enabled, would have been defined by Marx as a method of increasing *relative* surplus-value. Its economic meaning must not close our eyes, however, to the power struggle involved between the classes in the installation of new technology. Some Italian marxists have come to call this power-dimension the 'decomposition' of the working class, meaning that by the introduction of new technology existing organised centres of working-class strength are dissolved. In other words, the new process is not only cheaper and more efficient, it also uses a more pliant labour-force – which directly contributes to making the process cheaper for quite some time to come.

Thus only when the dockers' existing class composition had been dissolved – their communal cohesiveness, their capacity to overman, their ability to manipulate piece-rates for different cargoes and conditions in their own favour, even their scope for thieving from cargoes – only then could relative surplus-value be extracted at a higher rate without heavy and costly opposition. What happened in the case of the docks in Britain has also taken place in docking right round the world. The process of decomposition has equally operated in many other industries, printing, shipbuilding and steel being classic cases.

20

A central dimension of the invention of new technology, and of the refinement of controlling workers in the labour-process, is what has been called *taylorism*. Named after the American, F. W. Taylor, who campaigned endlessly for its merits, taylorism is the distillation of a whole mass of attempts in the later nineteenth century to organise faster, less time-wasting effort on the part of workers. Some of these were common in the re-organised steel industry which provided Taylor's own first industrial training. The practical manifestation of taylorism on the factory floor is the time-and-motion person (though they like to be called 'work-study engineers'). Not that taylorism is confined to the factory floor. In recent decades it has been extended into offices and hospitals, with work-study engineers measuring the time it takes to open and close a centre drawer (.053 minutes) as against a side drawer (.029 minutes).

There are two objectives at work in taylorism. One has been mentioned already, that 'time is money', the reason being that surplus-value is relatively increased through more detailed and precise use of labour-time. With ever more expensive machines, this matters enormously. Two and a half seconds may not be a lot; multiply by 60 times an hour, 8 hours a day, 250 working days a year and a labour-force of 600, and you get 50,000 hours extra work. *At the same wage as before*.

Over and above this objective though is the further aim of de-skilling. This is its other connection with new technology. The essence of taylorism is to reduce to the lowest point the independence or control of workers over the labour-process. Where management are dependent on workers' experience and skills, the task of taylorism is to study these skills, systematise them, make them available to management, and so rob workers of their ability to use them as a lever in their dealings with employers. The end result is the construction of more sophisticated technology embodying this knowledge, and so to de-skill, pay lower wages to the new workforce and control the labour-process more tightly.

Taylorism, new technology, relative surplus-value and de-composition are then intimately bound up with each other. Taylor

21

himself called his method 'scientific management', and defined it as a process in which

> The managers assume . . . the burden of gathering together all of the traditional knowledge which in the past has been possessed by the workmen and then of classifying, tabulating and reducing this knowledge to rules, laws and formulae . . . All possible brain work should be removed from the shop and centered in the planning or laying-out department.

Another characteristic of the development of capitalist production technology in the USA, was the development of continuous assembly-line production. It is associated above all with Henry Ford and the motor industry, and hence is sometimes called 'Fordism'. Its effect is to subordinate all workers tightly to the factory machinery. The speed of the conveyor belt governs their activity, along with a minute division of labour geared to the belt. Like the artificial job structures of the steel industry, like taylorised production, Fordism became typical of many other branches of industry in the USA and the whole capitalist world. Workers' autonomy is invaded ever more deeply, to the point where neither their understanding of what they are doing, nor even minute movements of their own bodies, are allowed to interfere with surplus-value creation.

Today the combined development of taylorism and Fordism is producing a further phase sometimes called neo-fordism. Its form is of highly automated process production, in which each machine-tool contains its own micro-computer to register feedback. If the feedback fits the programme, the robot machine-tool continues as it is; if not, the machine is programmed to adjust itself to get its operation correct. The few workers left are minders rather than producers, easily replaceable in most cases. A striking illustration is the electronic typewriter which corrects spelling errors itself! No pauses for secretaries to make corrections . . .

Technology, today symbolised above all by the application of the computer to production, is never neutral. It is frequently directed towards reducing the control of the producers, to fighting their ability *not* to work for part of the day. It becomes a living menace to the workers against whom it is directed, whether in printing, docking, shipbuilding, steel or the office. It is used to attack jobs, wage levels, and workers' organisation. The media often make workers out to be stupid and tradition-bound for their resistance to the introduction of new machines, and it is easy enough to put this line over to people who know nothing of the actual forms of work in question. Once the real story is known though, *which it rarely is through the media*, the picture is always the same. Wage levels may rise for the workers left with their jobs – this may be used as a carrot to divide workers' resistance against redundancies – but the firm's wage-bill will always go down, as a proportion of costs and in relation to surplus-value.

Often this de-composition of a given class is geographically based as well, like the shift of docking away from the docks. It can take the form of setting up new compositions of the working class in new towns and away from cities. ChemCo, the firm studied by Nichols and Armstrong in their *Workers Divided*, did precisely this. And today an important aspect of imperialist capitalism is setting up factories away from the high-wage metropolis countries, in tightly controlled countries such as South Africa, Taiwan and South Korea. Car firms in Britain, like Ford and Chrysler, quite often threaten to shift production to other countries unless workers behave themselves.

De-skilling, redundancy, lower wages, de-composition: this is the political economy of new production technology under capitalism. But it is not the only major offensive of capital against workers' resistance.

The 'keynesian' state

State intervention against the working class is nothing new, as trade-union history shows. As an attempted solution to the international capitalist crisis of the thirties, however, state intervention against labour has grown on a massive scale. Some writers have come to describe this era as that of the keynesian state, or of

23

keynesianism, after its leading theoretician, the English economist J. M. Keynes. Keynes himself was centrally concerned with the international implications for the future functioning of capital, of both the thirties' crisis, and of the Bolshevik Revolution. He was hardly alone in his concern, but his writings contained a strategy for the state to resolve the crisis at least for the immediately foreseeable future.

What Keynes offered, first of all, was the clear recognition that the motor force of capital accumulation was the working class. Not only was there no production without it, but its wages were the only guarantee that what was produced could be bought on a large scale (and thus the system kept running). Furthermore, the Bolshevik Revolution had proved the working class did not need the capitalist class, indeed that it might leave the capitalist system at any time. The thirties' experience was hardly likely to cement its adhesion, so the problem lay in how to channel the energies of this highly independent sector back into capital accumulation.

His solution to these dilemmas was to accept workers' demands for better living standards, but to use their buying power – which he termed 'effective demand' – to guarantee capital that its products could be sold. Thus the irresistible pressure of the working class for better wages could at the same time be the guarantee that capitalist production could function and grow. The art in the strategy was to be able to indentify at any one time the point of balance of forces in the class struggle, to channel this upward pressure on wages within orderly routines and predictable levels. He never offered a permanent solution – 'in the long run we are all dead' is his most famous aphorism – but he did provide a set of basic guidelines within which to negotiate temporary solutions in the face of a constantly shifting class dynamic.

These guidelines amounted to what we would now call capitalist economic planning, whose core – distinguishing it sharply from socialist planning – consists in the establishment of a permanent working relation between state, capital and trade-union leadership. Again, this was not invented by Keynes, but in

24

the keynesian era took on immeasurably increased significance. It meant in practice a relation between capital and unions in the most strategic industrial sectors, which in turn meant in the largest firms that dominated these sectors and thus the economy as a whole.

These guidelines have been legally fixed in the USA since 1947, by the Taft-Hartley Act. I am taking the USA briefly as the first example of keynesianism in action, because the objectives of keynesianism can be seen there with the starkest simplicity. The methods vary considerably, as the contrast with Britain will make clear, but the basic targets remain the same. They are the disciplining of labour and the establishment of a centralised union hierarchy involved deeply in capitalist strategy-making. The second, naturally, contributes directly to the first.

The main mechanism within the Taft-Hartley Act for achieving these goals is the labour contract, a legally enforceable two or three year written agreement between a firm and its workers, in which the workers guarantee not to strike in return for regular increases in their wage packets. The firm can then plan ahead with some confidence, able to prepare far in advance for any strike disruption at the end of the contract's period, and to forecast its wage-costs over that period as well. The significance of this pattern for the US economy as a whole can be gauged from the fact that as long ago as 1961, no fewer than 1.9 million workers were covered by just nine of these contracts with the biggest firms. Upward movements in buying power through orderly and pre-dictable wage increases make the process of national capital accumulation in the USA a process which can be forecast and planned.

To the labour discipline which these legal contracts provide, is added an increasingly centralised and remote union hierarchy. The negotiators of these contracts are permanent union officials, whose own organisation has increasingly come to correspond with the hierarchy of major firms. These officials negotiate for – and without – their members. The actual number of people centrally involved in these key posts within the unions, the state or the major firms is relatively small, and surprisingly stable over the years. A

25

hallmark of the keynesian epoch is the involvement of trade unions rather than their outlawing; but this involvement takes the form described, which diminishes the responsiveness of the union establishment to its members.

The mechanisms for achieving these goals have been quite different in Britain. The two attempts at a British Taft-Hartley, namely Labour's 1968 'In Place of Strife' and the Conservatives' Industrial Relations Act 1971–74, were both torpedoed by organised labour, which indicates how a keynesian strategy in Britain has been forced to operate more indirectly, with greater attention to the twists and turns of the class struggle, than in the USA. Institutionally, the vital difference lies in the strong relation between the TUC General Council, representing the trade-union establishment, and the Labour Party leadership. In these circles there is much more ambivalence about naked capitalism and its social debris (pensioners, the sick, children of poor families) than in corresponding circles within the Democratic Party and the AFL-CIO leadership in the USA. The trade-union base is twice the size, proportionally, and within that base anti-capitalist perspectives have much more currency than in the US working class. Thus only a capitalism managed by social reformers at the helm of the state, and attentive to welfare, is fully acceptable to the leadership of organised labour in Britain.

The tone of the normal relation between state and union establishment in Britain is revealed clearly enough in these words of the then TUC General Secretary, George Woodcock, at its 1963 Annual Conference. He was attacking the advocates of street demonstrations and rallies in Trafalgar Square, as methods of pressing home union demands: 'We left Trafalgar Square a long time ago . . . We have to deal with the affairs of the moment in committee rooms with people who have power . . . The whole work of the TUC in my time has been centred on *developing* this process.' (My emphasis.) The flavour of union leadership involvement in the process of capitalist planning in Britain is well captured by this statement, with its underlining of the vision of power-sharing which was undoubtedly the main motivation in the

26

TUC's attraction to the capital-state-labour concordat. The statement's rejection of mass action as a relic of bygone days is precisely the 'responsible', 'moderate' demeanour appropriate to the keynesian embrace.

Admittedly, my emphasis on the centrality of ongoing negotiation between the partners in this relation does seem to underplay the British state's several periods of statutory wage control (1962–63, 1966–69, 1972–74), and their importance in capitalist planning. However, legally enforced wage controls in Britain have not amounted to a Taft-Hartley Act, despite their importance, for two reasons.

Firstly, a measure of this kind only ever lasts for a fairly short period of time in its sharpest form, the wage freeze. It does not permanently invade the organisation of trade unions, as do some of the Taft-Hartley provisions. Thus either side of the freeze period the union leadership can continue to play its part in organising a stable balance on wage issues.

Secondly, these measures have never been seriously challenged by the trade-union establishment. Its own preference is for a voluntary form of wage restraint, as in the Social Contract of 1974–78, but it has always accepted legal controls, grudgingly under the Conservatives, heroically under Labour. Any revolt in its own base, any demand for full-scale mobilisation against wage controls, has always been *expressed yet defused* within the TUC structure. At Annual Conferences, for instance, the union establishment would loudly denounce profit controls for their weakness, price controls for their ineffectiveness, welfare payments for their inadequacy. But it would nonetheless accept legal wage controls rather than mobilise against them. If defeated, it would be stopped for a while from open acceptance of them, but its silence would still betoken consent. This tacit consent has been vital to their success, for it meant the state's wage laws would never be seriously challenged. By the time resistance began to crystallise, outside the official movement, a new 'phase' or 'stage' offering more freedom was usually on the horizon.

Thus wage politics are no longer simply a struggle between

27

capitalists and workers in the keynesian era. To achieve its full independence, the working-class movement has to engage in three different battles, with capital, the state, and its own union establishment. It marks the explosive nature of its power that such a massive machinery of control is necessary. Tronti has bitterly summed up what the unions' involvement in planning the national economy has meant for the workers' movement internationally:

> The idea of making the workers' movement take on the political role of managing the national social interest has exposed us to a historic suicide. It has interrupted the revolutionary process which had its successive stages in 1848, 1871, 1917. It is from that moment on that the annals of the revolution are headed: *workers' defeat*.

Accurately as the achievement of keynesianism is defined by Tronti's verdict on the labour establishment, we cannot leave the subject there. There continue to be certain critical challenges to this achievement: the tendency of rank and file trade unionists to drift apart from their established officialdom; the tendency of workers outside the keynesian concordat altogether to engage in 'undisciplined' forms of struggle; and during the seventies' international crisis, the acute problem of meeting the constant upward pressure on living standards that was channelled by the keynesian state. Workers' resistance continues, sometimes in new forms. Examples are numerous, even though we can only briefly note a handful. They are examples of what Karl-Heinz Roth has called the *other* workers' movement.

The constant tendency of the union establishment to lose touch with its base because of its closer involvement with the state was shown in a remarkable way by the unofficial union that sprouted within the British docks in the fifties and sixties, the National Association of Stevedores and Dockers (NASD). It was probably unique in its impact for a union organised quite outside the TUC, but owed its strength, after due recognition of the dock employers' policies, to the moderate, responsible leadership of the TGWU's ports section. This model of what might be called a

28

keynesian union section was not powerful enough to contain the dockers' struggles.

A second example, once more from Britain in the same period, was what came to be termed 'wage drift' in motor firms and the engineering industry. This term referred to the way in which the unions' mass base was constantly forcing additional pay out of employers locally, on top of nationally negotiated pay-deals. So serious was this challenge to keynesian economic management that the state set up a royal commission on trade unions (the Donovan Commission) to seek ways of controlling the situation. Once again, unofficial action – 95 per cent of strikes were said to be unofficial – dominated wage battles to a considerable degree.

The second challenge to the keynesian concordat comes from workers outside it. In many cases this means black workers, migrant workers, women workers. From the Nazis' use of forced Slav and Jewish labour, through to the consistent use of migrant labour in western Europe and North America since world war two, the apparent enlightenment of the keynesian guarantee of workers' living standards has *continued* to have as its condition the classically 'victorian' treatment of migrant workers. Quite often, being outside trade unions, they have had no formal organisation of resistance – or, as in several black workers' strikes in Britain and elsewhere, their union membership has meant zero support from its sometimes openly racist officials.

On occasion it has meant an outbreak of wildcat strikes, like the strike explosion in West Germany in 1973. In cities such as Detroit, black carworkers' militancy has been linked to rebellions of the black unwaged, as in 1967 when a whole area of the central city was fired by slumdwellers. In Britain there have been long and bitter black strikes, like those at Imperial Typewriters Leicester, in 1973 or at Grunwicks in 1977. The real threat to keynesianism would be a major spillover from these sectors outside its concordat to rank and file workers within it. These divisions within the working class, whether the splintering experience of domestic existence for women, or the divisions of

29

nationality and 'race', are strategically vital for keynesianism's success.

Its third problem, as mentioned above, is its dependence on a continuous expansion of surplus-value. When this sags and threatens to collapse, as it did throughout the seventies and into the eighties, the capacity of the keynesian state to allow normal wage increases, and to maintain the 'social wage' (pensions, medical care, etc.) also sharply retracts. (The rise of OPEC and the crises of imperialism dealt capitalism a further body-blow, but they are beyond our scope here.)

The result has been a systematic retreat from keynesianism and a commitment to austerity budgets in every major capitalist state. This drama has had one of its most dramatic scenarios in the financial capital of the leading capitalist power: New York. There, after a series of successful struggles by state employees and welfare recipients to raise their incomes in the sixties and early seventies, the city was declared bankrupt by President Ford and the banks in 1975. Its elected government was set aside, and an Emergency Financial Control Board imposed on the city to run it. A wage freeze was immediately declared, large-scale redundancies set in motion, welfare payments sharply reined in. Just as the IMF (International Monetary Fund) has so often been waved about in Britain and elsewhere as the reason for austerity budgets, so in New York the banks' refusal to lend the city more money was the sole justification for this retreat from keynesianism.

However, the resistance of city-dwellers also made itself felt: on 13 July 1977 ('Black Christmas') there was a power failure that blacked out New York. Tens of thousands of people poured into the streets and looted clean many hundreds of shops. Lorries were stolen, chains attached to them, and so the steel bars ripped off shopfronts. Children reported police positions; snipers slowed down police movements; and even temporary warehouses were set up to hold the larger goods. Perhaps a thousand million dollars' worth was taken. If so, it would have represented something equivalent to the money cut out of the city budget since 1975. It was not a long-term political solution, but it was a rebalancing of

30

the budget. Such explosions, taking a variety of forms, are likely to accompany and deepen this crisis of the world capitalist economy.

Conclusions

In examining the wage, work-technology, class de-composition and keynesianism, workers' resistance has always been pivotal. 'Solutions' have repeatedly bred their own crises. In the next chapter we shall focus on how the main British media have usually interpreted this resistance. The political centrality of people's overall understanding of the potential in this resistance – namely, the potential for the working class to achieve independence of the capitalist class – defines the importance of these media thrusts into mass consciousness. Often of the silkiest, most velvety kind, they nonetheless help to construct iron categories in people's thinking. A different analogy would be to see capitalist media as operating like coral in people's minds, imperceptibly developing assumptions that are rock-hard. Let us begin to see how, in the case of strikes.

2. The Media and Class Struggle in Work

The media pay very little attention to the realities of class struggle in work as outlined in the last chapter. Journalists are rarely allowed to observe firms at will and write what they want. The West German 'muckraking' journalist, Günter Wallraff, has described the incredible lengths employers went to in order to deny or defuse his reports from inside their factories. Only the public relations department may speak about the firm. Even an advanced 'workers' participation' law such as West Germany's, which requires workers' factory assemblies on site in working hours, nonetheless bans outsiders or the discussion at them of political or union matters. Public democracy and 'participation' must always yield to the rights of capital.

Editors rarely allow workers to speak for themselves in the media. In a study I made of 345 news bulletin items on eleven major industrial issues in TV News in 1970, the workers themselves were conspicuous by their near-absence. Despite their involvement, they were scarcely even asked their views. The figures left no doubt on this score.

Ordinary workers were asked to speak 64 times, sometimes to express opposition to the strike. By contrast, spokespeople for the state were on the air 110 times, employers 73 times, top trade-union officials 163 times, and the journalists 345 times. (These last I counted as expressing a single viewpoint – as they themselves professionally define their role – and so as a single person per item.) Members of the general public, as affected by the dispute, were on the air 51 times (usually to express their grievances against the strike).

In actuality this meant a weighting of about 11 : 1 against the workers. The employers obviously used the opportunity to state their case. The state presented itself as neutral, as did the broadcasters, but that does not mean they are 50 per cent pro-workers, 50 per cent pro-capital. It means, as we shall see, that they argue in a different way against strikes, just as top trade unionists in the keynesian concordat do not actually condemn strikes outright, but merely seek to avoid them or end them quickly (especially if they move outside their control).

The first conclusion is that whatever picture the media present of industrial conflict, *the picture scarcely ever comes from the strikers* (and never from journalists who have personal experience of working in the situation up to the strike). The media are visibly a part of bourgeois democracy. Officially, anyone has the right to speak through them. Superficially, a variety of interests express themselves about strikes. Actually the producers on strike are the last to be asked their views. The press presents the same pattern in this respect as broadcasting.

Let us now examine what kind of picture does emerge of strikes, as the most newsworthy and politically problematic form of class struggle in work. We will look at the following questions: media explanations of strikes; the overwhelming media emphasis on their effects; the handling of workers' solidarity; the image of the state; the political ideology of interviewers; the interventions of top union officials in the media; and certain differences between newspaper and broadcasting accounts of strikes.

The mysterious origins of senseless strikes

Media explanations of strikes vary from the non-existent to the schematic. The 1970 national docks strike, for instance, the first since the General Strike, and of pivotal importance in the British ruling-class de-composition strategy against the working class, was scarcely ever explained by press or TV. It was said, occasionally, to be about the difference between the demand for basic pay of £20 a week, and the employers' offer of guaranteed pay of £20 a week. This sounded rather like hair-splitting by the dockers, but the crucial difference between *basic* and *guaranteed* wages has been set out in the last chapter's dissection of different wage forms.

What a £20 basic rate meant was (1) a major pay-boost for 7,000 dockers in small ports; (2) a powerful lever to the price dockers could get for agreeing to containerisation (described in chapter 1). Unlike the basic rate, £20 guaranteed had no ratchet effect on piece-rates.

Not only was this not explained, but neither was the four-year build-up to the strike. Nor were the massive property interests of the leading port employers in redeveloping inner London dockland. Ambrose and Colenutt have documented the way many hundreds of millions of pounds were made by closing down inner London docks. Because container-ships were too big to get that far independently of tides, all that land was available for redevelopment. The only person to point this out in the media *was also the only docker to be interviewed about the causes of the strike*.

This gap in explanation was not a peculiarity of media handling of this strike, as work by other writers on the media and industrial conflict makes clear. Hyman, and Lane and Roberts, found that only certain 'quality' newspapers offered any solid explanations for strikes. Morley discovered only two, extremely simplistic, explanations. One was conspiracy by left extremists, the hoary old spectre of outside Red agitators. Even the most effective agitators know they cannot create discontent. Only employers have that power. The other explanation was in terms of 'hardening attitudes' among workers, and to some extent among employers as well. Yet to explain strikes in these terms, begs the question of *why* they hardened in the first place. The strike is still a mystery.

Hartmann found 'dissatisfaction with wages' the most frequently named cause of strikes at the time of his study. *Why* this dissatisfaction all at once – because of galloping prices for example – was another mystery left unsolved. For the one-day national stoppage on May Day 1973, the most frequently named causes were opposition to government pay policy, or union instructions. The reasons for such opposition were not explored at all, and 'union instructions' can imply a repugnant union dictatorship over their members. The Glasgow University Media Group found barely any explanation offered for the Glasgow dustcart drivers' strike.

Since the origins of strikes in class struggle in work are left unstated, mysterious, the way is clear for their systematic presentation by the media as senseless and irrational. Hartmann cites the *Express* dismissing industrial strife as 'senseless', and insisting that 'we cannot live by tribal rules which classify employers as Us, and employees as Them.' Tribalism = irrationality = class hatred. He also cites the *Telegraph* as claiming that among workers 'there are big reserves of sanity and good sense waiting to be tapped'. By contrast, when nearly two million workers struck on May Day 1973, Young found that the dominant theme of press coverage was that the strike was irrelevant, mad, irrational and antiquated. The theme is standard: when the *Mirror* announced Labour's attempt at a Taft-Hartley in 1968, it blazoned across its front page: 'BLOODY GOOD SENSE!'

Strikes remain mysterious then. Perhaps the reason is that real explanations would force too much attention to the continuing realities of class struggle in work, or to the bite of rising prices. Certainly, without explanation, it is easy to present strikes as pointless, antiquated relics of class hatred from the nineteenth century.

The focus on the impact

What is absent from the explanation of strikes is amply made up for by stressing their impact. In the docks strike this was detailed out as the damage to the national economy; the rise in food prices; and the danger to the 'modernisation' of the docks. Attention to these effects dominated media coverage of the dispute. Its impact was the news.

A national docks strike obviously does have an instant, sharp effect on the British economy, especially given that Britain is an island. The media always assumed, however, that this economy was all 'our' economy. Insofar as everyone has a direct dependence

35

on it, this was accurate. It was not correct though to imply everyone has equal shares in it, either of income or control. Yet reason was held to dictate that petty class differences of this kind should be brushed aside, and the strike called off, in the national interest of 'the' (= our) economy.

We see here the ideology that there is a 'national social interest' overriding sectional disputes or class interests. We then see it used to accuse workers (occasionally employers too) of deliberately refusing to act for the welfare of their fellow citizens. Thus the workers are isolated as deviants, localised as a small group contemptuous of others' rights, trampling on their reasonable concerns.

The most tangible development during the docks strike that could be pointed to as evidence for its economic disruption, was the rise in food prices. It became a major focus of media coverage. What was noticeable was that it was blamed on the visible activity of dockers, who were refusing to shift perishable foods. They themselves had no ability to fix prices. The people who had were the unseen army of wholesalers, who found the shortage allowed them to jack up their prices. This though was not anti-social. It was the *law* of supply and demand. No point in the suffering public complaining about an economic law.

The danger to the future 'modernisation' of the docks was the other main impact of the strike that the media emphasised. The term 'modernisation' is an absorbing instance of the political redefinition of technological change. In chapter 1, the effects of containerised docking were set out precisely in order to illustrate the politics of new technology. Yet 'modernisation' has the same quality as 'motherhood': what decent person can be against it in public? Every single major media outlet, TV, *Mirror*, *Express*, *Telegraph*, gave 'modernisation' massive prominence as the goal that must be achieved, but was endangered by the strike.

What they meant but hardly said, was that it would cost the employers more to get the dockers to agree to it if the strike were successful. They gave no estimate of the continuous future gains from de-composing the docks labour-force, shrinking its size,

36

evacuating its acquired handling skills, and using cheap labour to unpack the containers far away from dockland. (Nor of the property gains involved.) In the light of all this, the dockers could have trebled their demand. Yet, they were presented as against 'modernisation', hopelessly snared in the past, unable to rejoice in the 'modernised' future, but able to block those benefits for *everyone* else.

The same overwhelming emphasis on effects has been noted in other research. The media built up picket-line violence to be a major issue in the Pilkington strike, despite its being far less dramatic than they made out. Morley picked up the same concentration on the 'national interest', together with the inconveniences caused to the public by gas-workers' and hospital workers' strikes. Hartmann found that disruption of the firm was the major effect the media named in his sample, followed by lay-offs and public inconvenience. In the Glasgow dustcart drivers' strike the main issue presented by the media was the health hazard, of uncollected rotting refuse.

This focus on effects and silence on causes feed each other, because the more drastic the public impact, the more senseless and irresponsible is a strike with no clear cause. *This* explanation of strikes is available in the crevices of media accounts, and may be all the more influential for its indirectness. Since it is not usually presented explicitly to agree or disagree with, in viewers' and readers' minds it is all the more capable of seeming to be their own spontaneous reaction, not foisted on them by anybody.

One final note: no one ever asked in the media what damage it would do to the dockers' interests if they gave up their strike. This was completely off the agenda.

The irrelevance of workers' solidarity

Media coverage of the dockers' strike showed some interesting definitions of workers' solidarity. On the one hand, there was an amused attitude to attempts to break the strike. Some small ships ran some food, mainly bacon and eggs, from fishing villages in Northern Ireland to similar villages in Scotland, in defiance of the strike. A Liverpool housewife announced to the media her plan to sign up five hundred housewives to shift perishable food from the docks. The *Express* headlined these as 'Row sizzles over "bacon-and-eggs" run' and 'Boss Burrell' (the housewife) 'gets set up to send in her dolly dockers.' A BBC TV current affairs unit was sent to do the crossing on one of the ships, and put in a report from its bridge.

The notion of strike-breaking was made merely amusing by this presentation. The fact the breaches were tiny made it all the easier to poke fun at such antiquated, rigid refusal to break strikes. It made the action of some Belfast dockers, in tipping some of the goods into a harbour, seem petty and overblown. Ms Burrell's report to the media of a man telephoning her to promise to drop her in the Mersey river, held the same mixture of comedy with the lurking menace of organised disputes.

Another episode in the docks strike which bore on solidarity, was whether all the British ports would come out, and whether foreign dockers would support the strike. The TV journalists were very bullish in predicting that Felixstowe, already containerised and in the brave new 'modernised' world, would not join in the strike; and that there would be no solidarity from west European ports.

They were confounded. Felixstowe joined in, and Dutch, Belgian, Swedish, Norwegian and French dockers refused to handle British ships. These events were mentioned in all three bulletins one evening, and then dropped like a hot potato. Unlike breaches, solidarity was not news. Nor were they very interested in the solidarity between dockers in big ports and small ports, nor again in the refusal of TGWU market porters to handle anything moved from the docks by troops.

Since strikers are isolated as deviants from the 'national interest' by the media, it is perhaps predictable that breaches in strikes will be presented as comic, and solidarity dismissed as irrelevant. Both reactions confirm that strikes are a local issue, in no way a moment in the movement of the working class as a whole.

This *isolation and localisation* are a major dimension of media presentation of strikes.

The state as umpire

The media systematically present the state as a neutral umpire in strikes, endeavouring to act on behalf of the 'national interest' without prejudice to either side's arguments, but without allowing them to damage the said 'national interest'. In the docks strike, this image of the state surfaced in a number of ways.

The state had been involved from 1965 in setting up the Devlin Commission and its Report to reorganise dock labour (referred to in chapter 1). This action was simply referred to by the media as a fact, that 'Devlin' had produced a report whose plan was being worked out in stages at the present time. 'Devlin' was simply a rational, 'modernising' programme being messed around by the strike. 'Devlin' had nothing to do with the state's economic planning for capital, or the TGWU's involvement in these plans. It was independent of any interests except the best future for the docks.

The second point at which the state came in, concerned the quickest way to end the strike. The government began by proposing arbitration, knowing this would legally bind the dockers to its findings, knowing then that they would be sure to refuse – but also knowing most people would not understand why they refused. When the dockers did refuse arbitration, the media were not informative on this score, so the government could be said to have won that round in the battle for public opinion.

The next proposal was a court of inquiry. The media discussion of who should chair it revealed some classic ideologies of the judiciary, which any good history of trade unions and the courts would confound. The *Mirror* referred to the 'impartial' court of inquiry. The *Express* spoke of the court's 'fresh view, free of prejudice'. But it was the TV News bulletins which relayed, without batting an eyelid, the fact that a possible chairperson for the court was Vic Feather (TUC General Secretary, firmly on the

Labour right, later Lord Feather), but that he had been stood down in favour of a high court judge. The political neutrality of the state judiciary was taken to be beyond question.

Media accounts of the strike then restated and reinforced the ideology that government commission reports, arbitration procedures, and industrial courts of inquiry, were independent of state and capital. But there was more to come, in the shape of a State of Emergency and in the threat to use the army to shift perishables.

In British law, a State of Emergency is a draconian measure. The armed forces are allowed to control unrest, many materials can be requisitioned, and indeed almost anything is open to be done by the state. Parliament is meant to renew it every thirty days, but its provisions would enable parliament itself and many civil liberties to be swept away by a government hellbent on doing so.

When the Conservative government announced the State of Emergency, the media universally presented it as simply a technical measure to protect supplies. As the *Telegraph* put it, it provided 'reserve powers only . . . solely to protect the nation'. None of the media followed up the criticism of its dangerous potential by some Labour MPs. The expression of dissent was swept aside by a deafening media chorus hymning the state for acting in 'the national interest'.

The government kept proposing through the media that the only answer to rotting perishables and rising food prices was to send in troops to clear the perishables. Protected by armed force, presumably, though that was discreetly left unstated in the media. If the army did go in, it was presented simply as acting to avoid wasting food and to protect housewives from rising prices. Like the rest of the state machine, it would be acting for the common good.

Weakening the strikers' power was never mentioned, except indirectly by the *Telegraph* which argued that to use the army might be provocative and lengthen the strike. Why provocative was left unsaid.

We have seen how consistently the state's forms of intervention into class struggle in work are presented as neutral actions in the 'national interest'. We have even seen how its various modes of operation (courts, official reports, states of emergency, even the army) are presented as detached from any major interest – except everybody's. This reinforcement of the supposition that the state is a neutral arbiter is valuable to capital for the successful resolution of major industrial conflicts. In Britain in particular, unlike Italy or even the USA, acceptance of this ideology of the state is quite widespread. Media support for the ideology is a long-term bonus.

Journalists' political interventions in strike accounts

Journalists in British broadcasting would usually flatly deny that they make any political interventions in reporting strikes. Their self-definition is as professionals who convey both sides as accurately and impartially as they can, without making their own comments like American TV reporters do. Industrial correspondents in the British press even have a reputation for being somewhat left-inclined, so that any political bias on their part would be expected to be pro-striker. However, these self-definitions, though interesting, are misleading. Let us examine some actual cases.

There is a strong affinity between the ideology of the state as umpire, and broadcasting journalists' self-definition as balanced reporters. Normally the journalists during strikes put themselves in the supposed position of the general public, and ask the questions they imagine this fictional, homogeneous general public would ask if they could. What emerges from this imaginative exercise is a chain of questions which might be summed up as concerned with industrial peace for the national health.

For instance, in the broadcast coverage of the national docks strike nearly 80 per cent of the questions interviewers asked were about how long the strike would last; about arbitration and the court of inquiry as possible methods of ending it; on the chances of its postponement, or of a temporary return to work; on its economic damage; on whether troops shifting perishable cargoes

41

would be seen as acting for the public good. These were all concerned with ending the strike – but in no way with ending it viably for the dockers themselves. One evening when it seemed the strike might be postponed, the BBC TV current affairs presenter opened the programme by saying 'Good evening. And I do mean *good*.'

What these questions establish then is a triad of interests: the workers involved; the particular employers; and the national interest, represented by the state *and by the journalists themselves*.

Broadcasting journalists speak for everyone, in their self-definition – yet it is noticeable that they often slide into a more attacking posture when talking to strikers than to employers. The following example from the coverage of a firemen's strike at Heathrow illustrates this point well. The TV interviewer was speaking to the airport personnel director and to senior TGWU officials. Notice how he began balancing 'both' sides, and then imperceptibly slid into identifying the employers' interest in ending the strike with the 'national interest' in ending it:

> Well now finally could I put this point to both of you? I think the strength on your side [ie. the firemen's] is that ninety men can hold up this enormously complex operation and can hold to ransom in many ways – thousands of people can't travel, and vast sums of money are being lost. This is your strength: it may also be your weakness, because I think on Mr Hewitt's side [ie. the employers], there's a strong feeling that guilt can attach to this small number of men . . .

He later asked the union officials:

> You feel no guilt about this? But suppose severe national problems arise out of this? Financial crises?

Not in spite, but because of their professional ideology, broadcasting journalists constantly make political interventions in their reporting of strikes. They are not simply mirrors on social reality, but actors in their own right. Into the relation of forces between strikers and employers is inserted the national weight of

42

the media, always to end the strike in the public interest. Just because they do not come on screen urging strikers to support their friendly employers, it does not mean that this journalistic intervention is neutral in such struggles.

Indeed, the basic categories of economic analysis journalists take for granted are slanted against labour. Journalists unquestioningly rely on the 'wage-push' explanation of price inflation beloved of British cabinet ministers. This blames workers' wage increases for pushing up prices, so that the workers are judged guilty of creating the very price inflation they suffer from most. Out of the several explanations of price inflation available, this and this alone is the gospel for the journalists' balanced presentations.

The trade-union establishment speaks

The main voice speaking ostensibly on the part of workers through the media, is that of the trade-union establishment. Established it is: of the eleven leading union officials who dominated media coverage of the eleven major industrial issues I analysed in 1970, eight were still in post as late as 1977. A feature of the keynesian concordat is the stability of personnel on the union wing. How did these officials acquit themselves on the media?

First we must recognise the authority to speak which the media unquestioningly confer on these people. An instance is the intensive use of Jack Jones (TGWU general secretary) and Tim O'Leary (TGWU ports officer) during the docks strike of 1970. Jones had recalled the delegates' conference to try to persuade them to *accept* the employers' offer of £20 guaranteed wage. O'Leary's politics were even more conventional. He said to the court of inquiry:

> I confess that I must have slipped up to be in the situation I am in now. I am more to the right than any other dock leader since 1926, and yet it falls to me to lead a national strike.

In general, the record of the ports section of the TGWU was a dismal one. Yet the media never questioned the real ability of these two men to speak for 46,000 dockers.

However, it is instructive to listen to what the union establishment says in specific detail. The first two examples are of the then TUC General Secretary, Vic Feather, first in a profile of his life and work, and then in his media reactions to the Conservatives' 'Taft-Hartley' of 1971, the Industrial Relations Act.

In the *World in Action* profile he was shown walking through the back streets of the Yorkshire industrial city where he was born, chatting to workers, carrying his own bags, using a public callbox to make a call, flying in a plane to a union conference, speaking to a managers' conference. In other words, he was presented as being at ease in all classes and situations.

His own comments on class struggle were similarly collaborative. He was against the Conservatives' Industrial Relations Bill – because it would increase conflict! The closer relations were between management and the unions, the better, he said, adding that as a socialist he was in favour of the elimination of classes, not class war. 'Life,' he insisted in the programme, 'is compromise.' (For Mao, life was struggle.) He argued that strikes were overblown by the media, instancing the sheet-metal workers who had had an average of one day's strike each that year. That, he claimed, was '99.6 per cent perfect'.

On the Conservatives' proposed law, he insisted that as British unions are never above or outside (bourgeois) law, they would use every method within the limits of legality and democratic practice to defeat it in parliament. However, Feather roundly condemned the perfectly legal and democratic extra-parliamentary struggle against the Bill, which the Communist Party had led with a day's national strike a few days after the Bill was published. He also expressed himself as happy that only about half a million workers answered the strike call. (This was the man thought too biased to chair the court of inquiry into the docks strike.)

The communication of this collaborationist ideology on a mass level is a vital element in the effective operation of keynesian strategy. This interaction between media and trade-union estab-

44

lishment is the daily flesh and blood of keynesian political economy. It is not a question of consensus politics, which implies a millpond sea, but a question of successfully riding out the storms – not of obliterating class struggle but of managing it in an orderly fashion.

The limited variety of the news media

The last element in media coverage of class struggle in work is their degree of variety in handling strikes. Fundamentally, only the *Telegraph* (out of my coverage of BBC and commercial TV news and current affairs, and the *Mirror*, *Express* and *Telegraph*), openly pursued class struggle. The basic theme of all the other media coverage was class conciliation.

To see the difference, let us observe how the *Telegraph* handled the docks strike. Interestingly, it was critical of the employers – but for their flabbiness in dealing with the dockers. It defined the main problem in the strike as the dockers' determined truculence. This it regarded as totally unjustified, because the dockers were at the top of the earnings table (for manual workers!), while their productivity was low. The *Telegraph* also saw the sinister influence of the left skulking in the shadows. The whole episode, it argued, was proof positive of the urgent need for the 'Taft-Hartley' the Conservatives had announced.

Its editorial headlines faithfully reflect its sense of class outrage at the dockers' presumption:

'Dockers' Challenge'
'Dockers' Ditch'
'Dockers' Relent'
'Up To The Dockers'
'The Dockers Accept'

Under this last heading it commented sourly: 'To put it in the vernacular, should the 46,000 dockers repeatedly be allowed to have the penny and the bun?' In this attempt to cut the arrogant workers down to size, we catch the impotent fury of the paper's petit-bourgeois shire readership.

45

Such open class antagonism is not to be found even in the *Express*, perhaps because of its considerable working-class readership. Instead, it constantly preaches the virtues of rational class collaboration between employers, unions and the state. The unions are only attacked if this collaboration does not seem to be taking place.

Thus, during the docks strike the *Express* had some waspish remarks about the union's conduct. For instance, it argued that a secret ballot of all dockers would have been better than their delegates' conference hastily recalled by Jack Jones to press them to accept £20 guaranteed. A ballot, said the *Express*, would have meant that 'at least' the nation could have been sure the decision to strike was 'a democratic decision, democratically arrived at'. There was an implication that the elected delegate conference was undemocratic, yet no hint that Jones had unsuccessfully tried to manipulate it into accepting the employers' offer. If he had succeeded, would the *Express* have had the same anxieties about due democratic process?

At the end of the strike, the *Express* congratulated the dockers for having resisted the militant minority in their midst, in a tone which managed to be both sour and patronising. It also emphasised the merits of a 'Taft-Hartley' to avoid such confrontations in future.

The *Mirror* was the closest of the three papers to the broadcasting definitions of the strike. It reproached both sides on behalf of 'the nation'. It stressed the value of industrial peace, of the orderly resolution of conflict, of setting limits to tactics which could prove provocative. It kept a completely low profile on the army issue, making no comment either way. Its major concern was with what it called the 'fragile' nature of Britain's economic recovery, and of course – like every other media outlet – with 'modernisation'. It defined this last as simply 'a fair day's work for a fair day's pay'! Not only is the existence of surplus-labour and surplus-value obliterated here, but so is the de-composition of the docks labour-force (which was to lead to another bitter national strike in 1972).

46

It is important to recall that until it was overtaken in the late seventies by the *Sun*, the *Mirror* was *the* working-class newspaper since the second world war. It never failed to urge its readers to vote Labour at general elections, the only paper to do so, and thus it had great political credibility with more than a generation of the British working class. Its brilliant inflexion of issues to remove their class sting was, along with broadcasting, one of the most potent ideological influences brought to bear against the working class. Above we noted its definition of the Labour 'Taft-Hartley' proposals as 'BLOODY GOOD SENSE!', and this accurately conveys its outstanding ability to express class conciliation policies in direct and effective terms.

All three newspapers were united in their refusal to give the dockers themselves a chance to speak, or to explain the roots of the strike. In each case, moreover, their headlines constantly repeated words like crisis, threat, and peace. These terms convey the picture that *our* economy is in peril, that *we* the nation are threatened, that peace between the classes is urgently needed for *all* our sake. Morley commented how for TV:

> the gas strike *meant* the danger of explosions, the hospital strike *meant* danger to patients, the rail strike *meant* inconvenience to commuters, the teachers' strike *meant* disruption of children's education, and the customs strike *meant* the creation of a 'drug smugglers' paradise'.

The effect, as we have seen in broadcasting, is the localisation of strikers, their isolation from the rest of the suffering nation. The fact that strikers suffer both as consumers and through loss of pay is never mentioned. With or without the left-wing inclinations of industrial correspondents, at this point all the media sing in unison.

Conclusions

Media coverage of strikes in Britain provides a gigantic orchestration in favour of class collaboration with capital. The

47

docks strike, to which I have constantly made reference, illustrated almost all the themes which regularly recur. There are seven basic features of media coverage of class struggle in work.

First, consistent silence about the specifics of these struggles. Second, effective denial of a public voice to striking workers. Third, refusal to explain the roots of any strike, instead focusing on its disruptive effects, so making the strikers' decision all the more inexplicable and unforgivable. Fourth, localisation of strikes, disinterest in solidarity action, dismissal of their *class* significance. Fifth, isolation of the strikers, not only from their class, but from everyone else, in the name of the 'national interest', 'the [= our] economy'. Sixth, enthronement of the trade-union establishment as the authentic voice of the working class. Seventh, powerful reinforcement of the state as benevolent neutral guardian of the 'national interest', with journalists as the voluntary voice of this interest.

Thus, capitalist media offer workers no help in developing communication within the class. They must communicate without *and against* these media. The media offer neither useful information (about their employers, the state, or their union authorities), nor imaginative stimulation, to aid their struggles. Into this political vacuum constantly floods a mass of communication with the seven characteristics summarised above. This presentation of strikes has two effects, one specific, the other more general and long-term.

The specific effect consists of the most combative groups of workers, namely those on strike. The more effectively the media isolate and localise them, the more pressure is brought to bear on them to end their strike. In such struggles, both political consciousness and organisation can develop new forms, and therefore their isolation is doubly important. The Conservative government's plans in 1980 to ban sympathetic picketing were only one index of the importance of isolation. Employers' hostility to factory-gate meetings and their enthusiasm for writing to workers and balloting them at home, are similarly based on the recognition that at the gate workers are *together*, whereas at home

48

they are split up and subjected to a media barrage against their strike.

The general, long-term effect is the enthronement of the trade-union establishment as workers' normal, proper leaders. The fact that union leaders can be put on the spot when 'their' workers are in action – 'Aren't your dockers concerned at all, Mr O'Leary, about the damage that will be done to the country's economy?' – only underlines their own strategic significance as the generals of class collaboration. This collaboration is not always smooth. On occasion it is more akin to riding the tiger, especially for the union establishment. Nonetheless, their responsible, moderate central authority must be underpinned.

The media, then, are a vital part of the daily flesh and blood on the bones of the keynesian state. I have concentrated here on their role in relation to strikes, though there is a mass of other material, ranging from attacks on welfare 'scroungers' to assumptions that the USSR is socialism in practice, which assists in maintaining the working class within the system, in subverting its constant reassertion of its independent power.

In the next four chapters, we will examine some of the interaction between racism, sexism and class exploitation. In this book, the terms 'class' and 'capitalist society' are not reduced to economic entities, any more than economic exploitation itself is reducible to purely economic relations. Those forms of oppression are part and parcel of the entire system, locking and interlocking with each other so that no independence, no liberation is possible if any of them is left unharmed. The stability of capitalism rests on them just as much as it has rested on the keynesian concordat.

3. Racism in Modern Britain

You're dealing with a man who has a language. Find out what that language is. Once you know what language he speaks in, then you can talk to him. And if you want to know what his language is, then study his history. His language is blood, his language is power, his language is brutality, his language is everything that's brutal.

And if you can't talk that talk, he doesn't even hear you. You can come talking that old sweet talk, or that old peace talk, or that old nonviolent talk – that man doesn't hear that kind of talk. He'll pat you on your back and tell you you're a good boy and give you a peace prize. How are you going to get a peace prize when the war's not over yet?

Malcolm X, 1964

To explain the nature of racism in modern Britain it is necessary first to go back into history and to trace the origins of racist ideology. At what point did Europeans first come to consider people with noticeably different physical appearance to be socially inferior rather than physically different? Why did they do so? And why has that social definition of group inferiority persisted? Only when there is some answer to these questions is it possible to grasp the precise nature of anti-black hostility in present-day Britain (though more than the past is involved in that). In turn, the ideological definitions of the nature of racial hostility and conflict, and the racist presentation of black people in the British media, can only be understood against this historical background.

The genesis and development of racist ideology

It is possible to trace the development of European racist

ideology through a succession of periods in which the actual version of the ideology changed considerably. It is of course the case that there are historically many forms of racist ideology beside European racism, just as the oppression of women has many other forms beside those found in medieval and modern Europe. In the medieval world, unflattering images of other ethnic groups were normal.

The particular components of the unflattering image of Africans in this initial period were colour, appearance (hair etc.) and religion. Of themselves, the first two at that time might have marked Africans off in Europeans' eyes as more exotic, but no worse than, say, the Bulgarians. The decisive difference then was their religion. For medieval Europeans, only monotheistic religions could be regarded as authentic. Yet the Africans were unmistakably polytheists, about the only feature of their religious culture the Europeans grasped. At that period, the difference was akin to later beliefs in different levels of civilisation, and thus the Africans' image in Europe was marked from the first by this damaging blemish. The key difference between this and later versions of racist ideology lay in the fact that any African was a potential convert to Christianity. However unlikely in practice, the possibility of Africans leaving their inferior status behind was everpresent. In most later versions of racist thought, this potential for 'escape' was totally denied.

The decisive twist came with the emergence of slavery as a crucial feature of European economy, albeit sited in the New World. The economic impact of slavery on the primitive accumulation of capital in Europe and North America, and on the underdevelopment of Africa (which in the centuries of the slave trade lost at least 15 to 25 million of its young men and women), has been written about at length. Its enormous economic significance can be gauged from many sources. Perhaps the most striking is that in the eighteenth century the British government for a while considered handing Canada back to the French in exchange for the riches of the Caribbean island of Guadeloupe (measuring 532 square miles), which like virtually all Caribbean islands had been transformed into a series of slave plantations. Or you could gauge the importance of slavery from the shock-waves of horror or hope – depending on where you stood! – when the Africans in Haiti took advantage of the preoccupation of France with the 1789 revolution, rose in insurrection against their plantation ruling class and established self-rule.

Particular versions of slavery in the New World have been exhaustively discussed, together with the bestial cruelty which for each slave began with the 'Middle Passage' across the Atlantic. However, arguments between historians about variations in repression between various countries' slave plantations tend to obscure the central issue: the gigantic revenues that flowed from this barbaric exploitation of labour in the New World, for the benefit of the ruling classes of the Old World (and from 1776 to the new ruling classes of the United States).

This in turn raised a plain and growing contradiction within advanced bourgeois thinking. What was to become of the ideals of liberty, brotherhood and equality which were enshrined in the French Revolution of 1789 and the American Revolution of 1776, if one section of the human population was to be enslaved in a manner still more ruthless than feudal serfs? The seismic tremors which these revolutions for equality and freedom had sent through the emergent bourgeois classes and their intellectual spokesmen, the excitement and anticipation of further victories to come against reactionary feudal and monarchical power, are hard to visualise today. Yet all at once, the revolutions presented the dilemma described above. To this problem there were only two possible solutions.

The first lay in the economic realm: the abolition of slavery and the emancipation of slaves. The second lay on the ideological plane: the declaration that freedom, equality and brotherhood were for full humans only. All lesser approximations, such as African slaves, were not a problem of principle because human rights could not apply to them anyway. As attacks on the institution of slavery became more and more insistent in the first part of the nineteenth century, so its apologists began to systematise and propagandise their racist ideology with even greater intensity. Thus when eventually on largely economic grounds, whose treatment space forbids here, slavery was abolished and the slaves emancipated in one territory after another, ending with Brazil in 1889, the spread and penetration of racist ideology was immense.

It was in tune with the intellectual assumptions of the time that the inferior social position of African slaves should be explained – and explained away – in terms of their inferior biological and mental status. The difference between this stereotype of Africans and the 'religious' stereotype which preceded it, is that mental capacity is regarded as a stable feature of someone's make-up. If then a person is defined as part of a group characterised by limits on the mental capacity of its members, there is no 'escape' from this definition. In the social context of slavery, the individuals such as the African-American Frederick Douglass who by extraordinary effort and luck succeeded in escaping its accumulated oppressions and barriers, could always be written off as freaks who proved the rule. The fact that the 'rule' was socially constructed *and* enforced was disguised behind the ideology that it emerged spontaneously from inate biological capacities. That natural inferiority should need such forms of enforcement as chopping off a man's foot or castrating him for attempted escape from the plantations, said nothing for the slaves' biologically spontaneous inferiority. But then not only the affluence but the whole way of life and world view of the planter class was at stake, along with the prosperity of important sections of European and North American ruling classes who were not directly slave-owners (ship-owners and textile manufacturers for instance).

So from the material basis of slave-plantation production, what might be called the second version of racist ideology was born and later elaborated: the assumption of genetic inferiority of blacks. It was further buttressed in areas of strong protestant belief by arguments that 'god' was the creator of differently endowed 'races', and so distinctly approved of slavery. Although slavery itself was abolished, the beliefs lived on, in part at least to 'explain' the continued miserable position of blacks as sharecroppers and poor peasants and urban marginals in the Americas after their emancipation.

By now however, a new form of European domination of what was later called the Third World had begun to gain ground (literally). In economic terms the most significant single instance was the colonial annexation of India by the British in 1857. The most significant in terms of landmass was the movement of European Russians east and south, so rendering Russia today a primarily non-European country. The process grew apace, with the 'scramble for Africa' which completely divided up that continent between the leading imperialist powers in the 1880s. Britain, France, Portugal, Germany, Italy and Spain between them laid claim to every part of Africa by 1900. The United States expanded its frontiers to the Pacific and south in a series of bloody battles with Indians and Mexicana, and later annexed Hawaii, the Philippines and Puerto Rico. Most of these annexations were fiercely resisted, but eventually were enforced by superior military technology.

Not every territory (e.g. Latin America) had a colonial government installed. However, these formal and informal empires were unparalled sources of cheap raw materials for the development of industrial production. They also operated as a protected market in which to sell a variety of manufactured products. At their peak they took on the key significance of providing investment outlets for surplus capital. Their benefits could be measured in terms beyond the direct income to the ruling classes of imperialist powers. As a result of the expansion in their own overall wealth, it enabled higher wages to be paid to the disruptive and potentially revolutionary industrial working classes. It provided instant promotion for an army of otherwise insignificant individuals from the petit bourgeoisie, who went out as colonial civil servants or as members of the armed forces. And it provided an instrument whereby the man-in-the-mass could derive some significance and potency for his existence. To be part of an imperialist power was to be someone on the world stage. Of course this ideology might and did clash with other preoccupations such as housing or job security, but it was nonetheless part of the ideological impact of imperialism which clearly assisted the bourgeois class in solving its problems of successful rule.

European attitudes toward colonised peoples varied a little from time to time and place to place, but the underlying ideology was constant: all colonised peoples were inferior, from Maoris to Burmese to Arabs to Zulus. The sharpest stimulus to this ideology always turned out to be an attempt at organised insurrection, most notably the Indian 'Mutiny' of 1857, the Jamaican revolt of 1865 and the Chinese 'Boxer' rebellion of 1899. The towering rages that these rebellions always induced in the British ruling class were because of their direct affront to what might be labelled the third version of racist ideology, most often termed 'social darwinism'.

This ideology relied upon a supposed parallel between animal evolution and national development. Strong intelligent animals and strong intelligent nations survive; weak and stupid ones don't. Colonisation is therefore valid because it recognises the inherent weakness of the colonised peoples, yet instead of extinguishing them, stretches out the hand of 'civilisation' to them, thus offering them a future on the planet. That this hand should be spurned and even bitten could only be the response of the ungrateful and inferior, underlining once and for all their complete inability to recognise the beneficence of imperialist exploitation and plunder.

This third version of racist ideology was perfectly able to co-exist with the 'biological' version, and indeed both can be found alive and thriving in the latter third of the twentieth century, from the crudest fascist poster to the elaborated pseudo-scientific treatise on socio-biology. Nonetheless, it is clear that 'social darwinism' was the dominant racist ideology of the colonial period, answering the need to justify unprecedented economic rapacity on a world scale. It also interlocked with the continuing debate inside bourgeois classes throughout the nineteenth century, as to how far the working classes could be 'included' inside the pale of full humanity. The gradual extension of the franchise, the development of welfare state provisions, the growth of universal

55

education, the 'respectable poor' vs the 'dangerous classes' were all common features of this bitterly contested debate. The existence of colonised masses over the face of the earth at once demanded and to some extent secured the political adherence of the working masses in the metropolitan countries, which meant a further push to the workers' inclusion within the pale of civilisation. But their turbulence and the turbulence of the colonised were also seen, especially at certain points of insurgency, as defining them all in a very similar fashion. 'Social darwinism' could then be used not only to illuminate hierarchies of nations but also hierarchies of classes inside nations. This dual domestic and foreign relevance helps to explain its currency in British ruling-class thought of the period.

The three versions of racist ideology surveyed utilised in turn religious concepts, biological concepts and evolutionary concepts to convey their basic message, the inferiority of non-whites.

Today we are witnessing new versions of racist ideology, essentially geared to explaining – and explaining away – the concentration of black and migrant workers in the most dispossessed position in the national working class. Capitalist forming remorselessly squeezes out sections of the peasantry; capitalist industry employs most of them in urban centres. In this way, the movement of southern Italians north; of Irish, Italians, Poles, Greeks, Japanese, Blacks, Mexicans to northern US cities; of Yugoslavs, Turks, Greeks, South Koreans, to postwar West Germany; of Algerians, Senegalese, Portuguese, West Indians, to postwar France; and the wave of labour migration to postwar Britain; all are part and parcel of the same processes of capital accumulation which erode rural life, enlarge cities and towns, and leap across frontiers.

However, when black or brown workers come to Britain, they arrive unknown, but not as strangers. Racist definitions are normal in British culture, and allow many whites to think they know what blacks are like without needing to know one. These definitions are in turn the outgrowths of the material social relations between Europeans and the non-European world up to the very present.

The era of metropolitan labour migrants: Britain as a case-study

Employment

In Britain the total black population by 1980 was in the region of 1½ to 2 million. The type of labour-power attracted in has been to fill those gaps in the existing workforce created by relatively full employment and the consequent exodus from unpopular jobs.

In Britain this has meant the concentration of adult migrant workers in the following branches of industry: transport, textiles, foundry-work, construction, the lower grades of hospital work, hospital and office cleaning. Their occupational level has always been unskilled or semi-skilled, with the exception of medical staff. Their recruitment has sometimes been direct, with employers canvassing in Asian workers' home areas, London Transport maintaining a permanent recruiting office in Barbados, and the Ministry of Health (under Enoch Powell) recruiting overseas medical staff. At other times it has been by the traditional method of having a word with the foreman and then writing to family or friends to let them know of a specific job vacancy. Up until 1962, when the first Act to restrict immigration was passed, this pattern of labour recruitment followed the then minor upswings and downturns in economic growth.

As well as their direct function of producing surplus-value, or of reproducing the conditions for its production (medicine, transport), migrant workers have had two other key functions in the sphere of production. The first is that migrant labour is cheaper than the cost of home labour. Migrant workers therefore help to keep down labour-costs in the occupations in which they are concentrated. The second is that migrant workers tended to form what Marx defined as 'the reserve army of labour', a section of the labour-force subjected most directly to the brunt of recessions, and yet whose existance on the margins of employment assists in keeping down wage levels generally, on the principle that there is always someone else to do your job for you. (In the sphere of consumption, the age structure of the black population has injected a once-for-all boost to welfare budgets via taxation, for not till there is a large number of pension-age blacks will they really begin to redeem their contributions.)

However, there have been other political and ideological effects over and above the economic ones. For instance, high levels of unemployment among black workers could always have their political sting drawn on the ground that blacks did not matter, while at the same time they could be accused of refusing work and living off other workes' taxes. Also the fact that a decreasing number of the worst jobs were being done by white English people, meant that there spread a general feeling of social promotion. Combined with relatively greater affluence than many of their parents had known, this form of elevation allowed a greater degree of tolerance of the existing social order during the fifties and sixties.

Entry to other forms of work is always difficult for any individuals in unskilled or semi-skilled jobs. However, neither personnel officers, supervisors nor shop stewards could normally be relied on to help black workers through this transition by recommending them for training or English language courses. The result was that adult black migrants' job status was more or less frozen by this important pattern of discrimination, which in turn froze them into a position of higher-than-average economic insecurity and lower-than-average earnings precisely because of the type of jobs they were in. They were also often the losers in any competition for overtime. Grievances they had with management were less likely to be taken up by shop stewards than if they had been white workers; indeed in quite a large number of firms white shop stewards would be the first to liaise with management to try either to exclude black workers entirely, or to concentrate them in the least desirable sectors of the work-process. In a number of strikes, district officials of the union totally refused to be involved, sometimes going so far as to express in public their racist reasons.

Representation of black people in professional or managerial posts was (and is) tiny. At this level job discrimination is at its most powerful, because it can no longer be hidden behind excuses about lack of qualification.

The only three changes since the early sixties have been the following. First, through the expansion of government employment, a number of new minor posts have been opened up, of which some have been taken by blacks. Second, some British citizens of Asian descent from East Africa have set up as small capitalists in enterprises such as petrol stations, cinemas, and small shops. Third, routine office work, normally performed by female labour, has been a source of some employment to second-generation black women.

However, these patterns of employment have not stood still in one most important respect: unemployment. At this point we encounter the second generation of the black minority, of whom it was said (often by their own parents as well as others) that they would start on an equal footing with their white peers. There are several reasons why this idealistic hope was unfulfilled, but the growth of unemployment demands prior treatment. Unemployment is particularly high among young black males. The fact that many do not register for unemployment benefits means that official statistics seriously understate the numbers involved. In one inner London borough in 1976, eighty per cent of over 200 unemployed young blacks were not registered as unemployed.

This increase in unemployment partly reflects international recession, partly the growing problem of 'structural unemployment' – the permanent shrinkage in jobs which has been a feature of major capitalist economies for well over a decade now.

Recognising the results of these processes is fundamental to understanding the situation of the black minority in capitalist Britain in the 1970s and 1980s. It means that one generation was drawn in as a crucial condition of continued capitalist development in the 1950s and 1960s, but their children are faced with the prospect of suffering from structural unemployment as well as from Britain's overall stagnation. Their concentration in unskilled and semi-skilled jobs, and the various racist practices in work, mean there is no abvious escape from this situation.

As an attempt to defuse political protest over unemployment, the state set up the Manpower Services Commission in 1974, which in turn set in hand the retraining of labour through the Training Services Agency and its occupational selection courses (OSCs). In abstract terms these agencies appeared to be set fair to 'do something' about unemployment, and therefore to offer an unprecedented chance to the young black unemployed, amongst others, to learn a skill and so get a secure job. The experience of the TSA in operation however indicates the folly of hoping for such miracles from 'new' policies when those policies are administered by the 'old' personnel, in this case from the Department of Employment labour exchanges (brightly retitled Job Centres). There have for instance been a number of reports of young blacks being provoked to break the regulations only to be subsequently refused the right to continue their training because – they have broken the regulations! Bureaucratic brush-offs and run-arounds from section to section were other instances of the superficial nature of this state exercise, particularly as regards young blacks.

To summarise: one generation of black labour was pulled in for highly specific economic purposes, but their children and grand-children are growing up in a situation where those purposes are vanishing. As well as the decrease in jobs, they face racist employment practices which strongly favour white job-seekers. Young black women are a little better placed than men. The key additional factor in the second-generation employment picture is the school system, which we will now look at.

Education

Education has a particularly significant role in modern capitalism. On the one hand it prepares the incoming personnel of the ruling class and petit bourgeoisie for their tasks in relation to the economy or the state, and guarantees their ideology of rule. On the other hand it serves to reinforce in the minds of the great majority of working-class children the view that they are specially fitted for proletarian work, whether 'manual' or 'routine clerical', precisely because school was not a sphere in which they succeeded. In many senses therefore, capitalist school education is much

60

closer to the function of defining the appropriateness of people to enter particular categories of employment than it is to actually training people for these categories. Even university and polytechnic education is often quite unspecific, with courses in quantity surveying or irrigation engineering being the exception rather than the rule.

Given this, it is all the easier to see how school and further education have finally sealed the fate of such a large proportion of second and third generation blacks. According to educational ideology they could have used school to advance beyond the Lazarus-stratum of the working class, as Marx once called it, occupied by their parents. They certainly received parental encouragement to do so. Against this was the growing realisation that the job market was very restricted so far as they were concerned, and their treatment in school.

Young blacks' recognition that the labour market was restricted by limited openings in any but unskilled jobs, and by pervasive racial discrimination, was important in forming their attitude towards schooling. It might have been a similar attitude even if all schools were staffed by sympathetic anti-racialists. The fact that such individuals were normally in a minority on school staffs, helped to crystallise many young blacks' hostile attitudes to 'education'. This response was not all that different from white working-class children, who quite realistically see that school has nothing to offer them for their later lives, with the result that clashes on discipline figure largest in their school lives. In the case of black schoolchildren there were extra reasons for this attitude. African and Caribbean history and culture were rarely taught. History and geography textbooks often contained racist material, but were maintained in use year after year. Asian religion or arranged marriages were frequently treated with incomprehension or cultural arrogance. Asian children in some areas were transported by bus an hour's journey from their home in order to promote 'ethnic balance' (often with the effect of exposing them to playground isolation and bullying). In particular, the language structure and codes of West Indian children were not officially

61

recognised as causing a number of them severe difficulties in adjusting to the official classroom language code. The individual racist attitudes of school teachers and meals supervisors should not be omitted in any understanding of the school as a hostile environment for black children. Finally, all these aspects of school organisation were embedded in the frequently disastrous setting of inner-city working-class schools, with overcrowded classrooms, low morale, high teacher turnover and running disorder. Intellectual success in this situation measured many times the achievement of intellectual success in fee-paying schools.

Lastly, on the structure of the schools, there is a dimension of the interaction between secondary school organisation and careers advice which is important. By and large, the state relies principally on parents as sources of job advice for the new generation of workers. If however, as in the case of black migrant workers, the range of jobs performed by parents and friends is rather narrow, so will be the range of job information. This throws the children into heavier dependence on the provision of information through the school staff or the 'careers advisory service'. This advice is universally recognised to be very weak in quantity and quality. There has been for instance a marked failure to explain the apprenticeship system to many black pupils, and instead to recommend they get a couple of CSE certificates which then debar them (by age) from an apprenticeship. The racism among craft union district secretaries in their selection of apprentices does not excuse this failure in the schools.

The only other avenue to redeem past failures – personal failures, not school failures, according to educational ideology – is further education, i.e. the Colleges of Further Education and Technical Colleges. Their normal policy has been that interested individuals should come to them through their open front gates. This has meant that their students have generally been white. Brixton College of Further Education, in one of the main London centres of West Indian settlement is an apparent exception. From the early 1970s it made determined efforts to recruit black·students, consciously dropping the usual 'We're here if they want us' posture. Yet its

Principal was unequivocal in explaining in a press interview in the London *Evening Standard* in 1976 that his aim in this policy switch had been to act as the leading agent in the 'pacification' (his term) of a turbulent area.

This example serves to underline the rationale of this sector's role in the education of the black minority. It is not a role which is geared to redressing the truly disastrous educational experience of many young blacks, but at its most 'progressive' to generating a larger black administrative class than might otherwise have been the case (either in Britain or overseas).

Now that the basic contours of British 'educational' provision have been outlined, it is possible to pick up once more the question of the most recent versions of racist ideology, IQ and 'cultural deprivation'. The most recent versions are directly related to the position of labour migrant minorities in the cities of metropolitan countries, and utilise spurious social scientific categories to convey their message. They are both directly related to the question of educational failure, for both versions accept that such failure is an intellectual failure which disqualifies individuals from any but unskilled work. What each version seeks to explain are the reasons for the very high *school failure rates* among urban black minorities. Each version does so by pinning responsibility for failure – brutally or sorrowfully – on the blacks themselves.

The brutal version is that blacks are genetically endowed with inferior intelligence, as shown by their characteristically low IQ scores. The whole concept of Intelligence Quotient has recently come under intense fire, both for its evidence and logical structure, and because of the political context (black urban migration in the US, Nazi anti-semitism) in which it was encouraged. There is only space here to present the conclusions of this scrutiny.

The concept's logical structure and statistical reasoning are badly flawed. Some of the evidence produced by the British scientist Burt, a key figure in its development, has been proved to have been sucked by him from thin air. Historically, it was developed by scientists politically committed to a eugenic policy, namely selective human breeding to promote the highest species.

63

Such scientists were active in trumpeting the superiority of whites and Aryans, the inferiority of blacks and Jews. Its immense influence is otherwise attributable to the growth of mass secondary schooling, and the consequent need to sort children out into categories for their future position on the labour market. It has become institutionalised in the school system of practically every advanced capitalist state.

The recent factor in the reassertion of geneticist racism in the form of IQ is the resurgence of black rebellion in US cities, and their resonance in Britain's black communities. Jenson in the USA and Eysenck in Britain have had massive publicity for their writings, in which they argue that black intelligence is low. The political implication is, why are blacks protesting when their oppressed position is their own fault for being dim? Stopping the process, the IQ ideology implies, cannot be achieved by educational reforms and greater sensitivity of black aspirations, because they are trapped by their weak intelligence. The only logical alternative to 'pacification' by education programmes is 'pacification' by more direct repression. It is not an alternative that Eysenck or Jenson discuss, perhaps feeling that in terms of academic specialisation it is the proper role of the police and the armed forces. It is however the logical consequence of their argument.

The sorrowful version of modern racist ideology is the thesis of 'cultural deprivation'. At first sight this isn't racist at all – rather a compassionate liberal attempt to overcome the disadvantages experienced by certain sections of society. Briefly, it proposes that the low success of black minorities and others is due only to their unfamiliarity with the mainstream culture of the society. They therefore enter school at a disadvantage, which can be compensated for so that they can succeed. Sometimes there is particular stress on language deprivation as a critical feature of cultural deprivation (meaning inadequate fluency in one's ability to speak).

This version varies from the IQ version in that it sees judicious educational reform as the solution. The problem of black failure is not insoluble, as it is in the IQ ideology. It is nonetheless a problem residing in black children which requires a generous, imaginative and public-spirited response from educators. It is not a problem of the capitalist labour market, of capitalist education, or of the racist practices enshrined in both. The ideology therefore diverts the focus of attention from the class and racist character of the society, however softly and sorrowfully, and redirects it on to the (redeemable) inadequacies of black minorities. Why mainstream culture is so obviously the home of wisdom, why official linguistic codes should be imposed in schools, why schools should serve to reproduce the capitalist division of labour, how this operation moulds their organisation and practice: all these questions are conveniently absent from this ideological diagnosis of black minority disadvantage.

The relevance of these two modern versions of racist ideology to urban labour migrant minorities in metropolitan countries should now be clear. Both versions explain, and explain away, the minorities' especially oppressed position and their particular relationship to capitalist production (as outlined earlier in this chapter), by reference to their educational/intellectual handicap. *So long as existing educational provision is defined as the acceptable route to sure success, they must adapt to it or lose.* The IQ ideology defines them as bound to lose; the cultural deprivation ideology as having to adapt. Either way the capitalist social order and its racist character is excused.

By now, it must also be clearer why such a high proportion of West Indian children are relegated to schools and classes for the educationally subnormal (ESN) and severely subnormal (SSN). They are placed there on the basis of IQ tests in the first place, but also to some extent on teachers' reports that they are uncontrollable, or listless or inarticulate. Once there, the chances are remote indeed of being reclassified as educationally 'normal'. This educational classification of black children is therefore made possible by the IQ test machinery, co-ordinates with their parents' concentration in the Lazarus-stratum of the working class, and ensures they will take up their parents' places in the course of time.

This represents the normal co-ordination between the labour market and education, overlaid by a racist refusal by educational administrators to meet the several specific needs of black children in racist Britain. The ESN dimension presents this co-ordination with the greatest force and clarity: the fate will be similar or identical of large numbers of blacks whose experience of 'education' has been very nearly as disastrous, for instance those concentrated in the remedial streams of secondary schools.

The state authorities and the black minority

The relation of black immigration to Britain's economy has been outlined, as has its meshing with the state's educational provision. There are four other major aspects of the state's involvement with black workers and their families to which we shall now turn: first, the development and enforcement of racist immigration laws; second, the housing policies of the state at central and local levels; third, the role of the police, in conjunction with the courts; fourth, the functions of bodies such as the old Race Relations Board and community relations councils, now under the single administrative heading of the Commission for Racial Equality.

Immigration laws. Up until 1962 there was no quota imposed upon immigrants from any source, although formally the possession of a 'Commonwealth' passport ensured the right of entry to its owner, whereas an 'alien' had no such right. It was of course possible to exclude or deport individuals considered undesirable by the state authorities. In that year, as a result of successful lobbying headed by a group of West Midlands Conservative MP's, the Conservative government introduced the Commonwealth Immigrants Act which would enable the state to divide migrants from 'Commonwealth' territories into three categories, those with skills in high demand, those with a job waiting for them, and those with neither (C category). In retrospect it is a telling instance of the acute dangers of yielding to mild racism; for although it did not affect white Irish migrants, its provisions appeared to cover

66

Australians and Canadians. So although it had been a racist lobby which had successfully pressured an Act into existence, many people conveniently dismissed this from their minds. Also, the fact that white 'Commonwealth' immigrants were in practice given more favourable treatment by immigration officials, was generally overlooked.

At the time, the Labour opposition vowed to repeal the Act upon coming to power. In 1964, they found themselves with a majority of four, and without the man expected to be made Foreign Secretary, who had been due to be elected for the normally safe Labour seat of Smethwick in the West Midlands. Patrick Gordon Walker, the MP concerned, lost his seat in a pro-Tory swing against the national tide to a candidate who for nearly two years had assiduously banged the racist drum in the area, with the assistance of the local press. (A leaflet the day before polling stated: 'If you want a nigger for your neighbour, vote Labour.') Afterwards, Walker failed to get elected as replacement MP for another safe Labour seat, Leyton in east London.

The Labour government's response in August 1965 was to utilise the Commonwealth Immigrants Act to cut off C category entry completely, and to reduce intake to 8,500 working males from the 'Commonwealth' in any one year, together with their dependants and the dependants of those already arrived. From then until 1971 the actual number of such working males entering was in the range of 5,000–6,000 annually. This was the first confirmation by the Labour government of Conservative policy on black immigration. More was to follow. Repeal was dead.

The next episode in what was to be a series of dramas about 'immigration' – the word had now come to mean 'black' – was set in motion by the decision of the Kenyan government to restrict a number of civil service posts and economic activities to its nationals. This meant the exclusion of many Asian non-citizens, who had been issued with British passports at the time of independence. The reaction of the great majority of Asian non-citizens in Kenya was to utilise their British passports in order to start a new life in the only country to which they had the right of

67

entry. Their arrival began to attract hostile comment from two MP's, Duncan Sandys and Enoch Powell, who stumped the country urging people to oppose this. (Sandys had been the Minister of the Colonies who had issued the passports in the first place.) The Labour government was thrown into a panic; and in one week in March 1968 they rushed an emergency Commonwealth Immigration Act through parliament which cancelled the automatic citizenship rights of Asians with British passports. Instead, 1,500 heads of families were to be allowed in with their immediate dependants in any year. A hypocritical fiction was maintained that colour was not at issue, since admission was on the basis of having a grandparent born in Britain. For the first time since the abolition of slavery in Britain in the eighteenth century, there was a formal legal ratification of racism in Britain, and this from the main party with a working-class following, self-defined as 'socialist'.

In 1969, ironically during the Commons committee stage of the Immigration Appeals Bill, introduced reluctantly to give a semblance of fairness to immigration procedures, James Callaghan (then Home Secretary) announced that from then on entry permits must be obtained in the country of origin. This permit was over and above certificates and documents proving age, family relationship, employment prospects, and on having cleared the 1965 and 1968 quota-systems. This simple fiat meant that especially in south Asia, many individuals would have to travel hundreds of miles to the notoriously unsympathetic British High Commission offices. During the run-up to the 1970 election the numbers of black entrants dropped magically . . .

There were still more 'immigration' dramas to come however. In 1971 the Conservative government introduced a new Immigration Act, which accomplished two main purposes. First, it shifted British immigration law towards a west European model, with the rights of new immigrant workers severely curtailed. Immigrant workers from outside the EEC were given annual work permits tied to specific jobs. If sacked they could lose their right to stay as well, so their labour discipline would be higher than usual. Changes of address had to be notified to the local police station.

68

They had no right to citizenship after five years' continuous stay, as blacks from the former Empire had had previously. The police were now in a position where they had an excuse for 'supposing' that any black person might be a post-1971 entrant, and so could officially question and harass black people on this score. The police could break into any house without a warrant if they had 'reasonable grounds' for suspecting it contained illegal immigrants. The fact the Home Office controlled admission-quotas meant parliament would rarely debate them, and that the state could avoid the build-up of black concentration by admitting Filipinos, Turks and other nationalities in tiny packets.

The Act also codified many of the most hostile practices of immigration officials which had grown up with Home Office encouragement over the previous decade. Thus, many black people seeking to enter Britain legally have been sent back to their country of origin; have been shuttled round the world's airlines for weeks at a time; have been subjected to virginity tests, and anal probes for 'suspected' drugs; have been insulted and shouted at; have been detained in near-prison conditions under the watchful hostility of Securicor guards; and have had their children separated from them and cross-questioned on their own on numerous matters of detail in order to create some discrepancy between their and their parents' accounts. Although immigration officials are overwhelmingly racists, their practice is a faithful enactment of Home Office policy, not a contradiction of it.

In the years since 1971, storms like those over the Kenyan Asians blew up again, first over Ugandan Asians in 1972 and then over Malawian Asians in 1976. The reactions of both Conservative and Labour governments followed the same tired pattern of pretending in the international context that they were doing their duty by refugees with British passports, yet being hostile toward them through their immigration officials, and covertly endorsing the racist responses forthcoming from the media and sections of public opinion. By 1976 the Labour government was at work on a revision of the 1948 British Nationality Act, in order to entrench further the legal differences between black and white.

This long series of state interventions in black immigration has a critical importance, for both major parties were seen by the public to be united in their opposition to blacks. The same twisted rationale was constantly trotted out, that more blacks meant more racial hostility! There is a long continuity in British state policy in this respect, for precisely the same excuse was offered to justify refusing the admission of more than a trickle of Jewish refugees from Nazi Germany and Austria before the war. The 'argument' assumes racism is created by the presence of its object, Jews, blacks, or whoever. The 'solution' is to minimise the object, hence immigration control. Apart from its neglect of the historical roots of racism in British culture, the fatal flaw in this argument is that all the evidence demonstrates that these concessions by governments fuel the racist flames. Mild racist ideology and practice always harden once they are underwritten by political authority. The basic ideological framework of public debate about the black presence thus became the *nature* of the threat posed by black immigration.

In addition, immigration officials' practice has communicated to blacks from the moment of their entry to Britain that they are unwelcome. In turn, the officials and the Home Office have relied on this information becoming widely circulated in the Caribbean, Africa and south Asia.

State housing policies. Many local authorities, Labour and Conservative, have discriminated in various ways against blacks. Sometimes they have established lengthy residence rules as a condition for being placed on the housing list. In a number of boroughs, blacks have largely been rehoused in old terraces minimally renovated by the council, or in dilapidated prewar housing estates.

The decisions of housing visitors, many untrained and junior, have been instrumental in this type of allocation. Sometimes these policies represented the Labour Party machine acting in response to racist working-class feeling, to provide its major plums to its traditional clientele. Housing policy at higher levels of the state, for instance the Department of the Environment and the

70

Greater London Council, has been obsessed with trying to disperse blacks from central areas in which they were concentrated, for instance from Ladbroke Grove out to Harlesden in London. The 'gentrification' process in many inner-city areas has assisted this policy through the dispossession of tenants in multi-occupied Victorian terraces. The GLC was very interested in research done at the Centre for Environmental Studies in the late 1960s on the possibilities for encouraging black workers to move to the new towns. The political foresight in attempting to avoid centres of black solidarity in the inner city corresponded to Enoch Powell's repeated predictions of the wrath to come should such centres develop.

However, the results of local council housing policy were very often seen differently by racist white workers. If for instance a black family was rehoused under a slum clearance order, the chances are very high that their being allotted a council flat would be bitterly contrasted by white workers (who heard about it from neighbours) with the length of time they and other white families had been on the waiting list. There was rarely any attempt to find out why the black family had been rehoused, and even when it was known, the response would often be that the black family had only moved in to the slum because they somehow knew it was going to be a quick way to be rehoused. (It goes without saying that no council has ever implemented a pro-black housing policy . . .)

So blacks have got the worst of both worlds – bad housing *and* white working-class hostility. Although from 1968 racial discrimination in housing became unlawful under the Race Relations Act, the state has never effectively acted to improve housing conditions for blacks. This is something largely achieved by blacks themselves through owner-occupation, often at exorbitant mortgage rates.

The police and the courts. The police have become notorious among blacks for systemically harassing and persecuting them. The reasons are various, but include the possibility of easy convictions on trivial charges such as suspicious behaviour ('sus') or 'obstruction' or 'insulting words' or 'assault on the police'

71

(which in its legal definition need only mean touching their sleeve). The police are also in a position of being differentiated from the rest of the white population in being entitled to arrest and charge people, so that the racist hostility existing in Britain is able to find superficially legitimate action in their actions. Some incidents have been written up; most are only known to the police and to blacks.

Essential to the scope the police are given is the overwhelming support they receive from court magistrates and judges. It is rare indeed for their testimony to be challenged by the bench, but not uncommon for weak evidence to be winkled at from that quarter. These observations are easily come by in the courtroom, especially in cases with which the observer is familiar. Of course, once a black person gets some 'form' it becomes all the harder to get a job. Stamford House remand centre in west London is one index of this trend. It is a clearing house for convicted male juveniles awaiting sentence. In 1964, when the writer was a constant visitor, few black faces were to be seen. By the end of the seventies the majority of the inmates were black.

By 1976, the friction between blacks and the police had become so great that the head of the Metropolitan Police community relations division felt obliged to explain the situation. He did so in a report to the House of Commons Select Committee on Immigration and Race Relations, in terms of a high assault-rate by young blacks ('mugging'), as reported by white victims, and the 'urban stress' experienced by young blacks. Without denying the existence of crime by blacks, the shift away from police responsibility for the exceptionally high arrest-rate is visible and predictable. The friction also led to a determined effort to recruit some blacks into the police, an effort which has met with almost total failure. If British police history is anything to go by, it is probable that the purpose behind this recruitment was not simply cosmetic, to prove the police were not racists, but went beyond this and was to enable more successful penetration of black political groupings. (The opposition to black recruitment inside the police came from its slower and dimmer elements.)

72

Parallels with the relationship between the police and similar class and 'racial' groups in other advanced capitalist countries, suggest that this relationship cannot be explained away as a purely British quirk. The most likely explanation is the need to maintain particular fear of state power among the most impoverished and disadvantaged sections of the working class, whether or not they are distinguished by 'racial' or ethnic origin. The additional dimension of 'race' may be an added spur, as perhaps may be certain effects of police roles on police personalities. The principal factor to account for however remains the universality of this behaviour and the higher state authorities' tolerance of it. It is clear in several advanced capitalist countries that rebelliousness is presently at its most visible in those sections of the working class which are facing structural unemployment. It is a rebelliousness which in principle raises profound questions about the nature of capitalist society, though these questions may not be seen as such by the groups concerned. For that reason, the state will nowhere tolerate their protest.

'Soft' state policy. The fourth facet of state policy has been its 'soft' side, especially the three Race Relations Acts (1965, 1968, 1976), and the establishment first of the Race Relations Board, then of the Community Relations Commission, and subsequently their merging into the Commission for Racial Equality. These various organisations embodied the second part of the ideology that the solution to 'racial' conflict lay in strict limits on black entry combined with internal policies for 'racial' integration. What such integration meant was often left unspecified, though perhaps the leading spokesman for this position, Roy Jenkins, defined it as 'equal opportunity, accompanied by cultural diversity, in an atmosphere of mutual tolerance'.

In practice, this pluralist nirvana came nowhere near to fruition. The Race Relations Acts operated in a purely piecemeal fashion, so that although each revision of the law covered more areas, the legislation could only ever produce the most gradual and reversible shifts in racist practice. In addition to this, perhaps the nearest the law ever approached to having 'teeth' was in the threat

73

of publicity, since its designers had consciously rejected the standard enforcement procedures used in US anti-discrimination legislation. The Community Relations Councils in urban boroughs were the face of the Community Relations Commission seen most often by the public (which is not to say often). Here the basic drive from the CRC itself was to establish the councils as a normal feature of the local Town Hall apparatus, presumably on the assumption they would then approximate to official status in relevant decision-making. To this end they sat heavily on any community relations officer, such as Ann Dummett in Oxford or Chris Mullard in Newcastle, who tried to put justice for the black minority at the head of their programmes, and so inevitably came into conflict with the statutory authorities (thus endangering the Commission's policy). The councils' role was clear: it was to act as buffers, not as local political prods or community organisers. The very concept of 'community relations' suffers from an essential vacuity, in that the nature of 'community' is left utterly vague.

The conspicuous irony of this situation was that these toothless entities were defined by the media, especially by the antagonists of any justice for the black minority, as fierce watchdogs for black rights. Many white workers, accepting this view through having no direct experience of these bodies in action, felt that black workers were being given an edge over themselves. Who could they complain to if they were sacked or refused training? – certainly not the Race Relations Board! The result was blacks were given no extra help of any solid kind, while incurring hostility from fellow-workers because they were thought to be unfairly favoured. It was yet again the worst of both worlds.

Responses and resistances

Economism and racism. The versions of racism that were surveyed earlier all emanated directly from the policies and practices of ruling classes, as can be argued also for the IQ and cultural deprivation ideologies which 'cover' the inability of capitalist state policies to eradicate racism or structural un-

74

employment. They have undoubtedly trickled down to other classes, as in a standard British working-class explanation of underdevelopment, which is the national backwardness and ignorance of Indians or Africans – social darwinism without the civilising mission!

However, the position of the (white) working class stimulates yet another version of racist ideology; or perhaps more exactly, provides a material basis for racist hostility which then uses existing ideological frameworks derived from other classes' ideologies. The racism peculiar to the working class can be seen historically in Britain vis-a-vis Irish migrant labour in the nineteenth and twentieth centuries, to Jewish migrant labour in the 1900s, to Welsh migrant labour in the 1930s, to Polish migrant labour in the late 1940s, and most recently to black migrant labour. It is born out of the scarcity of basic resources which the working class has always experienced. There is competition for housing, jobs, decent schooling, transport at rush-hours, and a number of medical and social services, the reason being that there are simply not enough of these basic resources provided in overcrowded working-class urban areas. At any one time the competition for one of these resources, such as housing, may be to the fore; at a time of high unemployment, it will be the competition for jobs that comes first of all. The uneven development characteristic of capitalism concentrates jobs and population in certain areas, and drains others (such as the north-east or north-west of Britain): it is in the main urban centres that this competition will always be at its height.

Now it is very often the case that the more conscious workers are of *economic* class struggle, while limiting their definition of class struggle to that arena (economism), the more likely they are to express hostility toward their working-class competitors than against the capitalist class or capitalist state policies. Economistic opposition to capitalism normally defines capitalism as permanent, so that the *only* element in the situation which is subject to change is the quantity of competition. The argument is that the capitalist class (a) will never go away or be pushed out, and (b) will only

75

hand out so much in response to working-class demands. If the working class is suddenly expanded by immigration, there is less for everyone. The logics of economism, nationalism and racism all coincide.

It has been this ideology which has most characterised British working-class racism. Resentment of the Race Relations Acts and fury at apparent favouritism in council house allocations are clear illustrations in point. Anxiety about competition for jobs, which has confused numerous sociologists and commentators with its surface irrationality during the high employment periods of the fifties and sixties, reflected the bitter experience of the working class that full employment is always precarious under capitalism. The seventies proved the working class correct. Anxiety about foreign workers commitment to shopfloor solidarity was another factor to be taken into account.

Thus the overall effect within the working class is twofold. Black workers see little point in solidarity with white workers, who are prepared to connive with employers at their being refused jobs, at their low pay, at their worse conditions, at their blocked promotion, at their easy redundancy, and who are prepared to use the union to bolster up this state of affairs. At the same time as white workers fear black competition, they can be encouraged to see themselves as a step nearer respectability, a grade further identified with the top, with the people who matter.

This pattern can be seen in many cases. At its most violent, it can be seen in so-called 'race riots', such as the ones which took place in Harlem in 1900, in East St Louis in 1917, in Chicago in 1919, in Liverpool in 1919, and in South Shields in 1930.

Racism exists and operates independently of the workplace, but its presence there is an extra bonus for capital. Which, naturally, capital seeks to use to the strategic maximum. Edward Greer cites one executive of the US Steel Corporation, as declaring back in the 1920s: 'It isn't good to have all of one nationality; they will gang up on you . . . We have Negroes and Mexicans in a sort of competition with each other.' What is true of two minority ethnic groups can as easily be true of a workforce composed of a majority and a minority. Racism does not offer itself as an avenue for a divide-and-rule strategy because it is artificially invented by capitalists for the purpose, but because it is often so easy to maintain at simmering temperature.

Powellism and fascism. It is not in the first instance Powell himself who has to be explained, but powellism. He is only of account because he is unusual among bourgeois politicians in commanding a strong personal following among the working class. At the same time, the close overlap between powellism and fascism of the National Front variety must be taken into account in this analysis. (It follows from this focus that Powell's various disclaimers that he is neither a racist nor fascist are of secondary interest.)

The most important observation by far is that the working-class basis of powellism and fascism in Britain is directly related to the economism-racism pair of ideologies just discussed. It is because Powell and the National Front have articulated working-class anxieties about competition for scarce resources, about the erosion of feeling that there exists a minimal degree of control of one's locality, that they have achieved their degree of working-class support. Disillusion with existing bourgeois politics and politicians has assisted in the portrayal of Powell and the National Front as embattled and courageous spokesmen against 'Them', the established and complacent politicians at national and local level.

However – and this observation really is of the highest importance – Powell and the NF were *only* able to achieve this political resonance because the necessary ideological framework had already been established by the bourgeois state in its immigration laws and policies. Powell, it must be recalled, made his first infamous 'rivers of blood' speech a month after the 1968 Commonwealth Immigration Act had been rushed through parliament. The NF, though formed in 1967, did not make any real impact till the early 1970s. The seeds had already been sown; Powell and the NF merely did the watering.

77

One other element may also be vital in this complex of forces, namely the coincidence of outbursts of racist feeling with two periods (1968 and 1976) when standards of living were being reduced by a Labour government with the advice and consent of the leadership of the trade-union movement (or most of it). On one level, public opinion polls can discover that workers agree firm action must be taken to control inflation or steady the pound. On another level, workers find it is they as usual who bear the costs of this 'firm action' When that harsh experience is okayed by all or most of their own representatives, there is no apparent scope for expressing their resentment in that direction. Yet resentment there certainly is; and in 1976, the newspapers' enormous publicity for a family of Malawian Asian refugees living temporarily in a luxury hotel for free (though at £600 a week to taxpayers) was perfectly timed to channel this resentment against the blacks. In the absence of a major mass-based workers' party with a well-expressed position against racism, this type of feeling is quite likely to flourish spontaneously even without backing and stimulation from bourgeois media.

The last point to be made about the whole complex of economism/racism/nationalism/powellism/fascism, is that contradictory states of consciousness are the rule and not the exception. Monolithic ideologies do no hold sway within the working class, or any class in an advanced capitalist society, and those elements in overall working-class ideology which are not racist represent the elements on which a socialist strategy must build.

Black responses. These have varied very considerably. It is often glibly claimed that West Indians have been vociferous and pugnacious, and Asians quiet and withdrawn. The realities are more complex, and cannot be adequately discussed here. First, there is a crucial generational difference in both minorities, with a very strong tendency among those born here to be more prepared to fight actively for their rights than their parents felt appropriate. Secondly, there are within each minority particular groups who play a leading role. Among Caribbean blacks, those of Jamaican

78

origin represent toward two-thirds of the total, which is reflected in the dominance of reggae and its associated Rastafarian ideology. In turn, rebellious elements in Rastafarianism have acted as the main, but rather loosely defined ideology among many young West Indians. Amongst Asians, two groupings predominate, the Sikh Indian Workers' Association, and petit bourgeois leaders of East African Asian groups.

One final comment is in order, namely the extent to which authentic spokespersons for the black minorities are normally unknown to the white majority. There is a tendency among journalists to select individuals who are prepared to create news by making hair-raising statements about racial and political discord, as 'their' leaders of the black minorities, the late Michael Malik (Michael X) being a leading case in point in the late sixties. Those solidly grounded in the life of the black minorities are often reluctant to discuss matters with journalists, as a result of their observations of the normal 'dip-and-run' practice of media professionals. Information about the state of feelings and organisation of black minorities therefore tends to be much more unreliable than is often thought.

Conclusions

We have traced the deep roots of white racism, the way it has interlocked at many points with capitalist exploitation and development, and its pervasive penetration of every aspect of British social structure. It is obvious that the normal liberal view of racism, that it is an uncharacteristic blot on an otherwise pleasing landscape, must be rejected. The landscape is not pleasing, and racism is everywhere in it.

At the same time we must reject a characteristic marxist misconception, that racism is marginal to class struggle. This misconception is expressed in different ways. Sometimes marxists define racism as a 'thing' injected into the working class in order to divide it. Sometimes they argue that racism cannot be the cause of anything, because to admit 'racial' groups exist in reality, is to use racist categories – only classes exist in reality. And sometimes marxists argue racism will vanish after the revolution.

Our analysis has shown the falsity of these views. Racism predated capitalism, but has developed in interaction with it. The working class is not magically insulated from this racism, and so has no need to be magically injected with it to be affected by it. Divide-and-rule strategies do not create such divisions, they use, bend and reinforce them.

Similarly, to say racism has no causal power is to assume ideology is just a set of ideas. Racism is ideology *and* practice. It is a perverse distortion of marxism to deduce from it that black people are not oppressed by whites, but only by capital. As for the notion that racism will vanish after the revolution, this assumes that socialist seizure of state power leads to instant communism. Neither the marxist classics on this subject, nor twentieth-century history, can be used to support this argument.

To grasp the struggle in Britain against capital and the state, and for the socialist transformation of social relations, it is essential to understand the nature of white racist oppression. In turn, this oppression cannot be understood if it is divorced from an analysis of capitalist development. Both are all too real and all too supportive of each other to be artificially separated in revolutionary analysis.

4. The Media and Racism

In analysing media coverage of strikes, we found workers categorised as offending the 'national interest' while they are on strike. Actions are the focus of attention. With media coverage of the black minority, the subject is the very presence and existence of black people. They are defined for the most part neither individually, nor as members of classes, but – following Britain's imperial heritage – as blacks, both nationally and internationally.

The media have been very powerful in shaping white definitions of blacks in Britain. Studies of white attitudes to blacks in different areas (of substantial black presence, of low black presence, and of no black presence) have demonstrated a uniform spread of reactions in every case. The *only* common source of images and information about blacks in every area is the mass media. Admittedly there is the historical legacy of racist beliefs, but that does not account for the common recital of objections to black people specific to their presence in Britain since the second world war.

Here we will analyse media output in the following order. We will see how far the media ask black people their views on issues which affect them (black journalists being very few and far between). We will note the most important category within which they were presented: 'immigration'. Next, we will examine some of the rare instances in which their oppression has been discussed in the media. Then, we will comment on some cases of the international presentation of black people in British media. Subsequently we will contrast press and broadcasting accounts of these issues. Racism and entertainment media will follow as the next topic. Finally, we wil observe the growing importance of crime as a category for defining the black population of Britain.

Has the white cat got your tongue?

In a study already published, I examined how far blacks were invited to speak on TV about issues directly affecting them. The issues in question were racism and immigration in Britain, the Nigerian Civil War (1967–70), Zimbabwe and South Africa. (In the last three cases, I was concerned with the voices of black nationals of these countries, not with blacks as such.) The only case in which they were more than a third of those expressing a view was Nigeria, an all-black country. Even on Nigeria, blacks were *less* than 40 per cent of the speakers. In the case of both southern African countries, they were 10 per cent or less of the voices.

This concentration on white opinion is overwhelming. Just as striking workers were rarely asked their views, so blacks – both in Britain and in Africa – are similarly avoided by the media. (And so, we shall see, are women.)

What is sometimes very noticeable is the type of black person who was allowed to spread themselves in the media. Two figures stand out. One was the late Michael Abdul Malik (Michael X – *not* to be confused in any way with Malcolm X), a self-styled Black Power leader with a particularly vicious criminal career. The other was a Manchester West Indian, Enos Beech, who claimed to have detected a loophole in electoral law which allowed him to flood Manchester City Corporation with Black Power advocates.

Both these rather sick personalities were treated with deadly earnestness by the media. Beech's absurd waffle has been stimulated by a locally well-known Mosleyite fascist acting as agent provocateur. Yet all three major TV news bulletins relayed without comment his claim to be a *colonel* in the Black Power movement, and his assertion that Manchester was just the first 'to come under the hammer'. Malik was given a 25-minute interview all to himself (in which he talked uninterrupted rubbish), as though he was a significant black spokesperson, though nearly all black people died inwardly whenever he was featured in the media. As for white workers, which of them could get on the air by talking shit?

82

If these individuals were not brought on in order to discredit Black Power, then at best they were brought on as news-commodities. Their presence highlighted the normal absence of black people, even in material about them. Let it not be said the TV arc-lights have ever set on the British Empire.

The balanced white view of black immigration

Wherever the media picture of blacks comes from, it is not from normal black people themselves. The dominant ideology used by the white media to define blacks in Britain was 'immigrants' or as the 'immigration problem'. In chapter 3, we saw how this was the principal term used in political debate, so that in this sense the news media simply adopted the word and diffused it wholesale as the framework within which to refer to the black minority.

In my study three-quarters of the TV items concerning black people, and two-thirds of the air-time, were under the heading of 'immigration' or Enoch Powell. Hartmann and Husband noted in their analysis of the British press that during 1968–69 a sixth of all 'race'-related items were about Powell. Even the schoolchildren they interviewed evinced knowledge of his name more than any other politician's. They commented that it 'seemed as though once Powell and his views become incorporated into the frame of reference within which race in Britain has come to be reported, the press found it difficult to mention the subject without bringing Powell into it.' Still in 1976 Powell was automatic news on this issue. He was given massive coverage that year when he chose – as champion of public information! – to leak a dissident Foreign Office report (the so-called Hawley report), which claimed large-scale evasion of immigration controls. Certainly in my own study of who spoke in the media he dominated the scene, with other white politicians often appearing on TV simply to react to his views on 'immigration'.

The implications of this concentration on 'immigration' and Powell can be stated as follows. The hypocritical euphemism of 'immigrant' (compare 'New Commonwealth') was given maximum currency. This helped to excuse the white public in expressing hostility to the black presence. Their status as recently arrived (and so, soon to be repatriated?) foreigners underlined their lack of right to belong, the irrelevance of their status as workers, taxpayers, or plain individuals. Even the West German euphemism, 'guest-workers', recognises that they *work*. By contrast, emphasis was absent on white racism, on discrimination in jobs, housing, education, by the police and courts.

The other dimension of this matter is that the vacuum where black voices should have been heard, was filled not only by whites, but by the most prejudiced whites. Critcher and his associates, in their study of race in the West Midlands provincial press over 1963–70, summarised the implications of this national and local pattern very well. They wrote:

> The 'structure of access' . . . operates against black experience. There is no way any black group or individual could come to have the same status, and thus press access, as Enoch Powell. Not the least consequence of this is a massive failure of provincial press to communicate any sense of what it is like to be black in the United Kingdom . . . The discussion of race is largely left to white opinion leaders, who for the most part move throughout the period 1963 to 1970 to progressively more hostile stances and policies.

Later in the seventies, something of the same pattern could be discerned in the media's openness to leaders of the explicitly fascist, extremely violent National Front. In 1977, the day after a bloody demonstration in which they were involved in Lewisham, south London, their chairperson was interviewed on TV News. He was interviewed, moreover, courteously and at some length, sitting in his English country garden and patting his dog. Later the same year another leading NF figure was interviewed at length on BBC TV, with no exposure or criticism of his political actions or beliefs. (The interview was reprinted in the anti-fascist magazine, *Searchlight*.) This media treatment was in keeping with the half a million pounds also spent that year to provide police protection for the same fascist to march by himself through the streets of Hyde, near Manchester.

These patterns of coverage and access have been in formation over many years. Although the detailed studies by Hartmann and associates, Critcher and associates, and myself, concluded for the most part at the end of 1970, the patterns they revealed are not, regrettably, a part of the past. White racist consciousness has crystallised from its relatively fluid state in the early sixties to its resilient condition at the beginning of the eighties. The media have not been alone in bringing this development about, but their part has been a significant one. They have relayed, not questioned; they have used whites in overwhelming preference to blacks to define the issues; and the whites they have used have often been those determined to expel the black minority from Britain.

White racism? Yes, it does exist

Let us now examine what happened when the news media actually chose to investigate racial discrimination. This was rare indeed. My own year-long study – analysing three-quarters of main TV output – turned up with only 43 items on discrimination in housing, employment, or education; street attacks on blacks; police–black relations; and black resistance. The information about white racism was *occasional and fragmentary*, and continues to be so, as any systematic study will show.

The second point is that discrimination as such was a fairly small part of this small slice of TV time. Most of the items concerned either the police or black resistance to them, or street attacks against individual blacks. It can be said that the white population of Britain was more or less let off the hook, then, for its entrenched racism. Instead, the more dramatic confrontations between black protestors and the forces of law and order were at the forefront of attention.

Even the items which did surface on discrimination were seriously flawed. I will dwell in a little detail on five of them to illustrate this judgment, and to show that it is not a jaundiced

85

verdict. They were the 'shock' of a Housing Minister on finding black people in appalling housing conditions; the publication of the annual reports of the Community Relations Commission and the Race Relations Board (now merged into the Commission for Racial Equality); the coverage of a black march on Caledonian Road police station in Islington, London; the character of the items on the police; and lastly, an interviewer's questions to a white man whose skin had darkened due to a kidney complaint.

By expressing *shock* at overcrowding in London housing, the then Housing Minister, Peter Walker, publicly exposed his total ignorance of housing conditions for many blacks – conditions which he could have read about in government reports while he was being driven about in his limousine. Equally noticeable was the ignorance or deference of the reporters, who none of them questioned Walker on his 'shock'. It was a small but indicative episode.

The second case concerned the publication of the CRC's Annual Report. Its then chairperson was invited to discuss it on BBC TV News. He delivered himself of the opinion that the real race problem in Britain lay with Enoch Powell and others like him, who inflamed people's prejudices. (Was his implication that at certain levels racial prejudice was acceptable?) He also annouced that attacks on Pakistanis by young whites had nothing to do with race relations, because it was only a minority of hooligans involved in it. He even asserted that the alienation of young blacks from the police was due to the tiny number of blacks who joined the force.

It constituted a dim but dangerous view of racism, to insist that it would vanish – or at least reduce to a level acceptable to the CRC chairperson – if only Powell were to hold his tongue, if only a hooligan minority were convicted, and if only more blacks joined the police. Naturally, no black person was asked to comment on these assertions, nor did the interviewer pick the chairperson up on them.

He was not faced, for instance, with the point that blacks joining the police would mostly be outcasts in the black community. The reporter said to him: 'This view of the police is

86

obviously something you'll have to tackle – how do you propose to do it?' Note the implication of the question: the police are not at fault, but the blacks have a 'view' that they are. In turn, the job of the community relations apparatus is not to expose or condemn police violence, but to 'tackle' the blacks' peculiar illusions. The reporter was integral to this comfortable view of racism on the part of the CRC.

It is worth comparing for a moment the *Mirror* and the *Telegraph* handling of this issue with the BBC's. The *Mirror*'s editorial was headed 'Colour Unconscious', and more or less echoed the report's messages. It said that only 'colour-blindness' could overcome racialism. It claimed this 'colour-blindness' was normal among young blacks and whites. Young whites' Paki-bashing was defined as non-racist because, said the *Mirror*, they attacked the defenceless without discrimination – a claim that was both untrue and irrelevant. The editorial claimed that what racial hostility there was was due to whites' fears for their jobs and living standards, but argued that the *solution* to this lay in the schools and the community relations apparatus. Our analysis in the previous chapter indicated the absurdity of this argument.

The *Mirror*'s approach was consistent with its perspective on industrial conflict. So was the *Telegraph*'s. It was commenting on the annual report of the Race Relations Board. Its editorial was headed 'Colour Obsession', and attacked both anti-discrimination law ('silly and potentially mischievous') and the report. It was infuriated that the report publicly regretted the low number of discrimination complaints it had received. The *Telegraph* said this could lead to a situation where 'some official could go round bawling to every coloured immigrant that he should examine all his failures in life to see if colour should not be the cause.' The Peter Simple column was headed 'Think Bigot!' on the same theme, and further claimed the Board was dedicated to totalitarian thought control, stopping the ordinary man from thinking what racists thoughts he wished.

The third instance is the handling of a black march on Caledonian Road police station. This followed the arrest of some young blacks at a nearby fairground. It was sparked both by the injustice of the arrests, and concern that the arrested should not be beaten up inside the station. *News at Ten* reported that the march had taken place, and the charges of obstruction, abusive words, wilful damage and assault on the police. It added that from the courtroom gallery there had been shouts of 'fascist pig' and some Black Power salutes. There was *no* explanation of why the march had started, nor was any black person asked to comment.

BBC TV News asked a moderately well-informed white journalist who lived locally to interpret it for the viewers. He presented his own view, which was that in a poor neighbourhood blacks and whites tended to vent their frustrations on each other. This did not explain the march because it said nothing about police violence against blacks. (Whether this was the journalist's omission or editorial censorship makes no difference.) Why could no black person be found who knew what was happening?

It was noticeable that the *Mirror*'s report on this march was in a completely different tone to its editorial on the CRC Annual Report. Its headlines ran:

> 'MOB RAID POLICE HQ – 11 HURT'
> 'PCs HURT IN LONDON BATTLE'
> 'SIEGE AFTER A FUNFAIR SWOOP'

When the chips were down, the *Mirror* was plain and to the point: the police must be defended whatever. The basic message was, state and racial harmony good, black protest bad.

These patterns emerge out of the strong links which exist between news media and police, links which have been strengthened since 1972 with the establishment of a more sophisticated police public relations operation. Extraordinary consequences can follow from this media–police relationship, such as a major splash story in both *Express* and *Mirror* which had large photographs showing an Asian police constable marrying a white policewoman, and both walking arm-in-arm through a police guard of honour at the church porch. The police, racially prejudiced?

Recognising these links, and the importance of the ideology

of an impartial police force, let us examine media handling of the relation between police and blacks. There were three within my sample, two of them linked to each other, and cast in the usual format of a huge studio discussion with leading experts. A leading expert in two of them was a white sociologist who had written a book on the subject. Nothing wrong with that in itself, but it underlined the old, old message: if blacks say the police beat them up, there is no reason to assume they are telling the truth. So check with an impartial white person. Only the third programme actually set two policemen in front of a small group of young blacks and asked them to discuss the issue. This was a model format, but was never followed up again.

So, the characteristic presentation of the issue was as described. Black protest was hammered; but the police public relations department bent over backwards to produce material showing how nice the police were. Like a news item showing some black sixth formers being shown around New Scotland Yard as part of a recruitment drive.

The last instance of presentation of racial oppression in Britain concerned a middle-aged man whose skin had darkened following a kidney disorder. He was invited on to a BBC TV current affairs programme, because he had commented in a newspaper that his experience had shown him British society in a completely new light. He told viewers how strangers had stopped him in the street and called him 'wog'; how in a club he had visited one member refused to play snooker with him; and how his attempts to get a job after coming out of hospital suggested to him that he was being discriminated against there too. He and his wife admitted to going out together only in their car, to avoid the stares people gave to an apparently mixed-race couple. His wife painfully confessed to her own racial prejudice and the torture she experienced through being defined as the wife of a black man. He said that he had not had the slightest idea of how much racial prejudice blacks experienced in Britain until he involuntarily came to seem one himself.

This experience had a pivotal importance which could have

been explored thoroughly in the discussion. It was worth ten books by white sociologists because it was an immediate and personal experience which could be directly communicated to shake many white people out of their smug indifference to white racism. Yet the interviewer diverted the main discussion on to the side-issue of what they thought about racial intermarriage. This smacks of controversy, so was newsworthy to a 'trained' journalist. The real significance of their experience was lost.

We have seen how even in this occasional and fragmentary recognition by the media that white racism exists, the presentation is often seriously flawed. There are exceptions, such as Thames TV's *Our People* and London Weekend's *Babylon*, both series shown in 1979. But both were shown at inconvenient times, *Babylon* for instance on Sundays at 1.15 p.m.; and there were ferocious attempts made to kill or doctor the use of *Our People* in schools broadcasts. Husband has written of the myth of English tolerance which permeates official pronouncements on English racism. Media controllers do not rush to unmask this myth.

Look at the countries they come from!

In order to grasp the full dimensions of the image black people are given in the media, it is necessary to recall the international context of racism. There is a clearly defined white racist world view, to which we made reference at the end of chapter 3, which claims Third World underdevelopment is due to black stupidity and barbarism. In this ideology, the Nigerian Civil War or the turbulent condition of India are taken as evidence for the benefits of white control in a country like South Africa.

Media coverage of the Third World and southern Africa presents a great deal of material which neatly fits this ideology. The very fact that Third World nationals, though living in London, are rarely given scope to speak about their countries, produces a racist picture in itself. The focus in Third World coverage is usually on disasters or coups d'etat. Whole nations flash like comets through the screen, to vanish until their next

90

disaster. A BBC TV News reporter with many years' experience of overseas reporting said drily to the writer that the editors 'like disasters wherever they occur; they like particularly wars showing that anyone who's skin is not white is capable of acts of irretrievable savagery'.

Conversely, South Africa is presented as a seeming paradox. On the one hand it is a white land of cricket, tennis, golf, rugby and fabulous weather for holidays. On the other hand it has a viciously anti-black government. In the racist world view, the second is the condition for the first. Whatever the view, reactions to the liberation movements of southern Africa are never enthusiastic. In 1970 the media barely touched on them. By 1980 they could no longer ignore them. Instead they concentrated on favourable portraits of pro-western leaders (Muzorewa, then Nkomo), and hostile portrayals of people like Robert Mugabe as anti-white, violent and power-obsessed. In turn this built up public readiness in Britain for South African intervention 'to save Zimbabwe from chaos'.

The other foreign instance of black-white relations which is given a good deal of coverage is the USA. There, shoot-outs, riots and hold-ups seem to be regular themes, with black crimewave accounts a regular horror story to grip the reader or viewer.

Critcher and his associates usefully summed up the implications of these patterns of foreign coverage for British racist thinking:

[Material] from multi-racial societies stresses intermittent violent conflict without historical cause or future solution. That from immigrants' home countries gives little information about ordinary everyday life, but stresses the dramatic and the violent. That which contributes to an image of black self-government stresses the primitive and disorderly nature of politics and culture in such societies . . . Rhodesian and South African whites are struggling to avoid such a situation; the United Kingdom will become the United States. The easy solution to prevent racial conflict is to avoid any racial contact at all. Apartheid appears in its international form: immigration control.

Let us analyse some illustrations of these points from my sample of TV coverage. A classic case of the comet-treatment, this time applied to the USA, was the rapid portrayal in two news bulletins of an armed police–black confrontation in New Jersey. The episode was given less than a minute each time. How the confrontation had arisen was unstated, as was its aftermath. It was presumably a handy filler.

Yet it fed into that definition of the future of black/white relations current in British politics, enunciated by Enoch Powell on the right and Roy Jenkins in the centre, which sees the British future in the present USA. By the year 2000 said Powell in a widely reported speech, 'there would be several Washingtons in England . . . With the lapse of a generation or so we shall at last have succeeded – to the benefit of nobody – in reproducing in England's "green and pleasant land" the haunting tragedy of the United States.' Jenkins explicitly referred to the black city riots in the USA at the time when he introduced the 1968 Race Relations Act, as the reason for bringing it in. The New Jersey item is an example of one of those countless tiny media pushes to the memory which keep alive these assumptions.

Coverage of Nigeria during the year of my sample abundantly confirmed the newsman's 'irretrievable savagery' hypothesis. The country had massive coverage for just nineteen days at the end of the civil war in January. The TV screens were full of malnourished and starving children with their rectal canals hanging out between their buttocks. It was horrifying, and it was right that war should not be glamourised. Yet anyone who failed to recognise its contribution to the image of African barbarism had to be exceptionally naïve.

Two documentaries on India in the same year illustrated much of the same treatment. One was by the Indian-born poet Dom Moraes, long resident in Britain. He focused on every division in Indian society with the exceptions of class and sex: Hindus vs Muslims, North vs South, castes, language-groups, tribes, the two Congress parties, the fragmented communist parties. Moraes' script claimed India's problems were 'like those of any emergent African nation'. This elegantly underlined the chaos-image of Third World countries, and so fuelled contemptuous stereotypes of Asians. The BBC's selection of Moraes to do the documentary was obviously based on the view that what was needed was someone who could translate one culture to another. The analysis of imperialism and class, which would have made sense of Indian society, was not what they had in mind.

The other documentary on India was one of a whole series called *Phantom India* by the French film-maker Louis Malle. They were all characterised by their obsession with the exotic and the dramatic, this being the only linking theme. The example in question was true to form, switching from religion to contraception to the Tamil-Hindi language clash to dance and drama . . .

On southern Africa, the 1970 coverage focused mainly on whether their all-white cricket team should tour Britain, and whether the British government should sell arms to the South African government. It was a unique opportunity, which by and large was not taken, to analyse South African society and development. What was instructive was to see the treatment of representatives from liberation movements on the rare occasions they were invited to speak. Four, to be exact. After all, their very existence challenged the myth of white rule's advantages, the myth of black powerlessness, and imperialist control of the Cape sea route.

There is only space to cite two of the cases. In the first a representative of SWAPO, the main Namibian liberation organisation, was invited to speak. The Interviewer, in a very short interview, asked him three main questions. All displayed a ludicrous level of understanding. Why was so little heard of the liberation movements? (A question for newspaper and TV editors.) Why could fifteen million Africans in South Africa do so little to help themselves? (He seemed to have forgotten the massive international support enjoyed by the South African government.) Had SWAPO any 'dramatic plans' for the near future? (As though they would announce them over BBC TV.)

The second case had a representative of the Pan African Congress, who had shot a sharply critical documentary of South

Africa called *End of a Dialogue*. This was the subject of discussion between himself, the interviewer, and de Villiers, white South African author of a book praising South Africa. The interviewer's intervention in the discussion was highly revealing of many white journalists understanding of white racism and black liberation.

As the white supremacist began to pick holes in the film's message under the guise of questioning its facts, Mahomo (from the PAC) became angry and challenged de Villiers' basic purpose behind his words. From being a reasoned English debate with virtue the middle, political reality suddenly exploded into life. The presenter desperately tried to rescue the debate and then, failing, insisted on putting forward *his* understanding of Mahomo's position *for* him to de Villiers. This is what he said:

> Mr Mahomo, we're talking about *facts* at the moment – no, you're talking about opinions – and I must ask Mr de Villiers – I'm sorry, but time is – it's very interesting, and I must ask Mr de Villiers – I'm sorry, I must ask Mr de Villiers if there are any more things he feels are basically untrue about the film that we saw?
>
> The point I think Mr Mahomo is making here is that you are perhaps living on borrowed time; and I think the point he's making, which a lot of people do feel, is that the tide of history at the moment is working perhaps in a shrinking world towards greater racial integration in the world, towards a greater mingling of the races; and are you not in South Africa going against the tide of history?

Paternalism rides again! The interviewer clearly still thought that there was room for argument about apartheid, and that the film's aim was to create racial integration, not racial justice. The very title of the film, *End of a Dialogue*, should have been clear even to the most bone-headed liberal.

In this survey of international coverage, two final items deserve comment. They were the TV coverage of the death of Iain MacLeod, British Colonial Secretary at the period of African de-colonisation; and the TV coverage of a massacre-confession in the *Sunday People* by some ex-soldiers, that when in the British army in Malaya during the 'Emergency' in the late forties, they had gunned down about twenty innocent villagers in cold blood.

MacLeod's death could have been the occasion for a hard-headed retrospective on the realities of British colonial rule, and the factors behind the fast de-colonisation programme of 1959–64. What happened was rather different.

The Zambian High Commissioner was wheeled on as a token African and said what a good person MacLeod had been with whom to negotiate independence. Lord Butler, another former Tory Cabinet Minister, came on to declare how intelligent and far-sighted his colleague had been.

In *News at Ten* the reporter claimed MacLeod had put an end to 'White domination' in Africa, so confusing neo-colonialism with genuine independence. A clip showed MacLeod at a Tory Conference speaking in high moral tones about the brotherhood of man. De-colonisation was apparently an act of British niceness. It was never mooted that it might have been based on calculations of the astronomical costs of containing independence movements in all the territories, both financially (the military presence required) and politically (communist support for liberation). The mechanisms of neo-colonial rule were not hinted at.

What colonial rule meant was more precisely illustrated by the Malayan massacre, in which one villager had miraculously survived. It opened up the possibility of asking whether colonial rule really was all hospitals and schools and civilisation, or whether it was for profit and power, backed by armed violence. Were 'they' better off 'under us'?

Malaya, Kenya, Cyprus, Guyana, Aden, Oman, to name but six, pointed to profit and power as the factual answer. The media however, conveyed the picture that the British both colonised and de-colonised for the noblest reasons.

We have noted several aspects of the media's international coverage which contributed to racist thinking in Britain. The links between imperialism and racism have never snapped.

Press and TV: from the right to the centre

The variety provided by different media in relation to racism can broadly be defined as moving from a liberal position (witness broadcasting and the *Mirror* on the CRC Report, and on the police station clash) to an uncompromisingly reactionary one. The clearest examples of the latter are sections of the press. The *Express* and the *Telegraph*, with their determined support for Powell, are cases in point.

At one stage in 1970, for instance, both these papers became obsessed with illegal black immigration as a major threat. Since according to the *Telegraph*'s own editorial reckoning, the numbers involved in the decade 1960–70 amounted to 6,000 (= 0.0001 per cent of the population), the headlines below, from a single five-week period, can only have been dedicated to inflaming racist anxieties.

Take some from the *Daily Express*: 'Swoop'; 'Ghost ship hunt'; 'Smuggling racket'; 'Immigrant hunt swoop'; 'Migrant alert'; 'Pakistani smuggling plot'; 'Police clamp on migrant coast'; 'Channel police link to foil immigrants'; 'CID "sailors" swoop on boatload'; 'Illegal migrants "pay with drugs"'; 'Asian queue-jumpers'; 'Police seize "smuggled Indians" boat'; 'International gang'; 'Police step up hunt'; 'European check on Asians'; 'Menaced by blackmail'; 'Protection link'; '2000 Indians smuggled in'.

Or again from the *Daily Telegraph*: 'Migrants plot'; 'Immigration controls "inefficient"'; '68 more'; '3000-a-year illegal entry'; 'World ring'; 'Stronger action on immigrants'; 'Police talk of migrant register'; 'Doubt cast on migrant figures'; 'Coast blockade for immigrants'; '4 countries tackle immigrants'; 'Indian "tourists" flooding into Bavaria'; 'Bavarians and "Indian invasion"'; 'Big increase in Special Branch'.

The *Telegraph* even managed to find a member of an obscure Indian organisation in Wolverhampton who urged that Powell be put in charge of a special Race Ministry . . .

Studies have shown how certain local newspapers are also regularly extremist in their handling of the issue. One Yorkshire paper implied all Asians were smallpox-carriers in its handling of a smallpox outbreak in 1962. One West Midlands paper lent active support to the racist campaigning of a Conservative candidate in

1963–64. One Essex paper virtually incited racist violence against two Asian families living on an estate. A former president of the NUJ once characterised a south London newspaper as the 'Muggers' Weekly' for its obsession with the subject.

When it comes to fighting racism, no major media organ can be relied on for support. The nearest they will get is to commend the community relations apparatus. Many however are a direct part of the attack against the black minority. A comparison of the role of the racist local press in fomenting anti-black riots in the USA is a sobering exercise.

Blacks in entertainment media

This aspect of racism in the media has received much less attention than it warrants. However, Husband has produced an important essay analysing ethnic jokes and comedy shows on British TV. He concludes that so far from making whites laugh at their own prejudices, which is the media establishment's rationale for putting this material on the air, the evidence is unambiguously that laughter confirms and reinforces racism in these situations. He includes evidence the BBC suppressed from its own audience research on the Alf Garnett series that demonstrated this impact.

The other main work in this area is on blacks in US films. Available studies concur that they have scarcely ever been treated as normal individuals. The early American cinema was content by and large to present blacks within the most racist categories of the Southern states: as primitive beings, at their best and most acceptable when dancing, singing and grinning. Apart from their treatment in occasional films about 'the race problem', in which a favourite theme was the tragic impossibility of racial inter-marriage, blacks generally surfaced as waiters and other extras until the black rebellions in US cities in the sixties. There ensued a crop of films starring black superheroes and even superheroines, sometimes on the side of law and order, sometimes not. Although blacks starred, their image was equally remote from social reality – and in its reference to their stunning sexual potency, drew on a

97

long racist tradition. Apart from these, there is the huge mass of 'Westerns', which mostly define Indian Americans as dangerous primitives, enemies of the peaceful whites.

A great many of these films have been shown on British TV or in British cinemas, though British films themselves have not been studied systematically in this respect. Films with a Third World setting most often seem to select it for its exotic input. The local people are simply a foil for the action. The theme of impossible racial inter-marriage also comes up from time to time. Certainly films such as *Zulu* or *North-West Frontier* have no critical reflections on imperialism or racism. They simply present a dramatic conflict, with the Europeans in general outwitting and outshooting the natives. French films made about North Africa and surveyed by Boulanger show these same features yet again.

From 'immigrant' to 'mugger'

As time has passed, it has become less and less feasible to go on referring to the black population as 'immigrants', even though it is still a common term. A new catchphrase was needed, just as in the 1968 US presidential election 'law and order' meant the blacks, whereas in 1972 the term had changed to 'bussing'. In the seventies, 'mugging' became a standard newspaper term to refer to black crime. It was coined by the police in the first instance, and borrowed from the USA, (whose image in Britain as a society of black violence we have noted above.) The term was tailor-made to be the new media stereotype of the dispossessed, alienated young black male. It would implicitly justify his repression by police, courts and prisons. Whereas Paki-bashing was not racist, according to the *Mirror* and the CRC chairperson, from the first 'mugging' meant blacks.

One of the concerns of the British ruling class is that the Republican struggle in Northern Ireland could reproduce itself in an urban black struggle in Britain. Powell, whose analysis if not specific policies they have often made their own, has drawn public attention to precisely this threat to their interests. In the era of microprocessors, they know that unemployment in the new black generation will soar to new heights. Its criminal image has been gradually established in the public mind, even before petty crime and intra-community violence became a blind response to its oppression. The violence syndrome analysed by Frantz Fanon took root and shape once more, this time in Britain in the seventies, as two writers in the sixties had presaged, one the present author. It means that the 'mugger' image is a fixture, and will slowly replace the category of 'immigrant'.

Conclusions

British media supply whites with a series of racist images of blacks. Blacks, however, are practically obliterated from the public debate about themselves. The media have sustained certain features of that debate very strongly, notably the definition of blacks as 'immigrants', 'a problem', 'muggers', parts of the barbaric former colonial Empire, representatives of a backward and disorderly part of the planet. White racism, however, is a minor focus in the media picture of Britain.

The solution to the 'race problem' becomes a question therefore, in the media, of how to respond to the black presence: pacification? (education, community relations) repression? (police, prisons) or deportation?

Media output actively discourages black workers from communicating their situation to white workers. The media are a *white* public arena. In addition, to racist jokes, the 'immigration' hysterias, the white experts pontificating about blacks, the openness of the airwaves and newspaper columns to Powell and the NF, the overt bias of much sports commentating and radio phone-ins, add publicly to the mass of individual discrimination and insults black people face in Britain. Expressions of black anger have been rare in public, and are usually typecast as 'the militant with a chip on his shoulder'. There are very rarely programmes – certainly not popular ones – which show the contemporary or historical dignity of black people, their creativeness in

99

resistance to oppression, their cultural or scientific contributions.

This absence of media communication between black and white workers underscores the tendency to segregate black workers into particular streets, shifts, sections, factories, jobs or unemployment itself. The implications of this lack of communication are not simply confined to ignorance concerning cultural traditions. They also include the fact that the real pressures black people live under are not part of the taken-for-granted world of white workers.

Furthermore, as episodes like the Grunwick strike and some Ford strikes show, the tenacity and organisation of black workers in the 'other' workers' movement are often a model for the class. So is the militant resistance of many young blacks against the police a model of class belligerence. But while these struggles are confined to the black minority – for every Grunwick there are hundreds of lonely struggles by black workers – it is easier for them to be suppressed. The media constantly reinforce this political isolation, in which all segments of the working class lose out.

For the images of blacks as a threat to 'our way of life', as 'colonial' buffoons, or as pushy and stroppy, help to reinforce the social identity of white workers as white and British first, working class second – the easy step from economism to racism. The more powerful this nationalist self-identification, the weaker their class identity. The more blacks can be used as a reminder of 'Great' Britain (*It Ain't Half Hot Mum*), of the good old days of a white British population cheerfully united in oppressing the rest of the world, the more tolerant white workers will be of racial oppression, the more hostile to black people. The transition to the fascist definition of blacks as source of all problems, is close at hand.

The isolation of striking workers which we saw as the major drive in the media portrayal of strikes, is then reproduced overall in media treatment of blacks. Just as workers are urged to identify with the 'national interest', so white workers are encouraged to identify with the white British nation. Blacks who wish to communicate with each other must also do so *without and against* the established media.

100

5. A Dissection of Sexism

At 10 a.m. on Tuesday January 9 1979 a group of fascists, masked and armed with machine guns and molotov cocktails, broke into the broadcasting studios of Radio Città Futura, an independent radio station of the Italian revolutionary movement.

Five middle-aged women were alone in the studio at the time, making a broadcast about contraception for the Housewives' Collective.

The fascists set fire to the studio. It was totally gutted and one woman was badly burned. As they ran out of the room, the fascists opened fire with their machine-guns, hitting the women in the legs. One woman was forced to raise her skirts, and a machine-gun burst was aimed at her legs and genitals. Her pelvis was broken in several places, and in hospital her womb and parts of her intestines had to be removed.

> *Interview with Sandro Silvestri of Radio Città Futura,*
> *by Christopher Walker of* People's News Service

The forms of chivalry and deference, which are actually borrowed from feudalism, inevitably turn into brutality and a sort of sexist contempt when the women (delegates) become independent and express their own political opinions.

> *Woman delegate speaking to the*
> *1929 Congress of the German Social Democratic Party*

The power relations central to sexism are thrown into sharp relief by these two incidents. The first was a murderous, sexually focused attack against feminists. It was carried out by individual fascists, but it was a part of every day's violence against women, whether the physical violence of enforced childbirth, enforced sterilisation, rape, or physical battering by husbands and 'lovers';

101

or the violence of mental assaults by advertisements of the ideal woman, or by the Hundred Contradictory Commandments of child psychiatrists. The casual, smirking dismissal of sexism by men as an also-ran in human affairs flatly contradicts its expression in vile acts of aggression, and its actual power to box in the development of half the human population.

The second comment by the German woman socialist is only one of many on record in which radical or revolutionary men can be seen to be completely conservative and complacent sexists. The power and penetration of sexism in men's minds is tellingly demonstrated by its stronghold in the thinking and behaviour even of those who are supposedly determined to uproot all oppression and exploitation.

Just as I have analysed the foundations of class exploitation in work, and of racial oppression, so in this chapter I will dissect the bases of sexism in advanced capitalist societies. It is proper to begin, however, by explicitly rejecting some current explanations of sexism. I do not accept that – any more than racism or ageism – sexism is a trivial problem as compared to class exploitation. Nor do I accept the mirror-opposite position, that the real antagonistic classes in human society are males and females. The development of modern industrialism, pervading every aspect of our lives, has not emerged from the sex war.

There are two other quite widely held explanations which are not completely wrong, but certainly insufficient. One is that sexism is a powerful force because of its long historical roots. I accept that the formation of sexist culture over an extremely long period established its penetration of social relations at all levels. Nonetheless, other forces such as religious beliefs, with an even longer pedigree, have suffered decline. The contemporary forces sustaining *and developing* sexism must be our prior concern.

The final position I reject as insufficient is that the source of sexism lies in the (freudian) Unconscious. Again, recognition of the deeply irrational and emotional dimension of sexism, to which the freudian tradition gives perspective, is essential. But this dimension is not peculiar to sexism: racism, class prejudice, religious

102

prejudice also have it. The fact that the images produced in dream-work often have a sexual significance does not require us to acknowledge the Unconscious as the major regulator of sexual oppression.

Any general account of sexism must seek to give indicative answers to the following questions: what is the specific structural position of women in society? What are the ideologies which emerge within sexist society and justify it? What are the origins, historical and contemporary, of both women's position and these ideologies? What, in other words, is the nature of the historical dialectic between class exploitation and sexism?

Women's position in advanced capitalism

The two main issues here are women's domestic existence and their labour-market roles. After that we must examine the reinforcement of these forms of oppression in schooling, in language and by the state. The media are also extremely important but are dealt with in some detail in the next chapter.

The splintering experience of domestic life is reflected in the general aversion of men to exchange this role with women. Whatever the hardships of wage-labour, it is a rare male who prefers his wife to go out to work and leave him to be 'housewife' and 'mother'. When there is an extended family, with childcare and domestic chores shared between women relatives, the particular burden on any one of these women is more bearable than in a nuclear family, where one woman is totally and single-handedly engrossed in these tasks. Nonetheless, in either case it is the women who are usually reckoned to have prime responsibility for domestic labour.

This labour is very time-consuming. A French study in 1958 estimated a 60-hour week for the average housewife, while a US bank put the figure at 99.6 hours a week. Devices such as washing-machines, vacuum-cleaners and other home implements may save some effort, but rarely time. Any activity demanding well over half someone's working hours is bound to crowd out the possibility of other, more life-enhancing pursuits.

This invasion of women's available time is not fully under-

103

stood, however, without attention to its mind-numbing and isolating character. Petty housework crushes, strangles, stultifies and degrades her, chains her to the kitchen and to the nursery, as Lenin once put it, and without any exaggeration. The impact of this experience can be seen in a particularly visible form when women graduates, confident in the powers of their mind, find themselves confined to these routines during their child-bearing years. For a time the experience can destroy their feeling of being able even to join in discussions on current affairs. The emotional pleasure they may experience in relating to their growing infant is trapped inside a welter of communication with an insistently demanding, dependent, unformed person (or persons), and this is quite capable of engulfing ordinary adults' thinking, blotting out their normal alertness. If women such as these can feel themselves reduced to near-cabbages, then the experience of domesticity must indeed be overpowering.

The nature of the home, the very physical construction of houses and apartments, conspire to isolate women in this experience. To be subjected to it in isolation, to be deprived of other adult stimulus, to be locked into a domestic ghetto and only allowed out to shop or mind the children while they play in the park, boxes in women's own development *and* their social contribution. In short, domestic life and labour is harshly oppressive, not sheltered and snug. The family would bring this experience to men or women, yet the latter are overwhelmingly stuck in it. Thus the nuclear family in particular constitutes a major source of women's oppression, to which only the socialisation of domestic labour is a full answer.

This is not all. Young girls in the family are usually brought up to help their mothers with these domestic routines. They are given dolls to play with rather than toy soldiers, or if they are really lucky, a doll's house. Some studies have shown that parents use a quite different tone of voice even to babies, depending on their sex, and relate to them in a different manner. Girls are not encouraged, are even actively discouraged, from independent planning of their future, whether in employment or sexual relations.

Then, in later years, so bound up are many mothers with these domestic routines, that they have intense difficulty in adjusting to their own children's independence and leaving home. It is akin to the shattering experience of retirement for many workers. Grandchildren – in other words, a repetition of the original experience – are often welcomed as the 'solution' to an otherwise inane existence for older women.

It might seem from this that the genuine pleasures forthcoming from committed relations between men and women, from the children they have, from inter-relating with their own parents, are being swept away on a tide of jaundiced emphasis on the shadow-side of domestic life. Certainly these pleasures exist, for if they did not, it is hard to imagine how many women would continue to bear it. What happens is that this softening of the impact of domestic oppression is used to justify it, *as though the two* – love and oppression – *were inseparable*. Harnessing them together in this way is a major rationale for women's subordination.

Defenders of divorce, for instance, sometimes cite the large number of people who remarry after divorce, and supposedly 'get it right' the second time. What their argument neglects in its sophisticated defence of marriage – still the normal gate to a woman's domestic oppression – is the intense cycle of emotional expectation and cruel disappointment that so often emerges within the nuclear family. Emotional burdens are placed on its members that they frequently find intolerable. Most often it is the mother who bears the brunt of these impossible demands by being their target, or by making them as she is supposed to do, or being called on to resolve the antagonisms that inevitably arise from their non-fulfilment. In the internal politics of the home, mothers often play the key role. Some use this opportunity to try to compensate themselves for their own oppression; others are simply stretched on its rack. Either way, the liberation of women is a long way off.

The second fundamental source of women's oppression in advanced capitalism is the exploitation of their labour-power. This takes a number of specific forms, whose overall effect is to pay women less than men. Given that in Britain, for example, at least a sixth of women workers are themselves the sole breadwinner, the sexist claim that women are only at work for the pin-money is revealed as doubly untrue, a particularly cynical evasion.

Till recently it was perfectly legal to pay women less for the same work as men. As this blatant form of discrimination came to be outlawed, so the employers promptly changed the definition of jobs mostly done by women, to fit the new situation. Thus, in the short term at least, capital's response to equal pay legislation has been to intensify the already existing practice of defining certain types of jobs as female: cleaning, cooking, nursing, shopwork, pre-11 school teaching are examples. Up to the Depression the classic instance was domestic service, now replaced by clerical work as the main type of wage-labour for women (40 per cent of the female labour-force in the USA is in this sector). These are typically low-paid occupations, and often have a content defined as 'feminine' within the sexist assignment of a domestic destiny to women. If men are employed in these sectors, it is generally because they are at their apex (chefs, doctors, college lecturers, administrators), or because they are migrant workers (e.g. the British textile industry).

However, this concentration in low-paid work is only one of the ways capital exploits women's labour-power. Many women are, like migrant workers, part of the reserve army of labour, so the first to be made redundant or put on short time. Many women work part-time, with all the immediate disadvantages in pay, prospects and security this entails. Once more, the hoary excuse is trotted out that they are only there for pin-money, and that they are always leaving to have babies or taking time off to look after sick children. So women's domestic oppression is also used against them in work.

In recessions, this treatment of women's labour as disposable is as marked as the enthusiasm with which their presence in factories is greeted during wartime. A textile union general secretary after the second world war once recalled the lengths women workers were driven to by the readiness of employers to sack them during the Depression: 'women were to be seen at childbirth at their frames, or were taken into lavatories to have their children'.

Another interaction between domestic oppression and exploitation at work is that after the experience of domestic isolation, many women are only too eager to get out and meet some other people, even if the work itself is dull and pay is low. Employers can rely on the availability of a large pool of such women. This can work independently of the economic pressure on women to take paid jobs to supplement their husbands' low pay, which is a standard reason for deciding to seek work.

The final main interaction between the two is that men often expect women to do a *double shift*, one at work and the other at home. This finally completes the vicious circle of women's oppression in these two crucial areas of their lives.

A particular case of the fusion of many of these processes is to found among the home-workers, the women who sit with their sewing-machines at home and supply the garment trade with its clothes. They have no insurance, no pension, no shield against redundancy, no safety and health protection, no union, and must supply their own machines, space and electric power. The gap between their pay and the garment's shop price is enormous (often twelve times), and thus their surplus-labour is practically a necessity for these firms to function at their present level. Naturally, their domestic responsibilities are also expected to be fulfilled.

The causes of this overall pattern of women's employment lie in the interaction between their domestic segregation, their typecasting in this role by men, and the logic for capital of using the cheapest labour-power available. If grossly underpaying women's labour is tolerated by the wider society, there is no logic in capitalist economic relations dictating they should be paid more. However, a key element in this equation has been the historically established sexism of male-dominated trade unions, often among the most vigorous defenders of unequal rights for women workers. The factors behind this will occupy us below, but the exploitation of women's labour-power cannot even be raised without mentioning its importance.

In charting the structural position of women in Britain, the two most important determinants are now established, along with their mutual interaction. They are reinforced at a number of critical points, of which one is schooling.

The very distribution of women in teaching – loaded at the pre-11 end, scarce at the post-school and administrative end – reveals the sexist nature of educational organisation. Consistently in Britain twice as many boys as girls have done undergraduate degrees. There is, moreover, the blatant or subtle steering of boys and girls into study of different subjects, supposedly sex-specific. Boys are assigned to woodwork and metalwork, girls into typing, home economics and domestic science. At a different level, girls are encouraged to do arts, sociology, teacher training, while boys are encouraged to do science, economics, undergraduate degrees. Even in cases where boys are taught needlework and girls woodwork, indications are that teachers define the purpose of doing so to the pupils as insurance for future emergencies when husband or wife is absent, rather than as preparation for various forms of 'sexually appropriate' work. Textbooks very often reinforce these stereotypes of sexual roles, and some studies suggest girls may often be discouraged from intervention in class, whereas boys are encouraged.

The effect of these practices is, obviously, to produce sustained pressure on girls to enter traditional categories of women's work. Since these are mostly so boring and poorly paid, the *further* consequence is to reinforce the ideology of marriage and babies, for these seem the only genuinely individual and purposive decisions girls have at their disposal. Their awareness of their own mothers' domestic oppression is usually brushed to one side at this stage.

The only ray of hope inside the education system lies in the contradiction between this reality, and its professed objective of enabling intelligent students to enter interesting work in adult life. The experience of those women who succeeded against the odds, got their degrees, and then found themselves pushed around as also-rans in the labour market, was a potent spur to the development of the women's movement in the sixties and seventies. Women with this experience were often at the heart of the

108

movement's many cells. In turn, the movement began to exert counter-pressure against sexism in education.

Language itself is a further source of subtle yet powerful and consistent sexist perspectives. Gender definitions are very important to many languages, though less so in modern English. Even so, English language use is drenched in sexism. The most obvious example is the convention of using 'man' and 'mankind' for humanity as a whole. Similarly, where gender is not specified, as in legal contracts, 'he' is always used to cover both sexes. Some occupations are explicitly defined as male, as in chairman, spokesman, linkman, draughtsman, cameraman. Conventionally, women's surnames at birth are their father's, and at marriage their husband's. The women's movement attack on these loaded language conventions is an accurate estimate of their daily influence.

It is constructive to consult any large dictionary and to discover the many prejudiced senses in which the following ordinary words are used: woman, girl, lady, womanly, feminine, female. He's an old woman; come along girls; now then ladies; womanly virtues; feminine wiles; the female of the species is deadlier than the male. Certainly the heaviest insults are usually sexual references to women.

Other writers have probed more deeply than this rather random selection of instances, and have argued that girls may be encouraged to use a more deferential and hesitant form of language than men. Some evidence suggests they may experience subtle pressure to use more 'proper' variants of language than men, as part of a general social pressure to render themselves more socially correct because they are women. Still others would claim language as a prime structuring force in shaping both consciousness and sub-consciousness, and thus as a pivotal determinant of sexism. Without being able to follow this up here, it is at least clear that language reinforces as well as reflects the power relations of male supremacy.

The last reinforcement of male supremacy that demands some analysis is the state itself. One of the first targets of women's organised resistance in nineteenth-century Britain was the state's discriminatory laws against them, for instance denying married women the right to hold property in their own name alone. Gradually, as a result of women's continuous pressure, one after another of these laws was repealed. At long last in 1929, all women were allowed the same voting rights as men.

However, the sexist character of the state has come nowhere near to being uprooted. The very concentration of males at the top of all its branches, civil service, military, police, judiciary, parliament, is an indication of its true nature. There is no need to surmise that sexist policies ensue as a result of this recruitment pattern, for it and they are inextricably bound up with each other.

For example, state tax and welfare policies have repeatedly been framed on the following assumptions: a married woman's place is in the home; a man is the natural provider, because his wage properly covers his dependants' needs (the 'family wage'). Beveridge, chief architect of postwar welfare expansion, explicitly argued that married women's commitment to wage-labour 'should not be the same as that of a single woman. She has other duties.'

Even up to 1980, a married man in Britain who chose to exchange roles with his wife was discouraged from this choice by the state's refusal to let her national insurance payments cover him. Similarly, if a man's wife is incapacitated, and he employs a housekeeper, he can claim some tax exemption on this score. Not so she, if positions are reversed. Looking after her sick husband is part of her 'normal responsibilities'.

In these and other ways the state in Britain underpins conventional sex roles, and so the oppression of women. A classic instance is the interaction between courts and social security. Divorce courts usually regard the mother as the proper person to look after the children. If she does so and does not work for a wage, she is dependent on pittances from the social security office to maintain herself and them. At the same time, the social security machine employs a larger and larger number of 'sex-snoopers', officials whose mission it is in the national interest to detect any sexual liaison these women may be having. If their sleuthing is successful, which can include searching bedrooms and examining bedlinen, then the woman may be docked part or all of her payment, and taken to court for non-disclosure of her income into the bargain. The male is assumed to be paying for something . . .

It might be countered that in the single decade 1967–76, the British state passed the Abortion Act, the Equal Pay Act and the Sex Discrimination Act, all encouraging women's liberation. Let us distinguish fact from fantasy in this contention.

The 1967 Abortion Act was the first British law to enable working-class women to have an abortion on social rather than physical grounds. Size of existing family, income level, husband-wife relations, even general personal preference, could be taken into account by the doctors whose decision it was. Petit-bourgeois women had usually been able to pay privately for this facility, and so had not been driven to compulsory pregnancy or attempts at self-abortion with knitting needles and other means, to the same degree. The Act was an advance therefore.

However, it still left the final decision over the woman's body in the hands of (mostly male) doctors. Women had to gain agreement both from their local doctor and from a hospital consultant, thus introducing both the hazards of delay in termination, and a double barrier. In some cities such as Birmingham and Liverpool, this barrier was almost impermeable. So despite its advance, the 1967 Act still does not allow women control over their own bodies, and thus it still does not ensure either that every child is a wanted child. It is only in relation to the repeated attempts to repeal that Act that it has become so very important to defend the relatively limited gains it has brought to women.

We made reference to the Equal Pay Act of 1970 above, in discussing how easily employers recategorised work so that men and women were not doing the same jobs. Whatever the Act's intentions, then, its impact has been slight. The 1975 Sex Discrimination Act, which in theory might have been framed to make this evasion costly, relies in actuality on a purely piecemeal case-approach, solving each case of discrimination at a time. Like the Race Relations Acts, its provisions are not designed for rapid or substantial change.

Any moves by the state underway during the eighties to rein in the Abortion Act, to re-emphasise marriage and the family against the growth of both divorce and single-parent families, and to cut back welfare provisions so that more medical and old people's care is organised at home, will further reinforce the segregation of women in their domestic prisons. There are many precedents for such state policies, especially in times of economic crisis.

We have examined the family, the capitalist labour-market, schooling and education, language and the state. We have touched momentarily on the sexist organisation of trade unions and medicine. There is only one conclusion possible, namely that women's oppression is systematic and entrenched. We turn now to see how this injustice has been justified.

Rationales for women's oppression

There are two main forms in which the structural subordination of women is explained, and explained away. One is a variety of assumptions and images which combine to elevate the status of men and demean the position of women. The other is in the social rationales for appropriate roles for males and females, which in turn rigidify women's oppression.

Thus men are conventionally defined as physically tough, emotionally stable, good at science and engineering or repairing cars. Women by contrast are customarily defined as having weak bodies, over-emotional responses, and a capacity for imaginative expression. The real strength of these definitions can be seen when they are reversed: the stereotypical male gay (the 'fairy', the 'queen'); the image of the Russian woman shot-putter athlete; the 'hard bitch'; the career-amazon. When conventional gender images are flouted, there is a very noticeable instinctive shock which proves their social importance.

These images are ultimately founded on what men and women customarily do. In this connection, women's domestic roles are at the heart of their image as the weaker sex, expert only in emotional self-expression. Conversely, men's roles outside the

112

home, roles of wage-earner and power-wielder, are the continuing source of their image as the stronger sex.

Once again, it is a reverse situation which demonstrates the point clearly. Studies of unemployed men and marital instability show that those men who leave the women they have had children with, are often much pleasanter to any children belonging to a woman with whom they start an affair, than they are to their own. The reason seems to be anchored in men's self-image as providers. If through unemployment they cannot provide properly for their own children, these stand as a daily reminder to them of their failure. This may often act as a pressure to leave home, in order to avoid staring their own failure in the face. Any act of kindness in their new relationship is not a matter of duty, and therefore can be thought of as generosity. Such gender role definitions are exceedingly powerful.

Many of these images and role definitions have a long history, buried in the religious ideologies of feudal Europe and the political structure of the early capitalist epoch. Let us scan some examples, for as we recognised above, these deep roots partly account for the tenacity of sexism in the present day. Furthermore, seeing how their specific content has changed over time, while women's oppression has stayed in force, shows – like the history of white racism – how alert we need to be in the present to alterations in women's definition. Not because they are cosmetic – far from it – but because they may herald a more sophisticated entrenchment of male supremacy.

The main ideology of late feudal Europe was Catholicism. Both it and the Orthodox churches of eastern Europe may have enthroned the Virgin Mary as practically a fourth god, and as more sympathetic a character than her three male partners. Nonetheless, she was a permanent virgin, only fully imitated by nuns. Thus women's sexuality was not religiously valued, indeed it was feared, and her menstruation regarded as disgusting and polluting. Mary's motherhood, a model for all womb-carriers, began without orgasm or penis.

By contrast, her notorious predecessor was Eve, who had led

113

mankind (Adam) into permanent separation from god by being more easily corruptible than he. Eve's sexual appetite was always a prime dimension of this historic disaster. The two faces of women characteristic of much later European folklore and literature have their origins in this contrast between the pure and perfect mother-goddess – on whom all women should model themselves, though all fail to do so – and the dangerously weak and suggestible bitch-on-heat. Shrews, vamps, witches and whores had their origin here.

The other religious traditions with any influence in medieval Europe were Judaism and Islam. Neither offered any alternative model to this. Once a day orthodox Jewish men ritually thanked their god he had not created them as women. The Quran portrays heaven as a place where righteous men will be served delicacies by dark-eyed *houris*.

Nor did the Protestant Reformation offer any change in this suffocating patriarchalism. Mary was dethroned, but preaching or taking services was kept as a male preserve. Only the wildest sects such as the Ranters at the time of the English Civil War, or later on the extremely sober but deeply suspected Quakers, were prepared to change this rule and allow women equal religious rights. Their contemporaries were usually scandalised. (A completely bible-centred version of christianity could not give women this scope because St Paul had expressly forbidden it.)

Thus the stranglehold of official religion had to be broken before there could be a real movement toward women's rights. However, the new social forces that were emerging to disrupt the feudal order – represented in the English Civil War, the American War of Independence, the French Revolution – contained no promise of this movement. On the contrary, their goal required, as one of its necessary conditions, women's seclusion from public life and so from power.

The bourgeois slogans of liberty, fraternity and equality are generally recognised today as only being relevant to the ruling segments of society. We saw in chapter 3 for example how the logic of these slogans led to the definition of Africans as inferior beings, only fit for slavery. It equally followed that women were not part of the fraternity.

If we study writers such as Locke and Rousseau, articulating commitment to a post-feudal order, we find that their definition of the extension of political power from the monarch's court to the notable members of society, meant the suppression of women's rights to political involvement in the public arena. In *Emile*, his analysis of education in the coming society, Rousseau is quite direct on this score. Women's education should solely be 'to please, to be useful to us . . . to take care of us when grown up . . . to render our lives easy and agreeable.' Locke denied the absolute authority of both monarch and husband, but the fact that the new dignity of property ownership was essentially only open to males, meant that the circle of political influence was bound to exclude women.

Thus the development of the public and private spheres of life at the dawn of the bourgeois era relegated women to the private realm. Even within that realm, they were relegated further to the domestic rather than the business side of that sphere. This trend could be seen at many points. The very organisation of houses changed, with private and public domain carefully separated from each other. The growth of influential professional associations for education, science and medicine were as male preserves. This sexual segregation also stamped the beginning of the newspaper, as we shall see in chapter 7.

This separation of spheres is no purely historical digression, but a structural feature of bourgeois life. The long story of women's demand for the vote, the overwhelming male bias in recruitment to top state office, show it to have been part of the foundation of women's oppression.

The contradiction between it and the ideals of bourgeois revolution was exposed by the earliest feminists, Mary Wollstonecraft in England, Olympe de George and Flora Tristan in France, the 1848 Seneca Falls Convention's Declaration in the USA. Yet to this day, the relegation of women to the private sphere alone has shown a remarkable resilience.

Let us see how in the nineteenth century the authority of

science was harnessed to support the domestic seclusion of women, just as in the same period it was dragooned into buttressing racism. This fresh development was extremely important, for it provided more prestigious and so more convincing rationales for male supremacy than were previously available.

Medical science, by now controlled by men like all other branches of science, was at the forefront of the new analysis of upper-class women. Its central assumption was that women were wombs-on-legs, *both* in respect of their social utility to the nation and species, *and* in regard to the governing principle of their own being. They were the reproducers of the future ruling class, and in turn were determined by this socio-physical function.

Such women were defined by nineteenth-century medical science as inherently delicate and sick. Their natural bodily phases, such as puberty, menstruation, pregnancy and the menopause, were stated to be periods of illness. The higher TB rates for women at the time were put down to their defective physical organism. Their entry into the professions or even to higher education was resisted in the name of the damage it might do to their wombs. Brain and womb were held by some to be mutually incompatible organs, the development of either bringing about the atrophy of the other.

The cure for this female tendency to 'nerves' and fainting fits was usually confinement to bed. The bedroom became a kind of high security cell within the prison of the home. Women's outbursts of rage and frustration at their repression were clinically diagnosed as 'hysteria' (from the Greek word for *womb*). For this fabricated disease, some doctors urged physical terror as the cure: speaking in a 'decided tone' of the necessity of shaving the woman's head; beating her with wet towels; suffocating her till the fits ceased . . . Sexual enthusiasm was regarded as another pathological condition induced by women's reproductive organs. There were cases of women being forced to have their clitoris cut out to aid them in domesticating themselves.

Such were the depths to which *upper-class* women could be forced by this scientific rationale for their domestic segregation.

116

While its more extreme features have not survived into the present period, including the specific theory that wombs govern women's entire behaviour, the notion that women's utility is primarily defined by their having one still prospers as the normal basis of state population policy. This directly affects the availability of abortion, contraception and sterilisation. Specifically, it is the basis on which middle-class women are discouraged from abortion and sterilisation, while their black and lower working-class sisters in particular are often strenuously encouraged in these directions, even sterilised against their will.

In the twentieth century the scientific establishment has branched out into new territory to provide rationales for the sexual division of labour. The housewife bent over the sink washing shitty nappies has been elevated into a Domestic Scientist, and the same person sweating through a supermarket trying to make ends meet, into a Home Economist. The germ and dust theories of the origins of disease justified a huge outlay of women's time in cleaning the house. Chores have been analysed to show women how to perform them more efficiently (shades of Taylor!), budget and other records stipulated, so that educated women might no longer see domesticity as unworthy of their minds. The threat to national civilised standards in slovenly working-class homes could be averted by middle-class women becoming themselves professional teachers of home economics and domestic science – to girls.

Child-rearing has been a particular focus of scientific analysis this century, with the mother–child 'bond' made sacred as the indispensable condition for the child's future emotional stability. Its maladjustment and misery could only be the mother's guilty failure to glue herself to it sufficiently. Armies of child psychiatrists and psychologists issued their contradictory commandments to mothers, all contributing to convince women that it was their unique responsibility to ensure their children did not grow up neurotic, psychotic or just plain dummies.

The final development of sexist ideology, especially in the latter twentieth century, has been in the definition of women, not

117

just as wombs-on-legs, but still further reduced to pure sex objects – vaginas-on-legs. Given the history of rape, this is hardly new. What is new is the public legitimation given it, as we shall see in the next chapter.

Women, by common impression, have much more sexual freedom than ever before. So far as it goes, this is an accurate judgment, but it misses out on the double-edged nature of this change.

Firstly, the advance is largely due to changes in contraceptive technology, meaning that women no longer need be left holding the baby; and also to the much more open discussion of women's sexual fulfilment made possible through the development of psychoanalysis. However, both these changes have a considerable sexist content. There is no male pill, and the ones women take are increasingly known to be dangerous to their health. Psychoanalytic practice, to say the least, has often been deeply sexist.

But over and above these considerations there is the dominant feature of women's increased sexual freedom, namely the male supremacist counter-attack. This has taken the form of an ever more aggressive depiction of young women's sexual availability. Its essence is the presentation of a contradictory set of ideals for women. They must be young, and by male conventions, physically beautiful. They must be sexually enthusiastic yet faithful to the man they are with. Orgasm is not an experience for them to revel in, but an acid test of their sexual competence. Little girls are usually discouraged in scandalised tones from sexual self-exploration, then later told the opposite in sexual advice columns and adverts: you must do what you mustn't do, your genitals are wonderful/disgusting. Women are to be interesting to talk to, yet submissive once captured. They must also continue to be what their mothers and grandmothers were, reliable cooks, washer-women, cleaners, child-rearers.

Thus one gain for women has in part been snapped up by another reverse, which has instituted this additional, impossible yet insistent ideal for younger women, and sharpened the division between younger and older women (for the latter cannot fit the

118

ideology of youth). Women's sexual freedom is redefined as their *easier sexual availability for men, in addition to their domesticity.* Rationales for women's oppression are not melting away under the onslaught of the women's movement; not yet.

The dialectic of class and sex

Our review of women's oppression and its changing rationales compels us to analyse the forces behind both. This book's argument is that their source is to be found in a historical dialectic between class forces and the forces of male supremacy. We have cited a number of examples of this dialectic, but to provide firm foundations for this contention, let us examine some further critical moments of the development of sexism within the period of capitalist development.

The first is emergent capitalism's operation within the patriarchal traditions of feudalism. We can observe this at a number of points, one being that as agricultural wage-labour grew, so from the start it was customary for women to be paid less for the same work. At the other end of the rural class scale, the yeomen (the new rural bourgeoisie) considered their own ability to make enough money to keep their wives from having to work, as a badge of their longed-for approximation to aristocratic life styles. Thus both the extra exploitation of women's labour-power, and the class prestige of a man who could afford to keep his wife at home, are to be found historically embedded in the marriage of patriarchal social structure and new economic relations. These were among the beginnings of class-specific women's oppression in the present epoch.

Secondly, we must understand the process by which women's labour – crucial to the early capitalist textile industry – came to be defined as unsuitable for industrial labour through the growth of laws purporting to control women's maximum working day. This was due to a different interlocking of class and male supremacist forces. I shall draw heavily upon Berch's account of this transition.

In Britain, France and the USA, although at different dates

119

and with specific variations, this exclusion of women from the labour market – and the consequent growth of the ideology of domesticity – was in the main the result of pressures from farseeing capitalists, supported by male trade unionists. Not, however, from women workers themselves, who protested their exclusion.

The capitalists wanted to drive their smaller competitors, who relied heavily on female labour working long hours, out of the market altogether. Limiting the hours women could work wrecked these small firms' profitability. Some manufacturers were also anxious that working-class women might become unable, through too much factory work, to reproduce a healthy labour force for the future.

Male trade unionists – the term male being almost redundant for much of this history – were happy to see women competitors taken out of the labour market, especially in the name of male concern for their welfare. Now employers would not have the same scope, they argued, to use women's lower wages to undercut men's. At the same time, the craft workers who formed the bulk of the 'respectable' working class, were actively adopting from the middle classes the ideology that their own wives' place should be in the home. Thus their manoeuvres in their economic class struggle with the employers coincided with the ideological penetration of the bourgeois view of women.

For this clutch of class reasons, officially expressed concern about women's working conditions in factories overlay neglect of their rights. This transition was crucial to the long separation of women from the trade-union movement, to their inexperience in organising around their own interests, and to the support for their domesticity within the working class. It brought into being a contradictory ideology, appropriate to the female segment of the reserve army of labour, as we saw earlier on in our survey of women in the labour market. This is the source of the argument that women should be in the home, therefore their jobs are worth less and can be taken from them more legitimately.

Lastly, these laws did not remove women from industrial labour, nor did they protect them in any major way. They were poorly enforced and tended simply to drive women into unprotected employment. Their main impact, Berch insists, was ideological: the reinforcement of domesticity as women's true destiny.

This leads directly to the third point in our consideration of the class-sex dialectic. Women's unpaid domestic labour, as we noted earlier, is extremely time-consuming. It is also of the greatest advantage to the continuance of capitalism that this labour be done. Some writers, perhaps to underpin this point, have argued that women's domestic labour produces surplus-value, or that the home contains a mode of economic production in which males exploit females for their own profit. There seems no need to insist on recognition of the necessity of this labour by attaching these concepts to it. It is obvious that the free labour women carry out in the home is a strong support for the present capitalist order. It is also clear that to tie women to this free labour is very oppressive. Most of it, if performed outside the home, is paid (nursing, cooking, washing, cleaning, child-minding, sewing). But this oppression should speak for itself, rather than being validated by superficially relevant concepts.

Lastly, the major threat to male supremacy, and so also to a foundation of capitalist stability, has come from independent organisation and attack by women themselves. This is shown positively by the history of women's suffrage, and the women's movement of the later twentieth century, just as the saga of 'protective' factory legislation demonstrates it negatively.

Yet automatic sisterhood is a romantic myth. Class and racist forces have penetrated women's consciousness like men's, and feminists are not any exception. A section of the American suffrage movement was happy to support the *disenfranchisement* of blacks as the price for white Southern states' endorsement of women's suffrage. The American-born women who had worked in New England's textile mills looked with contempt at their Irish sisters who succeeded them at the mills from the 1840s on. The French *internats*, convent forced-labour centres for young girls, and central to the beginnings of French industry, were ruled with a rod of iron by their sister-supervisors. The women's liberation movement itself has had an exceedingly small involvement on the

121

part of working-class and black women. Such scattered historical instances can stand for many more too numerous to mention.

They are cited, not to promote cynicism concerning the independent power of women, but realism concerning how to develop it. Romantic notions of working-class solidarity or black unity are equally harmful to the cause they embrace. The forces of male supremacy are all the stronger, the more the organised opposition to them can be diverted unawares from recognising the entrenchment of class and racist perspectives within its own ranks. Just as in chapter 1 I cited a manager of US Steel as recommending the advantages of having black and Mexican workers in competition with each other, so in the decades of the black movement and the women's movement it has been possible for the powers that be to set up a new competition between blacks and women for access to new but scarce resources.

Thus the continuous dialectic between class and male supremacy means that to reduce one to the other is to deprive the working-class movement and the women's movement, not to mention others, of the understanding they need to overthrow their oppression.

Conclusions

In this chapter we have examined some of the main elements in women's oppression. Their domestic segregation, the uses of their labour-power, the reinforcement of these patterns by schooling, language and the state, were the structural factors on which we focused. We then examined some of the changing rationales for sexism, from the emergence of capitalism to the present day: the images of Eve and Mary, the separation of public and private spheres, the medical science establishment's definition of wombs-on-legs the scientific redefinition of domestic labour and child-rearing, and the later twentieth-century shrinkage of women to vaginas-on-legs.

In the last section we used for aspects of women's oppression and struggle against it, to expand our argument that the dynamics of this oppression cannot be accurately grasped if they are thought

122

of as self-sustaining patriarchy. The discussion of women's images in advertising media in the next chapter will provide a fifth case in point. At the same time, the term 'the forces of male supremacy' has been constantly used. It is a preferable term in my view to 'patriarchy', since it does not imply fatherhood is the basic source of sexism. In practice, the use of either term is partly a way of insisting on the irreducible nature of woman's oppression, that it is neither trivial nor simply a spin-off from economic class relations.

However, avoiding that trap creates a different problem. What *are* these forces? What is their sustaining power, over and above the various stimuli capitalism provides to them? The question is crucial, for in alternative social structures such as Soviet-type societies, women still perform double shifts, still have their bodies controlled by state population policies on abortion, still are largely excluded from the upper ranks of every important job-sector. These societies may not be defined as socialist or transitional towards communism, but they are different in many respects from western capitalism – and women are still oppressed in them.

As I conceded at the beginning of this chapter, the dead weight of male supremacist tradition and the irrational-emotional forces of the unconscious are part of the dynamic of male supremacy. They are reinforced by the daily operations of child-rearing and numerous other social patterns and institutions. But is there an original kernel there explaining the *interests* involved? *In the short run* the answer is quite clear: women's oppression is men's interests as well as capital's.

It is a particular definition of interests that is at stake here. It is destructive to men's self-realisation to oppress women, just as sexism's support for capitalism helps perpetuate men's general oppression and exploitation under that system. But in terms of pandering to male desires for comfort, ego-massage, cushioning of their treatment at work, substitution for their lack of power outside the home, avoidance of domestic labour, being able to sport children as evidence of virility, and easy access to sexual action: in terms of short-run real interests such as these, women's subordination is patently of the greatest advantage. These interests

123

are economic, psychological and personal-political, the strands in the power relations between men and women. The logic and dynamics of personal politics in this realm as in others, cannot be read off as simply a reflex of class relations, *however mediated*. At the same time, it cannot be understood at all without reference to them.

We must end by recognising how women's experience accumulates a concentration of resentment and desire for revenge on the males immediately around them. This is not to suggest a spurious balance between male supremacy and female resistance. It is simply to recognise that where there is oppression, there is resistance, even if individual and unorganised.

Ten years ago I wrote of the colonial encounter in terms that equally convey the power relations in the home, once the actors are changed. I referred to the 'experience of the English colonists' (read *men*) 'who had to face fierce opposition and bloody rebellions, not to mention eternal pinpricks from the peoples' (read *women*) 'they subdued.' The difference is that this constant attrition combined with intermittent explosions, takes place in the *home*. According to one study, the most likely place for men and women in a relationship to kill each other is the bedroom or the kitchen. If true at all, everything in this chapter should help to explain why it is true; but let us note the obvious. The kitchen is the most dangerous place for the man, symbolising as it does the woman's domestic oppression. Furthermore, one possible revenge is to be disinterested in his sexual satisfaction, leading to the violent expression of charged resentments. The bedroom is the most dangerous place for the woman, apparently.

There are other forms of counter-attack, the woman personal assistant who defends her boss as a way of using his power to legitimate hers, women officials who enjoy citing the rules to recalcitrant males, women workers mercilessly teasing young male workers. Any account of male supremacy which does not incorporate this other term in its own dialectic, falls into the trap of thinking of women as essentially powerless in this struggle. Male supremacy, like racism or class rule, does not have to be all-conquering to be extremely dangerous.

124

6. The Media and Sexism

Analysing the presentation of women in the mass media presents different problems to the dissection of bourgeois and racist media output, for it is generally the case that newsmen usually define women's activity as not newsworthy, a direct result of their confinement to the private sphere of social life. The consequence is that there are far fewer *events* reported in the media that can be analysed for their sexist categories, than is the case for class relations or racism. Gaye Tuchman has defined this overwhelming absence as the 'symbolic annihilation' of women by the media.

Before commenting on the few exceptions to this rule, certain other features of media organisation have to be mentioned because of their bearing on this non-presentation of women. Principally these are the virtual absence of women from positions of editorial authority in journalism, as lecturers in journalism, and even from public service broadcasting, supposedly an innovation in the USA designed to supplement the inadequacies of the commercial channels! The mechanisms that exclude women journalists from Fleet Street newspapers in Britain range from crude discrimination, to the restriction of women journalists to the lowly regarded fashion pages, to the practical importance of the informal male bar culture among journalists in the construction of their careers. The BBC newsroom also has a powerfully male supremacist culture. The fact that in Britain during the 1970s, BBC News and ITN each hired a token woman newsreader (and a token black reporter), only highlights their virtual exclusion.

There are however two spheres of media output where women are, in a sense, much more to the fore: entertainment and advertising. These are highly significant dimensions of media to

125

which we have paid little attention in previous chapters. We may just underline the fact that although present in these spheres, women do not have the slightest scope to speak for themselves in them. Entertainment is scripted beforehand, and advertising is designed, not to provide open discussions, but to penetrate consciousness and subvert consumer preferences. Truisms, indeed; but the sheer size of the media vacuum where women's voices could be present, demands the statement and restatement of these truisms. A whole mass of women's concerns and of women's views on general issues, are off the media map.

The news media and women: the movement and rape

The handling of the women's liberation movement itself by the news media is indicative. It was disregarded as a news story till the middle of 1969. Initial reaction in the US newspapers was mostly frivolous; in Britain the first press response was to see the movement as an exotic foreign phenomenon. Neither the issues involved, nor the growth of a mass of women's organisations, were given any real space. At a later date, the US dailies came to define the movement as an attempt to adjust the social structure rather than change it radically.

Thus a major social movement, potentially affecting the entire population, was ignored, put down or redefined as a special interest. It cannot be said that media treatment of the movement has improved since then, although certain issues of women's rights are perhaps handled more sympathetically and in great depth now than previously – reflecting the impact of the movement itself, and the previous media desert, rather than the self-improving nature of media organisations.

If we turn our attention to an instance of women's oppression that has regular media coverage, namely rape, then we seen an equally distorted picture. The general ethos of the popular press softens the seriousness of sexual assault in the flood of sexually alluring photos, sexist cartoons and sexist ads, which all form the context for the stories. Certainly, papers like the *Sun* and the *News of the*

126

World highlight evocative details of rape cases, including the most salacious remarks quoted from the courtroom. Often the rapist's actions seem to be presented as the result of too much alcohol, sexual frustration, or both. The fact that rape is very often carefully planned, and committed against a women already known to the rapist, would not be understood from these accounts.

The impact of these stories is both to instil fear into all women, and thus to assist in their oppression, and to encourage men to fantasise sexual conquest. In turn, their fantasising is likely to have its effect on their everyday expectations of women, reducing them now to vagina-on-legs, beyond even the status of womb-on-legs. Sexual freedom becomes women's oppression.

Appealing to this male fantasy is obviously commercially profitable. In 1979, *Reveille* (a weekly with a 40-year tradition of this material) closed, having lost its readership to the *Sun* and the *Daily Star*, both new newspapers which handed out this diet daily instead of weekly. We should not underestimate the compensation that fantasies of sexual power, and of orgasmic release without social consequences, offer to male readers for their experience of being pushed around at work, dependent on their wage. It is a cynical betrayal by a commercially experienced press of the potential for sexual self-expression of men and women workers.

Resentment at exploitation is real, but apparently pointless. A male worker's resentment at his wife for not measuring up to newspapers' hints at the sexual qualities of young women models, brings the chance of expressing resentment closer to home. In turn, his wife resents his contempt for her, and may feel humiliated into the bargain by her inability to be 'a wife and mother', often a wage-worker as well, *and* a precocious nymphet. Sexual hostility within the working class is fanned by these processes, and probably helps to channel away the expression of the overall frustration workers feel against their exploitation.

Much remains to be done to analyse news coverage of pro- and anti-abortion demonstrations, as well as of the women's movement and of rape. Women workers' strikes would be another important topic, remembering how the striking women machinists

127

at Ford's Dagenham in May to June 1968 were presented by the press as being called in by Barbara Castle (then Employment Secretary) for a cup of tea and a chat. Once again the domestic imagery was out front, but this time to trivialise a strike which crystallised the long demand to abolish women's pay-rates.

Let us conclude by recalling the prime women's story in the local press: marriage. One of the staple features of local newspapers is the collection of photos of brides trussed up for their future domestic bliss. It is the only point at which they are ever likely to be news. Another one down. Nothing they do in the home will ever be in the paper, apart from murder or suicide – or being raped . . .

Entertainment media and women: macho, domesto, porno

No account of women's media presentation which set out to analyse more than a rather eerie silence could afford to neglect films, TV shows, women's magazines and the growth of pornography. The power of this type of media product lies in its appeal to the imagination and its arousal of fantasy.

Having said that, good material on the subject is hard to come by. There are accounts of the treatment of men and women in films, but they are usually written by film critics, in style that passes highly individual and rapid comments on a welter of films, mostly unknown except to film buffs. Of the rest, only women's magazines have been assigned a small number of studies of any detail. However, let us see what findings do exist.

Most film studies are of the American cinema. Given that so many American films are distributed in Britain and later shown on TV, this emphasis does not matter too much. It seems that the film portrayal of women has actually worsened since the emergence of the women's movement. As both Haskell and Mellen point out, the sixties and seventies have bulged with films that are effectively male only. Clint Eastwood, 'James Bond', Burt Reynolds, Charles Bronson, Jack Nicholson, Steve McQueen, Robert Redford, Paul Newman, Dustin Hoffman, are only nine names out of many who have both starred and customarily acted without women except as

128

occasional supports. There is, admittedly, the previous generation such as John Wayne (once Marion M. Morrison!), Gary Cooper, James Stewart, Rock Hudson and Alan Ladd, who were exemplars for this later trend. But in that previous period, there were also powerful American actresses, such Mae West, Lauren Bacall, Marilyn Monroe, Katharine Hepburn and Bette Davis. The later wave of actresses such as Jane Fonda, Joanne Woodward, Glenda Jackson and Vanessa Redgrave, while certainly powerful, have rarely been in films with a big box office draw.

Again, American films in the fifties could recognise real emotions between men and women. More recently, physical sexual relations have become very prominent, but emotional relations have withered as a subject. Emotional relations tend to be between 'buddies', Starsky and Hutch style, without a hint of homo-sexuality. Not since Chaplin, Keaton and W. C. Fields have male stars been comic, ridiculous, vulnerable. Certainly male stars are never to be seen washing up, ironing, cleaning or shopping. Their emotional insecurities either do not exist, or are quickly solved, often by the required fuck.

The British film industry is puny by comparison, but it is nonetheless instructive to reflect on two of its standard styles. Neither the 'social realism' films (such as *Room at the Top*, *Saturday Night and Sunday Morning*, *A Kind of Loving*), nor the endless *Carry On* films – especially these – are at odds with the images of men and women in American films! Incongruous as these two categories of film are together on one level, on the level of presenting the reality of women's lives they have more in common than might be supposed. Except for *A Taste of Honey*, and for Simone Signoret's role in *Room at the Top*, it is hard to think the women's parts in these films achieved prominence or complexity.

Thus although film portrayal of reality demands the presence of some representatives of the female half of the population, we still await a non-sexist or anti-sexist mass cinema. Indeed the trend may even be moving away from this direction rather than towards it.

TV entertainment confirms the situation in films. For example, one survey of 22 American family shows (quite a percentage of them shown in Britain), found that the 34 women characters in them were portrayed either as wives and mothers, or in comic roles. None of the married women worked outside the home. Only two women held prestigious positions, and so were independent of men, yet they tended to play them in a way that made them appear more subservient and less rational than their male counterparts. Women were normally tall, slim, attractive and well-dressed. The male characters, by contrast, occupied a diversity of roles and varied in their physical appearance. In general in TV entertainment men normally dominated women, though more so in crime series than in situation comedies.

It is normally the case that situation comedies and soap operas offer more scope to women's parts than the ever-increasing welter of police and crime series. With the exceptions of *Policewomen* and *Charlie's Angels*, these were another male preserve up to the end of the seventies. Not that either of these exceptions was a blow for women's liberation. 'Charlie's' three women characters were still organised by the unseen Charlie and his visible sidekick, and for obscure reasons seemed to be content with this childish charade. Their physical fighting capacity was not high, and part of the drama often consisted in the unspoken fact they were the weaker sex threatened by dangerous members of the stronger sex. Policewomen Angie Dickinson never pinned down her quarries alone, as did Kojak and other male cops. Her romantic existence also played a larger part than was ever the case in the big series, such as *Streets of San Francisco*, *Hawaii Five-O*, *The Professionals*.

As for *Bionic Woman* and *Wonderwoman*, female counterparts to the fantasies of male potency in *Six Million Dollar Man* and *The Incredible Hulk*, it was noticeable to anyone with the stamina to watch them that whereas Bionic Man was a former test-pilot with NASA, Bionic Woman was a former tennis star. In the episodes, their strength was combined with intelligence in his case, feminine beauty in hers. Wonderwoman was incapable of doing her amazing tricks unless she shed all her clothes except a one-piece that exhibited starkly her full figure. The continuing message of *Hulk* seemed to be that beneath the feyest male lurks massive power, even if *his* clothes-shedding somehow split his shirt but not his pants . . .

TV situation comedies deserve a much fuller analysis than they have so far received. I wish at this point simply to make one observation based on an interpretation of one of their recurrent features. Women are shown in them, quite often, as more intelligent than men, more subtle and imaginative, less rigid and wooden in their responses to immediate human problems. Some of the implied humour of the situation lies in this mockery of male pretensions. Yet there is usually a further underlying supposition, which is the incongruousness of female superiority even though it is based on her greater experience with interpersonal = domestic matters. A perfect illustration of this point was one series in which it was the axis of the episodes, a sitcom called *George and Mildred*. George was Mildred's husband, a rather small, mousy, sexless incompetent who was perpetually creating accidental havoc, from which he was constantly being rescued by Mildred. Mildred was larger physically than he was, sexually frustrated and voracious, and generally very much in command. Yet the motor which was presented as driving her was her deep longing that George could somehow be transformed into a MAN – at least sexually and in terms of his mouselike moral fibre.

In other words, sexual power-role reversal in sitcoms is often what provides the incongruity and so the comedy. Regrettably, there is little else in the way of studies of all the other TV shows, soap operas, variety shows, quiz shows and TV plays. One last comment however is in order. Studies of patterns of appearance of women and blacks in American TV entertainment found that from the early seventies blacks began to fade once more from the screen, to be replaced by more women. If accurate, this shows the sustained pressure needed to make the media non-racist and non-sexist.

Women's magazines present a paradox. Whereas men have a whole range of specialised hobby magazines written for them,

131

being a woman seems to be defined as a single hobby in itself. Thus women's interests are catered for in women's magazines, or on the Women's Page of dailies. In radio, *Woman's Hour* was always at – 2 p.m.! However, in Britain women's magazines have had a particularly wide readership since world war two, with a copy being sold to four out of every five adult women at one period. What messages are carried in them?

We may begin with a study of the cover photos of three leading British women's magazines over a 25-year period. These are important to their editors, since they are thought both to indicate the tone of the product and to be crucial in selling it.

The favourite style of face was what Ferguson described as 'Chocolate Box', signifying a 'blandly pleasing, warm-bath kind of warmth . . . half or full smile'. The next favourite style of face was what she described as 'Invitational': 'emphasis on the eyes, mouth shut or with only a hint of a smile . . . suggestive of mischief or mystery, hint of the female interaction potential rather than sexual promise.' The implication of these images was that all was right with women's world, proceeding stably and contentedly. No hint of Valium prescriptions here . . .

Overwhelmingly the women portrayed were in their twenties; none was ever over forty. This confirms the emphasis on young women which we have already seen in American family TV shows, and which we shall find to be the norm in advertising. It is an implied commandment that women must not grow old if they wish to be regarded seriously, or perhaps at all. As we saw in the dissection of sexism earlier on, in that ideology a women whose uterus no longer functions, no longer has a clear function. The counter-attack on sexual liberation has defined women as no longer sexually desirable after forty. Once both uterus and vagina are discounted, what are women for? It is a vicious, destructive ideology, but one of incredible potency. Then people wonder why middle-aged women sometimes cling on to their teenage and adult children . . .

Another study contrasted two American women's magazines, *Family Circle* and *Ms*, representing in turn conventional and

132

feminist perspectives (and so with echoes in British media as well). There were predictable contrasts between the two, but the women portrayed by *Ms* did not represent an altogether revolutionary change in perspective for American magazines. *Ms* focuses on people from the world of work, whereas since world war two American magazines have been solidly within the keynesian schema in their concentration on people who operate in the world of consumption and leisure. In this sense, *Ms* is a throwback, not a radical departure. At the same time its overall drift is that 'the world will be more humane when women hold important positions'. This is very reminiscent of the American suffragists' argument that women would be a gentling force in public affairs. Perhaps this kind of position, while an advance, does not represent a drastic switch after all. At least, however, *Ms* covers are not restricted to one age-group.

The magazine image of Jacqueline Kennedy/Onassis in American women's magazines, is interesting on other counts. The massive financial empire behind a $30,000-a-month clothes' bill was given no comment. Instead, readers of a dozen women's magazines were encouraged to identify with Jackie's emotional and domestic problems. Indeed, the working-class readership magazines hardly even referred to her wealth. Her problems could even be argued to be evidence of the irrelevance of personal wealth. Exactly the same treatment of the Queen and of film stars can be seen in British magazines.

This finding is important in confirming that the analysis of messages to women, or images of women, cannot succeed in its tasks by merely assessing women's images. These magazines were all saying that what women have in common is more important than what divides them, Queen of Britain, Jackie, or whoever. Yet by saying this, an extremely important political message was being got across to working-class and middle-class women. No serious study can ignore the constant elements of class ideology in these media, a communication designed to integrate the women of the working class with ruling-class women.

A debate between Pollock and Spence in the journal *Screen*

133

Education emphasises this point. Pollock insists that the analysis of photos of women is incomplete without understanding the corresponding images of men. In particular, she stresses the way in which the direct contrast of males photographed in the same way as women, illuminates the specific prejudices behind the presentation of women. She instances a woman photographed bare-breasted carrying a tray of apples, and a man photographed holding a tray of bananas just below his naked genitals. Through the comic contrast, it is possible to recognise the importance of women's bodies in their contemporary image, and the far lesser significance of men's (ancient Greece was quite another matter).

Spence does not disagree with Pollock so much as take her argument a vital step further. She argues that photographic images of women cannot be analysed purely on the plane of gender, but that class operates its own important dimension. She analyses the growth of advertisement photos of women at work in the 1970s as a reflection of capital's need to stimulate consumption and so to get women earning. The organisation of women's images is not then, she argues, simply founded on gender, even the dynamics of both genders together. Women's images are organised by class forces as well. It is an assertion central to this chapter, but not reflected in many studies of women and media.

The last comment on women's magazines comes from Frankl's survey of them, in particular the newer wave represented by *Cosmopolitan*. Here there is certainly a far great openness toward and emphasis on women's sexual needs. The tilt is even toward presenting men as sex-objects parallel to the conventional presentation of young women. However, *Cosmopolitan* assumes its women readers want to join the system, not to overthrow it. Frankl concludes:

> If you are obliged to *buy* all the props for your rebellion, if commerce provides you with the wherewithal of a new image, then your rebellion and your new image is bound to be a fashion, and will be subject to changes of fashion . . . Your ideas and life style become a market commodity and can be manipulated by business.

134

The question of pornography is a complex one, on one level it raises the question of whether most artistic presentation of erotic women has not been a reflex of male supremacy, whatever its artistic skill. Certainly in the seventies the dividing line has become almost invisible between 'public', 'soft' pornograhy, as in the *Sun*, and 'hardcore', 'adults only' pornography in magazines. The producers of pornography have reduced the presentation of women to minute, clinical and contemptuous detail: 'beaver' means the portrayal of women's pubic hair; 'split beaver' is their term for portrayal of the vaginal opening. Sales have boomed, and so pornography cannot be left out of the analysis of women's presentation in entertainment media. We will draw heavily on Frankl's valuable discussion of the subject.

In essence, the growth of pornography stems from commercial exploitation of the potential for revolutionary liberation in sexual self-expression, (and thus constitutes a reason for its present failure). The stress in pornographic magazines on photographs; their concentration on activities such as spanking, sadism, masochism, orgasm with artificial sex-aids; their rare articles; their tendency to substitute advertisements for sexual partners, for letters about problems of sexuality: none of these encourage sexual liberation. Frankl cites the advertisement of a two-week course in mutual massage and bathing as a method of sexual arousal, and drily notes the irony in organising puritans to become sensitised to their bodies through a list of pedantic instructions . . .

The result of their cynical pretence at sexual revolution promotes a:

> de-personalised and regressive sexuality . . . When the experience of subjectivity, the inner sense of being alive, when the communication of subjective feeling through love and friendship is not possible for the armoured and alienated man, he will either buy a sex symbol or commodity or he will make a scientific research project to measure human reactions, to discover in this way what he cannot know subjectively.

(In this last remark Frankl is referring to the related

135

development of sexology, and its own perverted assumption that any orgasm necessarily leads to health.)

When we recall the importance of pornographic photos of women in the factory, often to decorate and 'humanise' some corner where a male worker does his daily shift, then we can see at once the importance of this form of media presentation of women, and its relation to class. The frequency with which sexual experience is mechanically traded in teabreak discussions at work, the drawing-power of dinner-break strip-shows in pubs near factories, all testify to that compensatory function of sexual fantasy mentioned above, in overlaying the harsh realities of exploitation – for men workers. At the same time, as was suggested in the discussion of rape accounts in certain newspapers, the untouchable enemy at work (the boss) is joined by the betrayal at home, the woman who does not meet up to these sexual fantasies. She can not only be touched, but is liable to be beaten up as an alternative. The woman at home can become the accessible enemy, ignored and despised, if not actually attacked.

We have now provided a sketch of the range of communications to and about women in entertainment media. It it clear how they restrict the definitions of women, reducing them in most cases either to domestic serfs or to sex objects. The impact is often to induce in women a sense of inadequacy and anxiety about their social role and their own significance. The advertising industry is specifically geared to sharpening up that anxiety and to battening on it, and so it is to adverts that we must now turn.

Women in advertising: the slender young body

The presentation of women in advertising cannot be understood without first grasping some essential features of advertising in general. Advertising came into its own with the arrival of the keynesian state. Simply producing high wages, consumer credit and more leisure hours, were not enough to guarantee the right level and kind of consumption. What Ewen calls the 'psychic desire to consume' was the missing element supplied by constant advertising pressure. In constructing this psychic desire, certain leading psychologists were systematically consulted. One of the most famous, in the thirties F. H. Allport, was of the opinion that if people felt themselves to be under 'continual and harsh social scrutiny', they would be much more receptive to advertising which offered them some protection. This has been a cornerstone of much advertising, especially to women, ever since. Fear has been the propulsion to buy.

In this scheme, 'women were cultivated as general purchasing managers for the household'. A 1929 report of the American Academy of Political and Social Science described the housewife, in terms already familiar to readers from the dissection of sexism above, as 'an administrator and enterpriser in the business of living'. Thus women in advertising are more than simply attention-getters for the product, like the nude models paid to drape themselves across new cars in motor-shows. Women are targets because they spend the wages. For these reasons they are everywhere in adverts.

However, it is not women as such who are normally used in advertising. It is *young* women, just as in family TV shows and women's magazines. And it is not just *any* young women either. These are expected, as Lavoisier has found, to be young, extremely slim, and much taller than average. In other words, advertising tells all women they should conform to the rather unusual age and shape of a female model. To a surprising extent, the fashion industry also tends to produce clothes tailored for this shape, though only a minority of women can conform to it.

The rigid conviction among many women that they are too fat – even women who actually fit the advertisers' norm feel this – cannot be explained otherwise than by reference to advertisers' portrayal of women. Indeed, Lavoisier gives some instances of relatively lifelike ad drawings, rather than photos, in which this distortion was not constrained by any physical reality of actual women. The pictures of women are so elongated that the women might have come from a medieval torture-rack.

The reactions of many women to this anxiety, apart from

137

having to live with it and feel inadequate, are to involve themselves in slimming programmes, quite possibly eating less in the way of necessary diet than they should. These programmes are not embraced by men in the same way until they reach middle age and begin to worry about blood pressure and heart attacks. The different effect is obvious, and it is a tribute to the power of advertising media that women's weight-anxiety is usually proof even against their own men companions' standard conviction that pneumatic bliss scores against skeletal edges any day.

Let us turn in more detail to the ways in which advertising plays upon women's anxieties, or strives to create them, in order to solve the problem with its proffered commodity. The attempt is frequently blatant, and contains the following elements.

The first is the reinforcement of the body in the image of woman. Advertising lends enormous vitality to the feeling that this body must be fully acceptable to its actual or potential male users. Think of the numerous instances of adverts concerning skin, lips, nails and cuticles, hair, eyelashes and eyebrows, teeth, breath, corns, periods and breasts (size and shape). Even notes how in the twenties an even larger percentage of ads showed women looking in mirrors. He comments that 'women were being educated to look at themselves as things to be . . . painted and sculpted with the aid of the modern market.' This was not a new impulse of course, but advertising certainly expanded it on an unprecedented scale.

All these messages are pitched to cue in on women's concern for their satisfactory appearance to men (the parallel in advertising to men about their appearance is simply not in the same league). Thus women are systematically pressured to accept their reduction to being a body-for-men, and even to pay handsomely for the privilege.

Secondly, prodding women to compete with each other is never far from the surface in this kind of advertising. There is always the presumption that even the woman attached to one man must be careful to 'keep' him, or better bodies may entice him away. As for unattached women, how are they to end their pre-dicament satisfactorily, by riveting the attention of the man they

138

want, and not choking him with body odour or disgusting him with carelessly trimmed cuticles? In soap advertisements, efficiency in promoting cleanliness is hardly ever the message; it is rather the soap's potential for romance, or for averting romantic disaster, which is its key property. People may laugh at ludicrous associations like these, but are quite likely affected by them in their thinking about male–female relations even while remaining unconvinced about soap-brands.

Thirdly, women are advertised at to persuade them to spend on domestic appliances, cleaning aids, babyware and processed foods. Once more their anxieties are played upon. Domestic inefficiency on the part of a housewife obviously denies her utility as a human being. One advertisement cites a housewife's supposed 'damaging confession' that after spring cleaning the house had been getting dirtier. Solution? A vacuum cleaner. Another cites the relieved assurance of another supposed housewife that after using Saniflush, she will be declared 'Not Guilty!' of lack of toilet hygiene.

Clearly, advertisers feel compelled to warn women that the Sexual Inquisition is constantly on its rounds, ruthlessly investigating their overweight, their smells, their houses' cleanliness, their childcare practices, their cooking. Only expensive but necessary commodities will enable them to pass scrutiny.

This scrutiny is not just a figure of speech. Lavoisier devotes a considerable part of her book to discussing the relation between advertising and men's scrutinising gaze at women passers-by. Women know only too well how they are often reduced by this gaze to two buttocks, two mammaries and a vagina, without mind, personality or rights. It is not necessary to agree with Lavoisier that advertising is the only source of this type of interaction, to recognise nonetheless how it is massively encouraged by adverts. Lavoisier cites some of her women interviewees who admit to scrutinising other women themselves, to reassure themselves of their own bodily acceptability or superiority, and others who recount the crushing experience of being scrutinised in this way by other women, or doing so themselves, and then being convinced

139

they have lost the contest. Especially when they are in the company of their male friend. The pressures on men to compete with each other's bodies in this way are trivial by comparison.

The last point to be made about advertising images of women has been made to some extent already, but deserves restating. Advertisers are highly conscious of class differences in income among consumers, as they are of the significance of housewives in making decisions about consumption. Thus they will not produce images of women as such. Their images of women will be geared to the income bracket most likely to buy the commodity they are advertising. In one magazine the woman would be exquisitely dressed; in another, hard-pressed and a little flustered. In the case of hoardings, they will normally aim for the middle range of the market, not too far from anybody's buying power.

There are even indications of the covert effect of the women's movement in making advertisers' images of women more differentiated. Williamson cites two examples which seem to indicate this trend. One two-page ad has the same woman on both pages. On the left-hand page she says, 'As a bio-chemist, I recommend Skin Dynamics.' She looks crisp, efficient, has a white labcoat on, and appears authoritative. On the right-hand page is the same woman, now made-up, saying 'As a woman, I love Skin Dynamics.' Her appearance is less practically efficient, she is off duty, her lips are slightly parted, and she has exchanged her authority for a certain potential for intimate, relaxed conversation.

This advert states woman's capacity for a scientific career, only to transcend it in favour of her more vital and compelling total self, as a fascinating man's woman. The fundamentals of the message remain what they have always been.

Williamson cites another advert in which one woman is presented in seven pictures, at work, playing sport, interacting with a man friend, and so on, *and* – with her hair unset. The message is that a Eugene 10-Day Set will enable her to get through the many varied activities in her life, but still be a presentable woman at all times.

These last two examples are important because they illustrate the subtlety and sophistication of which advertising is capable, its ability to remodel its messages according to changing realities. Not only women's liberation, but alternative life styles and the ecology movement, have been used as themes in advertising during the seventies. Clothes and cosmetics for the liberated woman have been a particularly standard theme. At the same time, what this has often meant is the reduction of women's liberation to liberation in sexual matters, and the further distortion of that liberation into increased sexual availability of young women for male users, as we saw above in the analysis of trends in sexism. Thus liberation has been offered from *so much* housework by domestic appliances, equality has been put within reach by the chance of buying a second family car, and women's sexual self-determination has been established with see-through bras. Consumer power means women's power . . .

The economic effectiveness of these ads is beyond our scope for discussion here. What is beyond dispute is their reiteration and reinforcement of certain highly restricted images of women, even when these images are quite subtly conveyed to be in tune with contemporary social trends. These images are conditioned by different images of men, by social class, by skin colour, and have as a peculiarly important motif the bodies of women. Mother, Housewife, Wife, Lover: these constitute the sum of woman.

Conclusions

In this survey of women's presentation in the media, we have been forced firstly to recognise their 'symbolic annihilation' from certain important branches of media production. We have also noted their absence from positions of power in media organisations, as indeed their lower representation in media organisations overall. Thus in many cases it is not a question of the restricted presentation of women in the media, but of their banishment.

In the realm of news, such happenings as the women's movement and such events as rape, we found to be handled in ways

141

that varied from the poor to the sex-sational. It is not hard to trace the consequences of these patterns of presentation for the production of women's oppression and the dismissal of their resistance. In entertainment and advertising media we found wearisomely rehashed the ideologies about women that surfaced time and again in the analysis of sexism earlier on. Usually they were refracted into class categories. At the same time a number of the presentations were far from crude or repetitive in their actual wrapping of the message.

What we did *not* find was any comment on the segregation of women into domestic labour; their function as cheap labour in the factory and office and as home-workers; their place as disposable factors in the reserve army of labour; their activity as organisers on their own behalf, in and out of the women's movement; their status as sexual actors, but just recipients; or indeed their existence as humans with independent minds who are *systematically*, not just individually, oppressed. We did not find women's history of struggle, in public or in private, or the history of women's labour in industrialisation. We did not find the history of women's struggle against imperialism, past or present.

In the realm of women's oppression the media have therefore a dual affect. They encourage men in their assumptions of male supremacy, that women's place is in the home or the bed, and that they are the strong providers for them. They pressurise women to accept all this baloney.

Contrasted with the operation of media in relation to class or racism, the media's sexism is rarely concerned with sudden and dramatic political changes. Neither strikes nor 'immigration' have any real parallel in this area, which is concerned much more with the long term undertow of daily life. This directly mirrors the political significance of sexism in the organisation of capitalist society, over and above its immediate oppression of women as individuals. Domesticity, leisure and media entertainment all belong to the private realm, and thus to the slight involvement of half the population in the public sphere of social and political life.

142

Part Two

7. Capitalist Media: a Marxist Introduction

The birth of mass media: the case of Britain

To understand the media in the present, it is first necessary to know how they began and developed to their present form. There are plenty of histories of publishing, press, radio, photography, cinema, TV, which are more or less informative and/or boring. What they normally omit is the key question of the basic reasons for the emergence and growth of new media. Typically, a basic reason in these accounts is the sheer possibility of a new technology. *Why* this particular technology grew, is regarded as self-explanatory. They assume the new technology is itself the basic, self-propelling reason for the development of a new method of communication. Behind that concrete ultimate, they do not penetrate. Hence, the incredible insulation of histories of media from each other, let alone from the basic changes in human societies over the past two hundred years. The interaction of specific inventors and patrons, and the internal potential of the technical innovation itself, are reckoned to be a complete explanation of what happened.

Here we are not going to look at Caxton, Marconi, Baird, the *camera obscura* or even the electronics industry. Our initial concern is with what Jürgen Habermas, in a seminal study, has called the changing organisation of public debate. He traces the emergence of the distinction between 'public' and 'private' as capitalist relations began to dominate feudal relations in Europe.

In almost every late feudal state, the principle of absolute monarchy had to be asserted and reasserted against the rising demand for political influence by the emerging capitalist class. An example of this principle's assertion in its tightest form is to be seen in the reply by Louis XVI of France, rejecting the idea of a representative assembly. He declared:

> Those principles, which are universally accepted by the nation, stipulate that to the King alone belongs the sovereign power in his kingdom, that this exercise of power is accountable only to God; that the link which unites the King and the nation cannot by its nature be dissolved; that the mutual obligation of the King and his subjects can only ensure the perpetuation of this union; that the nation has an interest in making sure that the rights of its commander are not changed whatsoever; that the King is the supreme commander of the nation and is one with the nation; finally, that the power to make laws resides in the person of the Sovereign without dependence or division.

Now, the fact that monarchs always had their clique of advisers, some of them sometimes coming to wield greater effective power than the monarch himself, did not change this structure of power. However, in time, whether absolutist rule was swept away as in the United States or France, or whether it changed more slowly as in other countries, it yielded to the principle of extending involvement in political decisions downwards, and to developing this involvement structurally, not simply for individuals. It was a slow process: we have seen how African slaves never got near power in the 'land of the free', and how white workers and white women had acute struggles to achieve first base, the right to vote in parliamentary elections.

Nonetheless, the social base of political involvement was widened. The public realm began to stretch beyond the court, and the importance of the court itself shrank inexorably. It meant that political decision-making was able to be influenced by wider and wider circles. So, in those circles, they talked about politics and the issues of the day. Broadsheets and posters emerged in the tea-houses and coffee-houses (in France, in the salons) patronised by well-to-do men. Well-to-do women in London protested angrily, but were excluded (see chapter 5). In the single decade 1700–1710,

144

there were over 3,000 such coffee-houses in London, each usually with a regular clientele.

This changing structure of public debate was of course a parallel to the growing demand by the well-to-do for freedom from government interference in their economic activity. Just as market forces should be allowed to work themselves out freely, ran the argument, so should ideas about politics and government. It was a tenacious ideology, which took the ideas of the well-to-do and the politically dominant as expressing the interests of the majority. This emerging structure of public debate was the matrix for the eventual development of the newspaper. It was not advances in printing technology that caused the newspaper, but changes in certain economic and political relations which stimulated the need for news-sheets and newspapers to convey information quickly about politics and other matters to a large number of people.

This development was to backfire badly however once a literate and politically self-conscious artisan and craft worker class emerged: the growth of a whole mass of radical newspapers in the 1820s and 1830s put liberal ideology to the test. Would it allow the free play of *any* political ideas? The ruling class found itself caught up in its own contradiction: it had summoned into being working classes through its enclosures of rural land, through its development of industrial capitalist production, and through its major imperialist presence overseas. Workers were essential – yet the higher grades and the artisans could quite often read. What is more, printers were among them, who could therefore produce newspapers on a small scale.

There was a major struggle of classes in newspaper production in Britain in the Chartist period. In order to try to force the radical papers underground and close them down, the government slapped a tax on any copy of any newspaper. *The Times*, not surprisingly, accepted it and charged sevenpence for itself; naturally enough it was still read by the literate members of the ruling classes. Most small circulation papers dependent on a low-income readership would have priced themselves out of readers if they had charged the tax. Punishment for refusal was a fine or

145

imprisonment or both. Eventually, as a result of the determined resistance of the printers, including their readiness to risk prison, the government lifted its tax, but only when Chartism was past its peak as a political force . . .

At the time, the surcharge was described as a 'tax on knowledge'. It is a tribute to the contradictory ideological position the ruling class was in, that the government did not feel able simply to impose censorship, normal enough in the old absolutist state, and then still fully in force in Germany whose capitalist development was largely yet to come. Instead the government imposed an economic discriminator, technically leaving everyone free to buy a newspaper. One response to this was to make coffee-houses double up as newspaper reading centres. Another was to flout the law openly and advertise for illegal distributors. Plenty volunteered.

What the English example shows is that the social significance of mass communication in its beginnings derives from the development of classes namely in the historical transition from a late feudal to an early capitalist economy. With this transition went a changing organisation of political involvement and of public debate. The newspaper was a weapon in first one, and then another, class war; first in cracking the mould of feudal politics, then in the struggle against capitalism. It was the very breath of the day-to-day ideological combat between class and class, between state and subordinate classes. As one of many members of the English ruling class complained about the radical press in the 1820s: 'Dustmen and porters read and discuss politics; and labourers, journeymen and masters speak one language of disaffection and defiance.' The contrast between this period and the present in the leading capitalist countries is extremely sharp.

The growth of new media technologies, cinema, radio and TV is the most visible change in communication, but as previously their development has never been self-propelled. The decisive insight into their present operation, not as specific technologies but as socially and politically powerful institutions, belongs to Antonio Gramsci. It was he who made possible an explanation of

146

the transformation of media from potential instruments of liberation for working classes into instruments of dominance and leadership for the ruling classes in the later nineteenth and twentieth centuries.

Gramsci's theory of 'hegemony'

Gramsci did not spend time elaborating any theory of the media as such, although the roles of a socialist press and of popular culture interested him greatly. Rather, he developed a theory of class struggle directly relevant to understanding the operation of media in developed capitalism – and if it comes to that, the roles of education and religion as well. His theory incorporated the dimension of ideology, so covering in principle all the sources, mechanisms and relations of communication. We shall need to add quite a number of specific points about the media as such, but let us ground these by presenting his core themes in their own right: 'hegemony', embracing ideological dominance and class alliances; the contradictory consciousness of workers; the central role of mass hegemonic institutions. To begin with, though, we must understand the central political dilemma at the heart of his theoretical work.

Writing in the twenties and thirties, Gramsci's thought pivoted on the contrast between the success of the Bolshevik Revolution and the failure of socialist revolution in western Europe. It was a standard enough theme among communists at the time; when the Third Communist International was set up in Moscow in 1919, its leaders saw its Russian address as temporary, pending its likely location in Germany after the imminent revolution there. The waves of sharp working-class struggle in Italy, Germany, France, Britain, the USA and many other countries in the period 1918–20, made socialist revolutions elsewhere seem only a matter of a few months or years away. The isolation of the Bolsheviks was an unexpected and bitter outcome for them and for all communists.

Gramsci, then, focused on the problems of achieving a

147

successful socialist revolution elsewhere in Europe. He saw the vital contrast between western Europe and Russia as being the development of a whole institutional-ideological complex in western European societies of a kind that had scarcely existed in Tsarist Russia. This complex consisted of schools, universities, the church, media, publishing, trade unionism, the family: it made up a whole array of ideological supports of the bourgeois class which had to be undermined before a revolutionary seizure of state power was possible. To overcome the power of the ruling class in western Europe, therefore, would not mean just a rapid military operation in a period of crisis, in order to seize and immobilise its army and police power. It would be something closer to pain-staking trench warfare, gradually defeating this complex of ideological institutions while continuing with economic struggles and military preparedness.

In turn, this institutional-ideological complex was not a rapidly invented policy package by the ruling classes of western Europe. It had emerged over time, and the forms it now took had taken shape gradually, at different rhythms in different countries. The emergence of mass education as a method of disciplining the working class while meeting its demand for literacy, is the easiest example of these processes at work. The corresponding growth of newspapers as a small cluster of big-circulation dailies, owned by capitalists and increasingly dependent on advertising revenue, was a trend in the nineteenth and twentieth centuries.

This institutional-ideological complex is only a part of what Gramsci meant by 'hegemony'. For as well as the word fusing two English concepts, dominance *and* leadership, it also contains two basic components: the ideological dimension of capitalist rule, and the question of class alliances.

If we recognise that a capitalist class cannot rule by terror alone for a long period, that it must normally be able to win acceptance of its leadership of the rest of society, then equally we must see that it cannot rule all by itself either. Since the capitalists are always a small percentage of the population in any country, they need class allies to secure their rule. Their normal class ally is

148

the petit bourgeoisie – accountants, lawyers, doctors, surveyors, estate agents, management, administrators, social workers, educators, journalists. This is the class closest to the bourgeoisie in level of income, social background, life style, aspirations and general ideology. It looks to the capitalist class as the obvious rulers and to itself as the capitalists' natural allies and the obvious pool of talent from which individuals may be promoted into the ruling class or the upper layers of the state. (One study of modern France gave an estimate of the size of this class there, as roughly 17 per cent of the working population.)

A class alliance is quite unlike a party political alliance, patched up for tactical electoral advantage and potentially discardable at will. A class alliance emerges over time, and out of the mutual long-term understanding within each class of their respective past, present and future interests. In particular, it emerges from the ability of the ruling class to imprint on other classes its own view of itself as the natural leaders, to whom loyalty is only commonsense.

This imprint is never just the straight agreement to the simple practical question: shall *we* rule? It is because of its superior grasp of the movement of history, because of its coherent and encompassing world view, extending into science, literature, the arts, government and even personal relations, that the ruling class exerts its hegemony over other classes.

Whenever and wherever possible, however, it *also* attempts to exert this hegemony over the working class and peasant classes, over and above its stable alliance with the petit bourgeoisie. To return for a moment to the pivotal contrast in Gramsci's thought between Russia and Italy, the difference between the two in revolutionary success or failure did not lie in the organisation or combativity of the working class. A vital difference was that the Russian working class succeeded in 1917 in imprinting its hegemony cn the peasant classes. The peasants in Italy, however, were still firmly under the hegemony of the old ruling class, materially assisted by the ideological force of the Catholic Church in the countryside. And by itself, the Italian working class could not rule. Thus hegemony over class allies is central to capitalist stability and to socialist revolution.

However, ideological dominance and leadership over the working class and the peasant classes is not always enough. Whereas the petit bourgeoisie rarely revolts, workers and peasants do revolt against the system. Then, argued Gramsci, capitalist rule required physical force.

Hegemony and the sources of political instability

In his analysis Gramsci also insisted on the importance of the co-existence and even interpenetration of warring ideologies within the working class, and the tremendous strategic importance of what I will call mass hegemonic institutions, both capitalist and anti-capitalist (eg the British Broadcasting Corporation, and a mass revoluntionary socialist party). Let us look at each in turn.

Gramsci saw the consciousness of the working class neither as a passive mirroring of what it was told to think by the ruling nor as a triumphant socialist conviction only temporarily thwarted by reformist political leaders. Instead, he focused on the divided elements in working-class consciousness and on the varying situations of struggle which would call forth one or other element.

> The social class in question may indeed have its own conception of the world, even if only embryonic; a conception which manifests itself in action, but occasionally and in flashes – when, that is, the class is acting as an organic totality. But this same class has, for reasons of submission and intellectual subordination, adopted a position which is not its own but is borrowed from another class; and it affirms this conception verbally and believes itself to be following it, because this is the conception which it follows in 'normal times' – that is, when its conduct is not independent and autonomous, but submissive and subordinate . . . The active man-in-the-mass has a practical activity but has no clear theoretical consciousness of his practical activity . . . His theoretical consciousness can indeed be historically in opposition to his activity. One might almost say he has two theoretical consciousnesses (or one contraconsciousness): one which is implicit in his activity and

150

which in reality unites him with all his fellow workers in the practical transformation of the real world: and one, superficially explicit or verbal, which he has inherited from the past and uncritically absorbed. But this verbal conception is not without consequences. It holds together a specific social class, it influences moral conduct and the direction of will, with varying efficacity but often powerfully enough to produce a situation in which the contradictory state of consciousness does not permit of any action, any decision or any choice, and produces a condition of moral and political passivity.

The central point raised here is the divided state of consciousness of most members of the working class. This division is not just between individual members or sections of the working class, important as these may be, but within individual workers themselves. The ideological class struggle takes place as a daily reality inside the heads and guts of workers, with political apathy and fatalism representing a temporary victory for capitalist hegemony. At the most basic level of analysis, then, the individual's own consciousness is likely to be an unstable amalgam of spontaneous resistance to capitalist relations and of accepting capitalist society as 'normal', 'sensible'.

Examples of co-existing warring ideologies are not hard to find. A classic case is of the worker who is ready to strike if s/he thinks the situation at work demands it, but equally ready to condemn other people's strikes as selfish and silly, when s/he knows of them only what s/he has heard through the media. In Nichols' and Armstrong's study, *Workers Divided*, we meet Bill, explaining industrial conflict:

> 'Why d'you get bad relations? A few reds. You only need one bad apple to spoil the barrel.'
> 'But why do the others follow them?'
> 'I suppose it's partly because you become just a number in this kind of work. You follow the bunch. A lot of men on strike don't know the reason for it. If you were to go up and ask the average bloke outside a factory gate why he was on strike, he wouldn't know . . . Don't get me wrong. The unions have done a good job. The

151

working man wouldn't be where he is today if it weren't for them. But it's these stupid strikes that're putting the country in a mess.' Here are two co-existing, warring ideologies, one plainly mirroring a standard media handling of strikes (Red extremists), the other expressing working-class tradition and experience ('the unions have done a good job' – 'you become just a number in this kind of work').

Other examples of warring ideologies expressed as a single harmonious viewpoint are to be found in society at large. Parliamentary democracy as a central instrument for achieving socialism is one, EEC workers' participation schemes as instruments for workers to wield power are another. Both echo the desire of nearly all workers, at least from time to time, to control their own lives and work processes, and to do so peacefully. Neither strategy will construct authentic democracy for workers, but will help them to lose the wood in the trees by getting them buried in the detail of 'doing the best job in the circumstances'. In these ideologies of democracy, capitalist control and workers' resistance interpenetrate each other, superficially fused.

These ideological contradictions are derived from material sources. They do not suddenly swim up out of the void. They are witness to the power of mass hegemonic institutions to which we will turn in a moment, *as well as to daily experience of exploitation and oppression.*

Thus the political neutralisation of which Gramsci spoke is not fixed reality. Workers' resistance is not ironed out of existence. The warring elements never actually fuse. Even the keynesian 'long boom' of the fifties and sixties has not proved a stable resolution of class struggle, as we noted in the first chapter.

Because of this endemic instability in capitalist society, securing political stability depends all the more on what I have called mass hegemonic institutions. The jargon is dismaying, but it is hard to think of a term which effectively defines the common dimensions of the media, schools, universities, churches, social work, and so on. 'Mass' points up one of their key features, that they have an impact on large numbers of people (*not*, of course, that subject to mass control). Although 'institutions' is a term

152

implying permanency, which has led some writers to prefer the term 'apparatus', my own preference is against the latter term as implying something too easily contrived and manipulable.

So: why are endemic social and political instability and mass hegemonic institutions interlinked? At one level the answer is straightforward: the more the instability, the greater the need to develop mechanisms to contain it, and over the centuries of capitalism these mechanisms have been worked out by trial and error.

However, there are additional dimensions to this question which are worth exploring a little. Gramsci, in commenting on the growth of literary realism in the USA, made this point:

> The fact that America has a current of literary realism critical of its customs is a very important cultural fact; it indicates that self-criticism is growing, that a new American civilisation is being born which is aware of its strengths and weaknesses: the intellectuals are detaching themselves from the dominant class in order to unite themselves more intimately to it, in order to be a real superstructure, and not simply an inorganic and undefined element of the economic structure.

The notion of the intelligentsia detaching themselves from the ruling class in order to unite themselves more intimately to it as a key moment in the establishment of hegemony for a national ruling class is an insight of profound significance for any analysis of mass hegemonic institutions. It is clear enough on reflection that capitalists in a changing environment simply cannot afford to tie themselves to a wooden reproduction of the status quo, socially any more than technologically. The fact that some of them are stupid enough to think that if things are going to stay as they are they need not change, does not alter this fact. Trotsky once said of the British bourgeoisie, that it thought in continents and centuries. The last thing the ruling class needs is to be totally surrounded by last-ditch defenders of free enterprise or any other shibboleth.

One aspect of this is perfectly illustrated by the role of Reith, the founder of the BBC, in the 1926 General Strike. His policy was that for the BBC to be seen to be conveying independent news, was a crucial factor in favour of political stability. As against

153

Churchill, who was happy enough to issue a blatantly biased government bulletin in the absence of any newspapers, Reith could see the centrality of credible institutions in maintaining order. But, as he later wrote in his private diary, the government 'know they can trust us not to be really impartial'.

Now this degree of necessary independence, necessary that is both for flexibility and for credibility, produces certain contradictions. If these institutions are to be open to dissonant ideas and individuals, they are then open on occasion to being not merely penetrated but actually 'colonised' by revolutionary elements. Poulantzas, in his study of German and Italian fascism, has drawn attention to these processes of colonisation, as also to the massive purges and reorganisations which took place in these institutions under Mussolini and Hitler. They were considered to have become totally unreliable in assuring hegemony, and thus required drastic action to restabilise the situation.

For example, Catholicism was made compulsory again in Italian schools, by the largely irreligious fascist leaders, because of its disciplinary value as well as its merits in maintaining a good relationship with the Catholic Church. In Nazi Germany, the very language used in journalism was changed to express the reorganised ideology. Some words were given new meanings, such as the word for toxaemia or blood poisoning, which was assigned the meaning 'appearance of decay in people and races'; or the word for incest, which was changed to refer to sex between Aryans and non-Aryans. Other words appeared for the first time, such as *Aufnordung*: the enlargement of the area of the Nordic 'race', or *Aufartung*: the improvement of the 'racial' stock.

But there are many other instances of purges on these institutions when no longer considered reliable by the ruling class, which take place within liberal democracy. The classic instance here was the McCarthy period in the USA, when film producers, schoolteachers, trade unionists and an array of government officials were among those dismissed from their jobs and permanently barred re-entry, because of their Communist beliefs, sympathies, or alleged sympathies. The West German state to this day maintains a permanent purge (the *Berufsverbot*) on employing anyone as a state official who has any link with marxist politics. After May 1968, the French state sacked a mass of broadcasting workers; and from 1979, the Italian state began a major purge of university lecturers.

The changeability of mass hegemonic institutions is then related to a variety of factors – the instability of working-class commitment to capitalism, the need for the ruling class to be flexible in the face of rapid change, the corresponding tendency for these institutions to become unreliable, the problems of purging them politically. The media, as one such institution, cannot be simply written off as 'in general more likely to reinforce the existing opinions of its audience than it is to change opinion'. This was the view of empiricist media research in the USA in the fifties and sixties. On the contrary, as we have argued, any of these institutions, whether licensed to experiment, or under tight rein, is an important component in coping with the problems of maintaining hegemony.

It is instructive to compare Gramsci's concept of 'hegemony' with Max Weber's term 'legitimacy', (very much a key word in radical sociology in the sixties and seventies). Now 'legitimacy' is something a government or a ruler has or has not. If they have it, their rule is secure; if they haven't, it isn't. Hegemony, by contrast, does not describe a settled state of affairs, or an 'either/or'. It denotes the continuing effort of the ruling class to influence against rebellion and for loyalty or neutrality or at least for a limited form of opposition. It presupposes a struggle to maintain an enduring alliance with the petit bourgeoisie, at least, and influence over the working class wherever possible. But it does not presuppose secure or guaranteed success for its endeavour. People's heads are not just filled up with legitimacy or non-legitimacy. Furthermore, there are many ideological elements in capitalist hegemony, and they cannot be reduced to a single core. Ideological clusters and contradictions, class alliances, mass hegemonic institutions, political instability: these are the components of the concept of hegemony.

155

The concept of hegemony and theories of the media

The media, then, are an integral part of the institutional-ideological complex of capitalist rule, a part of the development of the ruling class in alliance or struggle with other classes. Their history cannot be accurately mapped in any country if divorced from these wider relations. Now the organisation of capitalist classes and of the state has changed dramatically over the nineteenth and twentieth centuries. Understanding media means grasping the main lines along which these changes have moved.

On the economic level, there have been changes in the growth of monopoly capitalist firms, to the point where the biggest are transnational in their operation. These firms dominate industry, banking and commerce. The trend was well established already when Gramsci wrote his analysis of 'Americanism and Fordism', but has moved at ever greater speed since his day. It is a development which has not passed the media by. At the turn of the century, great press magnates had emerged, as well as some of today's biggest advertising companies. By the seventies however a further change was evident: it was becoming increasingly rare for a press baron as such to exist. More and more media were being taken over by monopoly firms as just one wing of their activity, in the same way they might buy up a toothpaste factory. A standard British case is the company Reed International, a paper trans-national which owns the International Publishing Corporation which in turn publishes the *Daily Mirror*, *Sunday Mirror*, *Sunday People*, and a mass of the biggest circulation magazines. The Thompson Organisation publishes *The Times*, the *Sunday Times*, the *Scotsman*, ninety or more papers internationally, *and* organises mass package holidays. The barons do exist: Springer in West Germany, Hersant in France, Hearst in the USA. But they are no longer the norm. Electronics firms (eg International Telegraph and Telephone) and firms involved in aerospace, are notable for their interest in broadcasting media of various types.

In turn, this raises the link between contemporary imperial-

156

ism and the media. The operations of transnationals in the Third World have been surveyed by Schiller and Mattelart. They vary from satellites, to vigorous diffusion of magazines and comics, to the establishment of advertising and public relations subsidiaries, to selling US films and television series to Third World countries. The operation is thus both profitable and has a long-term ideological goal. The latter was well expressed by two US sociologists giving evidence to a Congressional committee in Washington DC in 1967:

> Another thing that people [i.e. in the Third World] crave is simply to see what a modern way of life is like – seeing *commodities*, seeing how people live, or hearing popular music . . . the broadcasting of popular music is not likely to have any immediate effect on the audience's political attitude, but this kind of communication nevertheless provides a sort of entryway of western ideas and western concepts, even though these concepts may not be explicitly and completely stated at any one particular moment in the communication.

To speak of the state is, lastly, to raise the other main change in the organisation of the ruling class. Earlier we examined the keynesian transformation of the state. We did not examine though the growth of workers' parties, social democratic and communist, and their degree of 'colonisation' of parliament. In step with this has gone a growth and concentration of power in the top layers of the Civil Service. It is a shift of power from the legislature to the executive which has occurred in every advanced capitalist country. The precise forms vary, but the centralisation and concentration processes are identical. A result of this has been the entrenchment of secrecy about government policy-making in all these countries. In Britain, the Civil Service hierarchy is solidly against liberalising the Official Secrets Act, which presently is signed by every civil servant, however junior, on entering and leaving the Civil Service. In the USA, which is usually regarded as having the most open of the major capitalist governments, despite the Watergate upheaval, executive privilege against testifying in front of Congressional

157

committees can now be claimed by the more than 6,000 civil servants who are in the President's Executive Office, White House staff, or policy advisers. This sector's growth was especially fast in the Nixon presidency. Its result is inevitably to choke the flow of information, with direct effects on the capacity of media organisations to circulate knowledge if they wish to do so.

These implications of the growth of monopoly, of imperialism, and of the modern state, for the organisation and use of media are also part of Habermas' study of the changing structure of public debate. For him, these changes have led to the 're-feudalisation' of society, the disappearance of the private realm of social relations carved out in the early period of capitalism. One index of this he takes to be the invasion of radio and TV into everyone's homes, which provides broadcasters, advertisers and the state with a one-way channel to beam messages in even to people's individual retreats. As another, he takes the spectacular growth of opinion polling by governments, at and between elections. This is a method of sounding out individual reactions, already formed to some extent by one-way media communications, first for the government to reassure itself, and then often to re-broadcast as 'most people agree the government should take a firm line to control inflation', or whatever the issue may be. Thus in Habermas' view, a mass of pre-moulded undebated opinions is gathered, used to check public tolerance, and if appropriate to tell the public what it 'spontaneously' thinks – a slick way of pushing it to bow to the 'majority view' and conform.

It is a perspective on media in contemporary capitalism which owes much to the radical mass society theorists of the Frankfurt School, and also in particular to C. Wright Mills' *The Power Elite*. It is a view in flat contrast to the US empiricist position that the media are a rather irrelevant force in society. Despite its far greater theoretical depth, it overstates. No one should deny the significance of these uses of political opinion-polling and their interaction with media, nor the one-way form of communication (at its strongest in the fast flow of broadcasting),

158

nor the significance of transmission into every corner of people's lives, their cars, their homes, their caravans. But it understates – in a way that does not characterise Gramsci's work – the contradictions that surface within the ruling class, and the different forms of communication to different classes, and the divided consciousness of the working class. It is a view veering towards the conclusion that late capitalist society is a seamless garment.

But there are conflicts in the ruling class: on whether, for instance, to attack the unions or to attach them. In British media the first view is to be found in the *Daily Telegraph*, the second in the *Daily Express* and the *Daily Mirror*. The petit bourgeoisie are communicated with in different ways to those generally used to the working class. Far more is explained to them, they are much more likely to be invited to think and reason for themselves (though always within the bounds of bourgeois ideology). The petit bourgeoisie are not fed sex, sensationalism, soap operas, sport detail, the *Sun*, but current affairs programmes, documentaries, serious plays, international news, arts programmes, book reviews, *The Times*, *The Economist*. Journalists are in their class, and what is more, if they switch on radio or TV they are quite likely to find other members of their class talking about some issue or another. This fosters a feeling of belonging to the circles whose opinion counts; it is nutritive of the class alliance between them and the bourgeoisie.

The pointless dilemma of media research – do media have overwhelming effect, or can they be brushed aside as marginal to the formation of consciousness? – is avoided in Gramsci's analysis. The answer is that it is a perpetual struggle. The media are obviously at their weakest when they deal with matter directly within workers' own experience, but at their strongest on topics outside it.

Thus to read directly from the growth of monopoly capital, imperialism, the strong state to a stably controlled consciousness via the media, is to overstate the links between ownership and control, and media effects. It is like assuming that the dominance of advertising in media finance, or state control of broad-

159

casting bodies like the BBC, has total audience or readership effects.

The case is better put negatively: what possibilities are *not* available through the media once they are effectively under monopoly capitalist or state control? Would the ITT public relations division or one of the US advertising transnationals active in Chile have advertised a statement in favour of the Popular Unity government? There is a whole mass of potential communication that simply will not take place, and – Habermas and Mills are right this far – any serious attempt to use media in *developing* democracy for the working class will not take place. All that happens is fake participation: radio phone-ins, reader's letters, voting for the most popular song of the week, managed TV debates with audiences too large to do anything but be utilised by the show's star interviewer.

Gramsci's work, while providing a valuable anchor-point for media analysis, does not however offer any account of the *specific* role of media in the maintenance of capitalist hegemony. To that we now turn.

The specific roles of media in capitalist hegemony

To understand the particular place of capitalist media, we need to pay attention to five points. First, their continuous and pervasive output. Second, their embedding of categories of thought and definition in the memory. Third, their relation to leisure-time activity. Once these dimensions of the role of media are clear, the way is open to study, fourth, the internal inter-relation of their various elements (TV, public relations, etc.), and fifth the main linkages and contrasts in their operation with other mass hegemonic institutions, notably the family, education and parliamentary parties.

Continuous flow

Of all the features of mass media, it is their continuous flow which stands out as most distinctive. Some radio stations operate every minute of every day, every day of the year. Many TV stations come close to this. Newspapers appear daily, magazines and comics every week or month. Films show every day at cinemas. Books continued to pour off the presses. And in many countries people devote a great deal of their time to these media: in the USA the average child of twelve has spent twice as much time in front of TV as at school.

This continuous flow is also lifelong. Parents and school are left behind, not as determinants of people's future but as guides in their present. The media are perpetually in the present as well as in the past. They are unique in this lifelong continuity. Of hegemonic institutions, only parliamentary parties come anywhere near this continuous role, but public attention to their operation is in no way comparable to public attention to the media. Indeed, most people derive all their knowledge of parliamentary parties from the media.

In the final analysis, then it is the very *daily* operation of media which is at the core of their role. Their problem is to keep abreast of changes, as I just emphasised above in the discussion of their instability.

Once this continuity is seen to be as central as it is, it follows that much of the empiricist research on media has to be junked. There, the conclusion is arrived at that media have almost no effect because effect is traditionally measured in terms of reactions to a single film or broadcast. To base this assessment on a one-off except from the media's continuous flow is to distort the reality of media beyond imagining. It is like a blindfold stab, hoping that a random single item will somehow explain the imprint of a million.

Definitional categories

The other crucial gap in traditional media effects research has been its refusal to look at media communication of categories and its perverse insistence on examining only the communication

161

of specific messages. From this angle, analysis of media content would focus for instance on whether a particular TV serial item displayed racial prejudice. It is a question worth asking, but it is less significant than the media categories customarily used to define black people.

This point is fully illustrated in Part One, in the analysis of categories for interpreting strikes and women as well as blacks, so I will not expand on it here. I have made it to illustrate the crucial place of categories of definition provided in the media. *It is the continuous flow of these definitional categories which constitutes the social significance of mass media, not the startling effect of a particular unit in media flow*.

This significance comes properly into focus once the connection between memory and media is clear. Much research into media effects has implicitly taken for granted that an item would be recalled consciously from media output, and would then feed into the audience's thinking when confronted with an event, say a strike. This is unrealistic. To have in constant recall all the programmes and newspaper stories that bear on any issue would tax a computer! Even though people can often remember a particular programme or story if someone reminds them of it, the normal response is for that item be slotted into the category or categories into which it fits, while at the same time revitalising and entrenching that category or categories. The categories are kept alive through being constantly refreshed in the media. It is these categories which are memorised, *painlessly*.

The vital point is then, that usually not only are the original media items out of consciousness even if available for recall, but so, *although powerfully at work*, are the very media categories of definition of social reality. People are often unaware of the origins of their definitional categories. They feel they are spontaneously responding to events; they repeatedly find their responses echoed in other people's, also it seems, spontaneously. This is a feature of the effectiveness of mass media which it is hard to over-emphasise: the feeling that it is your *own* thought, independently confirmed by others, constitutes *the* penetrative authority of media output.

162

Moreover, the categories in constant media use are rarely opened up for inspection in the media themselves (or elsewhere). There may be an occasional programme on 'What is news?' or 'The world of Fleet Street', but audiences are never regularly invited to examine or question the basic definitional categories in which particular stories or serials are framed, and which are equally subconsciously embedded in their own minds. Given the definitional category 'immigrant' in Britain, a single photo of Asians leaving a plane at London airport revives a whole mass of reactions in many people. It fits into and refreshes a definition of reality.

A point of significance is the variety of methods by which the media transmit these categories. They range from highly intellectual accounts, as in the business pages of the press, through to the evocative use of symbol and image, either verbal or aural or visual or a combination. Some writers on the media tend to focus on one of these to the exclusion of others, but it is surely their very combination which contributes to media effectiveness in the circulation of these categories.

One example of what I mean is the role of newscaster or current affairs interviewer in British broadcasting. This person's role is while communicating information, to convey an image of the desirability of political neutrality and 'balance'. It is constructed on the analogy of the Speaker in the British parliament. Before he or she ever opens their mouth, their role conveys the proper, rational, constitutional way of handling conflict. The newscaster does not open the news by announcing this neutrality: he or she *is* this. In recent years in Britain it has become a minor convention that on Christmas Day some newscasters drop their solemn public role and play the fool in some TV entertainment item or other. It is a modern version of the medieval All Fools Day, a reinforcement of their true hegemonic function.

So far then we have stressed continuous flow and the constant reproduction of certain definitional categories, by a variety of methods, as distinctive features of the media. No other hegemonic institutions have quite these features. But there is a

163

crucial third dimension specific to capitalist media, and that is their relation to leisure time.

Leisure time and media

Now the whole notion of 'leisure' can be argued to be highly suspect. It can imply that real activity is what you do for a wage, so that other activity is either frivolous or at best restorative. At the same time, there is little doubt that the entertainment industry, which today operates mostly within the media, is highly conscious of the desperate need of people to find satisfaction outside of their work. Thus, despite the confusion in the term 'leisure', there is plainly a large slice of people's waking lives in advanced capitalist society which is spent in 'consuming' entertainment via the media: sports, serials, comedy, music, and so on. Therefore no analysis of media in advanced capitalist societies can omit this question of entertainment and leisure.

As Dieter Prokop has argued, to see entertainment, which accounts for most of media output and which influences both news/current affairs presentation and advertising presentation, as a simple drug to keep the masses happy is both short-sighted and elitist. He insists that the popularity of media entertainment cannot be explained by the intellectual lethargy of the masses. This is valid, even if the class character of the school system is brought in as an excuse for their satisfaction with what they are fed. For one thing, it is often petit-bourgeois 'professionals' who are compulsive watchers of particular media entertainment products! Prokop also attacks the type of media criticism which concentrates *all* its fire on the absence in the media of critical questioning of political events. This assumes that political consciousness operates on a purely intellectual plane, and that political activism does not entail a transformation of every dimension of personal existence. No-one exists simply as a critic of transnational firms or of police brutality. They have wishes, desires, needs, fantasies, fears, loves, hates. And it is to these aspects of people's personal make-up, as they have been shaped and mis-shaped by capitalist forces, racist

164

forces, ageist forces, the forces of patriarchy, that media entertainment is directed.

Essentially what happens is that people's personal needs – for instance, to be loved sexually, to revenge themselves against repression – are part-met in the media by its entertainment offerings. Of course in meeting their needs partly, and in distorting them partly, the media are likely to make people's problems take longer to solve. In no way do they solve them. But they may *resolve* them for a little while. In a police series, for instance, it is possible for people to identify with the police on an emotional level as they 'legitimately' hammer some violent thug into the ground. Beyond all the discussions about TV making people more violent as against its spurring acceptance of a violent police force, there is the possibility that that thug *also* symbolises drives and desires repressed as impermissible by social constraints. People do take pleasure in sadistic attacks on what they actually long for.

Or take spy series: perhaps the licence to kill, the endless ingenious escapes in the nick of time, the miraculous successes against all odds, signify a social potency which is the opposite to most people's experience, locked up in a factory, office and/or domestic routines.

Certainly the popular series put out on TV networks in Britain, West Germany and the USA, featuring the 'comic' ranting racist (Alf Garnett, Alf Tetzlaff, Archie Bunker) all fall into this pattern. In chapter 4, we cited the official excuse for these series, namely that humour is a safety-valve, so that to laugh at an obviously absurd racist would exorcise racism.

However, the programmes were very popular, and were found to reinforce racism. This result had a lot to do with the fact that the ranting racist was not a landlord or an employer or a politician, but the archetypal 'little man', squashed and sat on by everyone, even in his own house. And in striking out against blacks, communists, 'hippy' youth, women's liberation, and in making outrageous remarks about them, he was a raspberry-blower, a defiant plaintiff. Given existing racism, sexism, ageism, 'communism' as practised, people identified with him.

165

Media entertainment output, then, cues into people's desires and fears, and offers a 'solution' to them in fantasy. But both the desires and fears, and the fantasy, are normally sufficiently based on reality for the process to work. It is not accurate to say that media entertainment 'lulls' people into political apathy. On the contrary, it stimulates certain deep feelings that would otherwise seek expression and satisfaction elsewhere, it gives them scope and play, and it provides for their short-lived resolution in fantasy. Such fantasy cannot be dismissed as abstract just because it falls short of the authentic satisfaction of people's needs. If media entertainment did nothing for anybody why would people spend so much of their leisure time watching it? Simply relaxing after the demands of work, cannot explain this intensive use of media, especially entertainment media.

The variety of forms of media

We now have three dimensions of the specific role of media in capitalist hegemony: their continuous lifelong flow, their constant provision of definitional categories, and their 'resolution' of people's needs in fantasy via entertainment programmes. What we have left out of account almost entirely up to now is the variety of functional and technical forms of media: radio, press, public relations, advertising, TV, photography etc. In some cases a particular technology is largely utilised by one type of organisation in terms of its mass audience. TV, radio and the cinema are obvious examples, where there is a whole organisation built around a particular technology, even giving the illusion of arising out of it. In printing, by contrast, newspapers and magazines and comics tend to have different organisations from book publishing. But as well as these forms of organisation, there are also advertising organisations, opinion poll and marketing organisations, and the public relations profession (sometimes a consultancy, more usually a permanent post with the firm or government agency that requires this activity).

This variety is an important feature of the media. In the case of the social roles of media technologies and organisations, however, just as with the methods of communication, this variety operates with a great deal of overlap. For example, two or several of these activities may be owned by a single giant firm. Also, the activities themselves overlap. The distinction between a public relations drive on behalf of some firm, and advertising, is marginal – witness the example of ITT at the outset of the chapter. Both advertising and public relations normally employ print and broadcasting as their major outlets, with posters as a much less expensive additional outlet. The overlap can also be seen to operate in different directions. Advertising has to be entertaining to catch and hold attention. It often works on the same fantasies as media entertainment, even if in a far more compressed form. Exploiting the need for sexual love and expression by means of sexual fantasies, is the most relied on advertising method of them all.

This overlap and intermesh could be commented on at length: the requirement for news to be entertainingly presented; the dependence of TV news on press scoops; the use of politicians' statements on TV by the press; the presence and importance of advertising in most media; the reinforcement of films by the book-of-the-film, of TV cartoon series by children's comics; the use of poll results and public relations material as news.

To develop an account of all these forms of media activity and their interlock would require a separate book or books. What I want to state here, though, is the importance that this variety-within-limits has for the effectiveness of media output. If three separate newspapers and three TV channels are prepared to highlight the same event as newsworthy, their independence from each other seems more real than their actual joint dependence on certain definitional categories. Not that most people are exposed to all these outlets regularly; but they all, using different outlets, often talk to each other afterwards about the reported event. A single media outlet, especially if known to be controlled by an agency with an axe to grind, governmental or otherwise, would never produce the same credibility as several 'independent' outlets.

167

Now if not only the event, but also its significance, are agreed on by six different outlets, then we have more than highlighting. We have the agreement of several *independent* actors on how an issue is to be interpreted and the plausibility of such an interpretation is, considerable.

Even if people are involved in the event in question and know first-hand the gaps in the media accounts of it, often they localise their criticism of the media to that one event they know for themselves. What else can people do in a situation where they are dependent on the media for their information on many issues? It is when there is a long-running struggle engaging in one way or another the majority of people, such as the Republican upsurge in Northern Ireland from 1969, that even the variety of the media comes to be seen by many as merely variations on a single theme. In Britain itself, however, coverage of Ireland has not produced any such credibility gap as yet (1980).

A classical case of this variety-within-limits, admittedly restricted to the press, was reporting of the war in Korea in 1949–53. By dint of very careful reading of all the press reports, and piecing together certain dissonant items that appeared here and there, I. F. Stone was able to put together an account of the actual prosecution of the war, of the barbarism of the US forces under the UN flag, and of the corruption and despotism of the Rhee regime that the USA was struggling to defend. This account was at sharp variance with the official account of a crusade against communist tyranny. Yet despite its extraction from the official press stories, the overwhelming burden of all the various newspapers taken together was of a sacrificial crusade for freedom, not of an imperialist war. A dozen voices in pure unison would have been suspicious. A dozen voices in overall harmony, with a quantity of discords, are far more effective. This is not to say that these discords are always marginal. The media may express opposition to British investment in South Africa or to the continued presence of British rule in Northern Ireland, or may ventilate an issue like Watergate. But the overall drift is evidently one of harmony, of dissent within a permissible spectrum of political and economic

168

views. Unity in diversity means strength. Pluralism however restricted, carries conviction; monolithicity breeds distrust.

Media and other mass hegemonic institutions

The fifth area to be examined in order to understand the specificity of the media, is their inter-relation with other mass hegemonic institutions, notably the family, education and parliamentary parties. Trade unions and the media were discussed in chapter 2.

The family, in conventional social science, is often taken to be the 'primary socialising agent', and the media join in later on as part of a ragbag of 'secondary socialising agents'. Since the media are also 'there' practically from birth, this time element cannot be the real distinguishing factor between them.

In fact the family can be said to have two major effects, the inculcation of patriarchy and – following the broad freudian tradition of analysis – the imposition of certain repressions which are the crucible of much of the future adult's emotional and sexual dynamics. The media reinforce patriarchy, as we have seen, and also cue in to these dynamics at many points, not least in the violence and imagery of children's cartoons. Looking at the reverse relation, it is certain that parental reinforcement of at least a large number of media categories is an important factor in media impact over time. How important parental challenges are to media categories is much more problematic.

When it comes to education, there are several points of interaction with the media. The most visible, namely the huge growth in educational broadcasting, now parallels and feeds the traditional linkage with textbook publishing. With the rapid development of audio-visual teaching programmes using audio-cassettes and video-cassettes, this trend is growing ever faster. US satellites have already been used for beaming US educational programmes to Third World countries, in the same way that the textbook publishers Pearson Longman have been engaged for decades and across continents in educational imperialism.

Moreover, the official freedom to do well or badly in the school system is paralleled by the corresponding liberty to watch what programmes or read what newspapers you wish. In practice, media organisations all carefully target their products for consumption by particular sectors of the public *as defined by their schooling*. Universities, *The Times*, *Panorama*, encourage people to think; the average working-class school, the *Sun*, radio newsflashes do not.

Language-use is a further carry-over from the school system into media. By and large, the language-use considered clear and acceptable by educators and media personnel, belongs to a fairly fluent regional (south-eastern) petit-bourgeois code. By contrast, 'strong' working-class or regional accents, let alone codes, are not considered right for extended use in school or media, especially the news media. 'BBC English' is its own definition of the approved code.

The result is that many people are excluded from explaining their own experience of society or of some happening, because their language use does not meet these requirements. The media organisations thus bar their columns or air-time to a very large proportion of the population, with the result that accounts of many working-class issues and events are usually given by middle-class observers or interviewers rather than by participants. In a sense it may even be the case that working-class speakers may be made nervous by a microphone which is only 'used' to registering BBC English, with the result that they become less fluent in that situation than they would normally be.

The role of the universities, pre-eminently, is to be the dynamos of bourgeois ideological production. That is where the original thinking is supposed to take place to assist capitalism to grow and prosper. In turn, these universities feed the lesser ranks of the bourgeois intelligentsia both with personnel and with ideas in print. This is fully visible in media organisations. Senior personnel are almost universally university-trained, those best equipped to reproduce and develop bourgeois ideology on their own. This pattern is evident in publishing, current affairs broadcasting, so-called quality newspapers, and among specialist journalists in politics, education, science and the arts. It is ideologically visible in the practice of newsmen, even when they have come up the hard way through reporting local funerals and have never been to university. The very definition of 'news' as objective discovery and presentation of 'the facts', owes its origin to the empiricist philosophy of science and history current in most twentieth century universities. (The same ideological currents are evident in the scripts of the increasingly popular tele-history series.)

Lastly, we must consider parliamentary political parties and the media. We have already pointed out how the interviewer and newscaster have a role closely resembling that of the neutral Speaker in the British House of Commons, and how both institutions support each other ideologically by emphasising that all conflicts in the political sphere should be resolved in an orderly and rational manner by debate. The eternal truth that there are two sides to everything, and that the accurate version lies at midpoint between the two sides, finds its expression even more powerfully in practice in broadcasting than in parliament, partly because so many more know the former at first hand, partly because broadcasting as an institution is supposed to be like the speaker. (In the USA, broadcasters often have a much more personalised, abrasive style, so the British pattern is not found everywhere.) In the press, of course, partisan politics are somewhat more common; but even there, papers like the *Mirror* or the *Guardian* are often surprisingly similar to 'balanced' broadcasting.

There are two further effects of the relation between parliamentary parties and media worth mentioning. The great stress in political reporting on parliament implies it is still the centre of political power. As is well known now, it is not. To that extent, the media invest parliamentary parties with more clout than they have possessed for quite some time.

On the other hand, the fact that balance in broadcasting is operationally defined first and foremost as the spectrum between the

171

main political parties, means nowadays a very narrow spectrum within which political issues can be defined as such and debated in public. Social democratic parties and communist parties in advanced capitalist countries have been steadily or rapidly drawing closer to the political centre; many right-wing parties have been doing likewise. In fact the British Labour Party and the Italian Communist Party in the late seventies were each responsible for administering or empowering heavy wage-cuts on workers via a combination of price inflation, unemployment, wage control and acceptance of the IMF's dictates. Yet things these parties say do not matter are exceptionally difficult for other socialist forces outside their ranks to raise in public debate. This means that the definitional categories of the media in Britain are powerfully restrained within this narrow spectrum.

If we examine the inter-relation between the media and these other mass hegemonic institutions, one thing stands out at once about the media: their *general* role. Political parties, because of the segmentation of politics in bourgeois thought as a restricted area for mass action (effectively the vote and referenda), are not felt to touch most aspects of life despite their continuing share in policy-making. The schools and universities mean nothing to the majority of the population except as institutions that once guided them into ordinary jobs through their own academic 'failure', or as institutions attended by a privileged minority. (This is not to say that the different components of 'failure' do not leave scars for life on many people.) The family, as the nucleus of patriarchy and of emotional repression, is a most potent institution but still has nothing near the media's remit. On the other hand, certain permanent things happen to people in these three institutions (perhaps least today through the parliamentary parties), which are then often relayed and reinforced through the media. The media are an *original* source of ideological hegemony to a limited extent only; on the other hand, other mass hegemonic institutions would have to function quite differently if they were absent. (Parliamentary parties would be most affected since the media act as their main grassroots communicators.)

172

Capitalist media: their production control

For a full understanding of media content, which is, because of its social impact, what everybody is ultimately interested in (and what this book mostly covers), there is one remaining major gap in this account: the internal organisation of media production. What types of organisation produce what kind of content? How do their forms of organisation relate to the ruling class and the state?

There are two problems in filling this gap. One is that the sheer diversity of media organisations, from satellite link-ups to international public relations to small publishers, cannot be covered. The second, which in a sense makes the first less onerous, is that production studies are very few and far between. There are occupational studies of journalists, of advertising agents, of film producers, but not to my knowledge of top editors, public relations consultants, publishing firm employees, camerapersons, and many other media roles. Even putting what exists in the second grouping with the first as clearly bearing on production organisation, does not produce anything approaching a comprehensive body of empirical studies.

What I shall do is to analyse the main components of the 'fit' between media production organisations and capitalist hegemony. Now in a strict and effective censorship, this presents no problem, *except* in the sense noted above, that people will come to distrust the media and so rob them of their effectiveness as mass hegemonic institutions. It is the mechanisms of indirect rule in a liberal democratic state that set up the puzzle: if no one is going to be fined or imprisoned for dissident media communication in countries such as Britain or the USA, how is it that the media are as routinely restrained as they are?

The first reason lies in how journalists are selected. If a regime has consolidated itself, or a corporation with media interests has done likewise, then the recruitment and training of media personnel is not random. Individuals will be selected as journalists, advertisers or entertainers who show solid signs of

173

reliability and commitment to the prevailing ethos. (BBC news personnel are almost certainly 'positively vetted' by the Special Branch before being hired.) These people will be grafted as individuals, into an ongoing organisation, itself structured to reproduce these patterns. The normal career rewards (money, power, prestige, security, job interest) are available to efficient and successful personnel, above all to those who can innovate within the proper limits.

An illustration of recruitment as a control mechanism comes from Portugal's dictator for fifty years, Antonio Salazar. In 1960, he publicly congratulated Portuguese journalists for their sense of responsibility and civic maturity. This, he said, made the state censor's activity scarcely necessary, and thus the Portuguese press one of the freest in the world! He did not mention the other result, namely the exceptionally low status of journalism as a career in Portugal . . .

Conversely to the carrots, a variety of sticks and stones are available for disciplining any dissidents outside these limits. Chief among these, perhaps, is the short-term contract, the bane of many film directors, documentary producers, current affairs journalists below editorial level, script writers and others. As soon as one of these short-term contracts of six to twelve months is signed, the worry about the next one begins. Moreover, many media occupations have high umemployment rates, intensifying this worry.

There are other instruments of control which mesh with this basic one. For example, reporters can have sub-editors repeatedly send back their copy as unacceptable. If this continues, the journalist in question is clearly not fulfilling his or her work duties. A bright future is certainly not in front of them. In order to get it right they usually read the editorials to get the general line (the approved definitional categories), and take pains to absorb the 'house-style' document that newspapers reproduce for their own staff. (This specifies terms to be avoided, euphemisms to be used, and so on.)

In the end though, even given these mechanisms of control, the basic daily controlling mechanism is the absorption of the ideology of the relevant professional activity, journalism, public relations, advertising, entertainment, or whatever. There are naturally variations within each sector, such as the distinction between campaigning and sober journalism, or between brash and decorous public relations. But ingraining a definition of professional excellence is the only effective mechanism for ensuring the *spontaneous* production of acceptable items. Usually by the time a media professional has got anywhere near the top of the tree (Fleet Street, the BBC national organisation), s/he will have thoroughly identified with the top of that tree. Continuous interaction with the organisations in question sustains this process. If all else fails, and some individual slips through the net with strongly dissident reports, s/he can be either isolated or shifted sideways. Only in times of turbulent change will such individuals emerge more frequently.

The spontaneous production of acceptable items is well illustrated in Schlesinger's detailed dissection of the elite corps of BBC TV News journalists, with their solid internalisation of the ideology of 'balance'. Prokop has described this kind of spontaneity as 'integrated', a spontaneity within tight boundaries which exclude the mass expression of a whole range of wishes, desires and needs. To unleash their full expression would require an authentic spontaneity, which he describes as 'productive' spontaneity. Prokop principally has in mind 'spontaneous' audience reactions to media output, but it is clear that media communicators themselves are mostly caught up within this integrated circuit. In this context he rightly points out that simply to restructure media organisations to make them democratically accountable to committees of journalists, printers/technicians, even readers, will not by itself change current ways of producing output.

The tenacity of this professional journalistic ideology, and therefore its importance in maintaining the media as hegemonic institutions within a liberal democratic state, is well illustrated in two examples. One is of a short-lived experiment in workers' control of a newspaper, the other from the practice of socialist journalists during the socialist Popular Unity government in Chile 1970–73.

175

In the case of the *Scottish Daily News*, the change in control structure brought about no very marked change in content and values:

> To run a series of committed, front page stories – on steel or Cambodia for example – alongside a lip-smacking report of a girl strangled after intercourse with her own bra . . . shows a naïve and markedly illogical political approach . . . The left-of-centre politics of the *Scottish Daily News* were sectionalised neatly into the top left of the leader and front pages, never being allowed to intrude into the features or sports pages.

The only point here which is inaccurate is to describe what happened as simply being 'naïve and markedly illogical', for even though some of those involved were alert to this powerful continuity between past and present in the paper, the overwhelming ethos was as described. The professional ideology did not simply evaporate under workers' control.

In the Chilean case, socialist journalists in broadcasting tried to observe a scrupulous balance and neutrality between right and left. This was designed to counter the right's onslaught against the media as biased and untrustworthy. The result was that when in the last year of the Popular Unity regime the right began what Mallelart describes as a 'Leninist mass agitation' against the regime by all media available to it, the socialist journalists were left out on a limb, still obsessively constructing balance. They were prisoners of the professional ideology, whereas the right, once confronted with its own crisis, junked that ideology without a second thought.

Mattelart also describes the penetration of this ideology in his account of the effects of taking Chilean workers to the journalism college in order to build up a corps of worker-journalists. Those recruited were usually unrecognisable on return to their neighbourhoods. Either they could no longer communicate directly as they had done before, and/or they were more than a little conscious of their newly bestowed status. The hegemony of journalistic professionalism could hardly be more tellingly revealed than by this unwitting transformation of socialist workers into would-be petit-bourgeois intellectuals.

Thus despite a change in the structure of control, despite a change in the personnel, despite a mass agitational communication by the right, in all three instances journalistic professionalism showed itself resistant to change. Control by publishers, editors, management, is possible because of this resistance, this tenacity of the professional ideology. Perhaps no instance reveals the mechanism of 'responsibility' and self-censorship more clearly though, than the case of British political correspondents – the lobby correspondents. In exchange for the right to be briefed before decisions are taken by the government, and for the right to accost and chat to MP's and government ministers about current political issues, these journalists and their editors maintain a voluntary self-censorship on matters or sources the government specifically insists are not to be disclosed. The circulation of important government information is therefore extended, but *only* to the three hundred or so journalists who make up this corps. They are able to feel in the know, that the government takes them seriously. They are content that they are allowed to judge what the general public needs to know.

Among journalists themselves, there is a further feature of their organisation which helps to lubricate the mechanism of control. The only real feedback that most journalists recognise is what comes to them from their fellow-journalists – either on the same paper, or in the same specialist corps of the supposedly left-inclined (industrial correspondents mentioned in chapter 2).

This, paradoxically, can give journalists with dissident or socialist views the assurance of integrity, in that their wording of a report, although indistinguishable to the average reader from any other report, will be picked up by their colleagues as evidence of their political outlook. This reassurance helps to soften any conflict they may feel between their socialist convictions and working for a right-wing newspaper. They do not *feel* hamstrung.

Once again, a limited diversity can be seen to be peculiarly effective in encouraging what Prokop calls an 'integrated

177

spontaneity', whether of media personnel or of consumers. It is an ethos which in journalism rests, nonetheless, on the marginalisation, even criminalisation, of serious political protest. This is defined as outside the limits of balance, and it is noticeable that it was the point at which the Republican upsurge in Northern Ireland could not be dismissed as either marginal or criminal that British journalists chafed most under extra controls on their Northern Ireland reporting. And that these extra controls were needed.

There is one further dimension of media practice which assists in the hegemonic process. No one should underestimate the place of art and skill in the presentation of media output, of graphic design or 'background' music in powerful media communication. We cannot investigate now these and all the other methods of capturing and holding attention – headlines, startling images, photos, order of presentation, colour – but they are part of the organisational definition of communicative skill, which help to validate the self-understanding of media personnel as creative and not dependent agents.

Media personnel do not work in a socio-political vacuum, but are bounded by a system whose fundamental achievement in liberal democratic societies (and even in Salazar's Portugal) is to develop in them a reasoned acceptance of the practice of *self*-censorship. Only when this practice cannot cope with abrupt political change, as happened in British broadcasting during the repression in Northern Ireland from 1968 onwards, do media controllers and the state come to intercept programme-making and news reports systematically. Control over journalists is thus in part a microcosm of capitalist hegemony in society at large.

Conclusions

Once we grasp even the first defining characteristic of modern media, their continuous flow, then their political significance is plain. They are part of an ongoing process, itself linked to class struggles, class alliances, the state and imperialism. They

178

intervene day by day and moment by moment, always freshly supplying definitional categories for interpreting the world about us, operating through information and entertainment. These categories, especially as expressed through entertainment, cue in to a whole range of needs and wishes which are often repressed as unacceptable. Media output does not solve, but simply momentarily resolves, the personal problems brought about by this repression. Their power lies in their variety-within-bounds; in their concession of apparent independence, both to journalists and users, yet their retention of strategic control; in their responsiveness without mass accountability; in short, in their capacity to shape public feeling while appearing only to express it.

The connecting thread is bourgeois hegemony. It is a hegemony of capitalist interests organised in huge firms that are often transnational in operation (which in turn means imperialist against the Third World). It is a hegemony operating through the more or less watchful eye of the state, through official secrecy and censorship. The so-called 'creative' side of the media is furthermore a range of petit-bourgeois occupations largely recruiting from that class. The media's organisation is a material element in the overall alliance of the capitalist class with the petit bourgeoisie.

Nonetheless, as is its nature, this hegemony is far from being stable. The contradictory experiences of workers, blacks and women in capitalist society – one derived from exploitation and oppression, the other from mass hegemonic institutions – often produce a contradictory consciousness within the working class. Certain key definitional categories would not be continuously communicated to it without the existence of the media. It is hard for the oppressed to match their patient reiteration of these categories, whose form and imagery is so often adapted to accommodate shifts in public mood and awareness.

The question we must now turn to is: under what conditions and in what ways can these hegemonic definitions be challenged and transcended in *our* mass communication?

8. Socialist Media I: Britain

The critique of capitalist media must not be segregated from a political assessment of the socialist media that are – or should be – their opponents. This means examining their effectiveness in subverting the stability of capitalism, imperialism, racism, sexism, and so on. But of equal interest is their contribution to developing communist consciousness, a broad and rich perspective on the transformation of social relations that will build the foundation of working-class hegemony.

In general, the classics of marxism only state certain scattered overall principles concerning media of mass communication in the service of revolution. We will briefly examine the work of Lenin, Gramsci, Mao and Brecht to illustrate the sketchy nature of marxist thinking in this area, fundamentally valid though it may be. We will then examine three socialist newspapers in Britain.

In *What Is To Be Done?*, Lenin argued that to start an all-Russian newspaper was the first priority to develop the effectiveness of their struggle. He was writing at a period when the Russian Social-Democratic Party was outlawed, along with other revolutionary groups and even trade unions, and thus had to operate in secrecy. The likelihood of raids and arrests by the Tsar's secret police saturated his argument, which centred on the need to work out an effective *counter*-organisation to combat this threat. We have the bricks and the bricklayers for revolution, he wrote, but the 'bricks are often so scattered that the enemy can shatter the structure as if it was made of sand and not of bricks'. He argued that 'the more perfect the finish of each little wheel [in the revolutionary organisation] and the larger the number of detail

180

workers engaged on the common cause, the clearer will our network become and the less will be the disorder in the ranks consequent upon inevitable police raids.'

A socialist newspaper would also, in his view, help to overcome the fragmentation of people's awareness of the struggles going on all over Russia. It would stimulate discussion of the true political situation, along with 'hints in the legal press, talk among the people, and . . . "shamefaced" government statements'. 'This newspaper would become part of an enormous pair of smith's bellows that would fan every spark of the class struggle and of popular indignation into a general conflagration.'

However, he also saw a precise linkage between the production and distribution of such a newspaper, and the developmen of a hard core of professional revolutionaries prepared to risk everything, even personal liberty, for the revolution. Distributing the paper would bring about personal links between party members in different towns, immediate political activity among the mass of the population, and so a process of contact with them and of learning from them. The paper would enable knowledge of trends over Russia as a whole, a generalised response to revolutionary happenings, and a network enabling effective secret planning of the tactics of an uprising.

Lenin has been accused of elitism and autocracy, particularly on the basis of this text. It is worth emphasising therefore that he insisted that the role of this socialist newspaper was not a dictatorial one: 'we wanted our line . . . to be respected because it was correct, and not because it had been laid down by an official organ.' He also fully recognised their existing paper's weaknesses in failing to cover conditions in the Russian countryside in particular, and urged more reports from readers living outside the towns.

The paper was not designed as the exclusive preserve of an inner-party elite. it was to be a weapon of communication to unify and develop the struggle more effectively agains the Tsarist state and against capital, to help to destabilise them and overthrow them. It would rely to an important extent on contributions from its ordinary members as material to feed the generalisation of class consciousness. And its distribution would build up a network more efficient than, and more or less proof against, the secret police. Thus it could be in a postion to fan every spark into an inferno, through the combination of its voice on paper with the voices of its distributors.

In the case of Gramsci, a major part of his revolutionary work in the period 1919–22 was bound up with his activity in the socialist newspaper *L'Ordine Nuovo* (The New Order). There is no point at which Gramsci produced any systematic account of the range of his thinking on this paper's role, or on the general possibilities of socialist mass communication. The nearest that can be got to this is to study Gramsci's activity as a revolutionary journalist in relation to the struggles at that time and I shall draw heavily on Gwyn Williams' *Proletarian Order*, which gives an account of Gramsci's political activity and development in the period 1911–21.

Certain major points emerge. Firstly, *L'Ordine Nuovo's* main area of circulation was the working class of Turin, a key industrial city in Northern Italy. Secondly, it developed as the expression of a conscious revolutionary alternative to the reformist Italian Socialist Party, an alternative based first and foremost on political commitment to the factory councils that sprang up fairly spontaneously in Italian industry in 1919–20. This commitment was to their expression of the new proletarian order, for effectively these councils, freely elected, took over the factories and ran them. Here, for Gramsci, was the beginning of *proletarian* hegemony, superior as a form of class organisation to trade unions and even to the revolutionary socialist party.

Although the paper was produced by a slender and ramshackle organisation, the deep involvement of most of its producers in Turin's working-class struggles, and their commitment to *and exploration of* the councils movement, made *L'Ordine Nuovo* for a time the key proletarian forum of the struggle and the means of its development. As the council movement began to decline, and the forces of reaction that were to usher in Mussolini

182

began their counter-offensive, so the paper began to lose some of its centrality to the immediate workers' movement. But under Gramsci, the paper 'was drenched in the spirit of state-building and squarely directed towards making the working class *think* like a ruling clas.' It contained articles on the international class situation, from the Soviet Union, Britain, the USA, Germany and many other countries. Its regular foreign correspondent was Sylvia Pankhurst. There were reviews of the politics of the previous week, articles by militants in self-criticism, a survey of the international scene, book reviews. Its style and subject matter seem to have been pretty heavy going at times, but this does not seem to have been a dampener in itself.

There are two main points to be drawn out of this experiment in socialist media. Firstly, the paper's roots were in the actual struggles of the time, specifically the factory councils movement, which was a great move forward in Italian history. Secondly, the paper's attempt was not merely to produce a critique of capitalism, but to develop a detailed and specific debate about the way forward towards communism within the Italian workers' move-ment – to *realise* proletarian hegemony. At his point, Gramsci's vision of the role of a socialist newspaper was wider than Lenin's, who saw it effectively as a mechanism of defence and attack in a strategic battle with the Tsarist state, rather than as a means of developing a new ruling-class consciousness for the working class. (Though as it happens, Lenin singled out *L'Ordine Nuovo* for praise at the second congress of the Communist International in 1920.)

From within yet another struggle, Mao, in his *Talks to the Yenan Forum on Literature and Art* and in his article *Oppose Stereotyped Party Writing*, set out certain key principles of organised socialist communication. Those who engaged in this activity, he argued, if they wished to be effective, were compelled to root themselves in a direct relation with the masses. Only so could they develop their work with any usefulness, even though it would involve them in 'much pain and friction'. 'Only by speaking for the masses can [they] educate them and only by being their

183

pupil can [they] be their teacher.' Thus far, the same basic principle as Lenin and Gramsci expressed.

He attacked a view current among self-styled socialist writers at the time that their task was always to expose, satire being a central device in this endeavour. Rather, he insisted, it is essential to distinguish in this respect between enemies, allies, and members of the oppressed classes, and not to cultivate a uniform style more in accordance with self-image as a writer than as a socialist communicator. Communist consciousness in the oppressed classes should be built up; its members should not just be savaged for their lapses as if by superior beings. His opposition to stereotyped political writing was in similar vein. He attacked it not only for its indigestible nature, but also for its constant use of dogmatic assertions rather than reformulating ideas to apply to actual struggles.

Mao also took the position that while political and artistic criteria were not the same, priority must ultimately be given to political criteria. Every ruling class operates similarly, he argued, and the more effective bourgeois communication artistically, the more seductive politically, the more its political assumptions and message need to be exposed. This raises the vital question of the continuing presence and effectiveness of bourgeois communication, which in one form or another is the central problem of all socialist communication strategies. Socialist media do not operate in a political vacuum, and how to handle the countervailing power of bourgeois perspectives is a continuing thorny issue. We shall have reason to come back to it.

These texts belong to the period of liberated areas and the struggles against Japanese and American imperialism. His later texts with a bearing on these themes belong to the period after 1949. His essays *In Refutation of 'Uniformity of Public Opinion'*, *On the Correct Handling of Contradictions Among the People*, and his 1957 *Speech* at the Chinese Communist Party's annual conference on propaganda work, carry forward many of the same themes. They make two points with particular emphasis however. One is the necessity for a variety of shades of progressive, anti-capitalist opinion to have free play, as in his famous aphorism, 'Let a hundred flowers bloom'. The other is his root-and-branch opposition to coercion as a viable method in socialist communication:

> It would certainly not be right to refrain from criticism, look on while wrong ideas spread unchecked and allow them to dominate the field . . . What is needed is scientific analysis and convincing argument. Dogmatic criticism settles nothing . . . You may ban the expression of wrong ideas, but the ideas will still be there. On the other hand, if correct ideas are pampered in hothouses and never exposed to the elements and immunised against disease, they will not win out against erroneous ones.

Mao's priority, like Gramsci's, was the construction of a new proletarian order. His analyses of the conditions for socialist communication, even more than Gramsci's, reflect the social relations that began to emerge after revolutionary advance. Everything was still to be achieved, and socialist consolidation clearly takes 'a long historical period'. Nonetheless, there is a somewhat different set of tasks implicit in Mao's comments since the tasks of consolidation are different.

Let us look lastly at one contribution by another socialist thinker who tried to develop new anti-bourgeois forms of communication, especially through theatre, namely Bertolt Brecht. Here we will simply focus on his remarks on the theory of radio. Writing in the period when radio was first developing in Germany, he called for a 'listener's revolt, his activation and reinstatement as producer'.

What he meant by this was that radio was being used simply as a distribution apparatus, to share messages, whereas it ought to be transformed into a communication apparatus. He comments:

> Broadcasting would be the most magnificent communication apparatus imaginable in public life, a colossal canal-system. That is to say, it would be this, once it understood not only how to emit but also how to receive; thus not only to make the listener hear, but also

185

> to get him to speak; not to isolate him, but to put him in a relationship . . . to organise the listener as a supplier.

He argued that in itself radio was a neutral technology, in class terms neither an advance nor a backward step. It was the use to which it was put that was decisive. He described its use in his time as comparable with that of literature or education, all three being organised so as not to have any de-stabilising political consequences.

He insisted, however, that radio had the capacity to ensure that any social change, however small, had a quite different, incomparably more powerful impact than it would have had without radio. Radio workers must learn that 'the technique to be developed in any such endeavour is directed toward the central task, which is that the public must not merely be instructed, but must also instruct'. He added emphatically that this process must not be allowed to be a drab affair: 'people's interests must be made interesting'. Even the opening of a new public building could be the occasion of public debate and interchange. Radio could make it an occasion for public political communication.

Brecht's remarks are fragmentary in nature, and perhaps unsurprisingly given their date do not forecast the possibilities of radio as an *appearance* of exchange of ideas and criticisms of the people and their rulers. Thus he instanced the possibility that radio could be used to grill politicians more effectively than the press, because they would have less time to think out their subterfuges. He also said that politicians should be called upon to explain their policies over radio. The appointment of safe journalists to do this 'for' the people, the use of radio by President Roosevelt in his 'fireside chats', lay in the future, as did pre-recorded interviews. Nonetheless, the possibility of radio given the political will of a working-class state, is well set out in his remarks.

Clearly then detailed principles (I do not mean technical handbooks) of socialist communication media are by and large to be worked out in the present and the future. What can happen when they are not properly worked out was evident in the case of socialist journalists in Chile during 1970–73, where their bourgeois

186

professional training often mastered their political judgment and communication practice.

From Lenin, Gramsci, Mao and Brecht emerge four inter-locking principles of socialist mass communication. it must be grounded in actual struggles. Those who communicate must not set themselves up as media controllers. The media must be used as a resource for the revolutionary movement to develop *itself.* Their specific activities must be determined by the political context (liberal democracy, fascist repression, socialist state-building).

Three socialist newspapers in Britain: economism rules OK

Out of the many socialist newspapers and periodicals published in Britain, I decided to examine the three with the largest circulation during the seventies. This meant the *Morning Star* (Communist Party of Great Britain), *Socialist Worker* (Inter-national Socialists, later Socialist Workers' Party), and the *Militant* (belonging to the Trotskyist entrist grouping within the Labour Party). My sometimes trenchant criticisms of them does not mean that every other such publication, *People's News Service, The Leveller, Socialist Challenge*, is open to the same attack. It does mean though, if my critique is valid, that the main socialist press in Britain offers a puny challenge to the hegemony of established media; and that its weakness *is directly in its content*, not in its small circulation.

It is a paradox that those responsible for these papers I have studied, have undoubtedly read at least Lenin on socialist communication, even though their practice diverges quite sharply from his model or the four principles above. This divergence is ultimately based on certain familiar misrepresentations of marxist politics. The political organisations sponsoring these papers work with political perspectives which seriously reduce the scope of marxism, veering from economism through workerism to human-ism.

These are not mere '-isms' in a doctrinal quibble. For instance, if workers' problems in capitalist society can all be solved

187

by giving them a better wage, then there is no need to abolish capitalism. The view that workers' oppression is purely economic hardship, remediable through trade-union action, is the most basic form of economism. Lenin once pinpointed some of the political consequences of economistic marxism, in *What Is To Be Done?*

> Inasmuch as this oppression affects the most diverse classes of society, inasmuch as it manifests itelf in the most varied spheres of life and activity – vocational, civic, personal, family, religious, scientific, etc., etc. – is it not evident that we shall not be fulfilling our task of developing the political consciousness of the workers if we do not undertake the organisation of the exposure (of the Tsarist system) *in all its aspects?*

Later on he added:

> Working-class consciousness cannot be genuine political consciousness unless the workers are trained to respond to *all* cases of tyranny, oppression, violence and abuse . . . For this reason, the conception of the economic struggle as the most widely applicable means of drawing the masses into the political movement . . . is so extremely reactionary and harmful in its practical significance.

Certainly in chapter 3 we saw how economism and racism are bedfellows in the working class.

Workerism is a different political view. It too is economistic in that it rests the solution for all social ills on the shoulders of the far-seeing and unconquerable working class, for they are visualised solely as economic producers who are driven inexorably to socialist commitment by their experience of wage-labour. Their strategic capacity to stop capitalist production whenever they so choose is also a centrepiece of this position. It is a mirror-opposite of a second version of economistic marxism, which holds that capitalist society is simply an economic machine automatically doomed to collapse and usher in socialism. This is mechanistic, whereas workerism is voluntaristic; but both views proclaim the inevitability of capitalist collapse, and both flatly dismiss the real power of capitalist hegemony.

Humanistic marxism is in turn partly a response to these two

188

positions. The 'Popular Front' strategy adopted by Moscow's Third International, after the consolidation of fascism in Europe and Japan, was at the root of its rejuvenation. Capitalism was obviously not going to collapse quickly as the Bolsheviks had first assumed, rather it was moving into a vicious new phase in which the Soviet Union itself might be crushed. Therefore a new approach was required. The International's previous policy of attack while refusing to ally with socialist parties, was turned upside down into a policy of defence and of trying to unite the widest possible array of forces against fascism (i.e. the popular fronts).

The anti-fascist strategy became transformed after the second world war, into a strategy of uniting the widest array of forces against transnational capital instead, as the first stage in a slow socialist mutation of the capitalist state. Either way the working class was no longer seen as the sole organised force opposed to capitalism, and inevitable capitalist collapse was certainly no longer the road to socialism. Thus humanistic marxism became germane to this political line, emphasising as it did the universal alienation of humanity. The unity of all the decent elements in society tended to become its practical goal, rather than the indefinitely postponed socialist revolution.

Thus these three reductions of marxism have a long history within marxist movements, which helps to explain their capacity to pass as authentic marxist politics in the present. (This sketch has simplified the issues involved, but will serve as an introduction.)

Let us now examine these three socialist newspapers and illustrate how strongly these trends can be seen at work in them. The examples which follow are drawn from two April issues of each paper for every year from 1970 to 1978, to try to be sure to cover a reasonably representative period. In the case of the *Morning Star*, all front page items (excluding 'fillers') were analysed, together with the lead item on every other page except the last (which is always devoted to sport). In the case of the *Socialist Worker* we did likewise, including the back page. In the

189

case of the *Militant*, since it is a smaller paper, we included all items for analysis.

Obviously, certain items are missed this way. However, the purpose in this exercise is not to say that certain issues are never handled at all, only to establish which issues are given *priority*. To this end we also studied the editorials, which in a socialist newspaper perhaps even more than in a capitalist one, are a clear index of the paper's priorities.

Straightaway it is obvious that every one of these papers gave massive priority to wage demands, strikes, trade unions, redundancy, unemployment, price increases, poverty, rents and housing. In other words, to economic issues, mostly the first three mentioned. Even the EEC only seemed to be mentioned as an agency responsible for raising prices. Curiously, medical care, which directly affects working-class living standards, was scarcely mentioned. Now the support given to strikers and wage demands is obviously a great improvement on the capitalist media handling of class exploitation. At the same time, the concentration of attention on these issues was overwhelming.

Socialist Worker and the *Militant* emphasised economic struggles even more than the *Morning Star*. For the two former, these struggles formed about half their main items, two-thirds of their outside page items, and nearly sixty per cent of their editorials. For the *Morning Star*, economic issues were still over forty per cent of its main items, rising to nearly sixty per cent of both its editorials and its front page news.

This pattern of coverage is unmistakably economistic. Readers are pounded with information about wages, wage negotiations, strikes, go-slows, trade-union affairs. The experience of capitalist *society* is effectively screened out.

Even when they do turn their attention to other matters, they tend to reduce them to the lowest economic denominator. *Socialist Worker* was especially prone to do this. In an item on the legal system, its headline was 'One law for the *wealthy*'. In an item on a leading English publisher, its headline was, 'Publish, *profit*, and the rest be damned . . .' In an item on the Scottish National Party,

190

it led off with 'When a Scotch *millionnaire* holds a party . . .' An item on Franco's Spain was headed 'Spain: MPs' *gravy train*'. And an item on advertising, 'Caring is whiteness, and fluffy puppies, and *rich* ad agents.'

I have emphasised particular words in these quotations to underline the way in which all other dimensions of the legal system, publishing, the Scottish independence movement, fascist Spain and advertising, are crowded out by an emphasis on greed. Gramsci once identified this tendency among marxist writers to explain everything by the 'dirty-Jewish' mentality of capitalists or public officials. Greed and corruption certainly exist, but they are not the motor of capitalism. They are symptoms not causes, and could be eliminated with capitalism still intact.

How they handled racism and sexism

If we turn to these papers' treatment of racism and sexism, we find something startling straightaway. They seem to pay as little attention to these forms of oppression as capitalist media! In this nine-year selection of April issues, the paper devoting most attention to racism was the *Socialist Worker*, with seven per cent of its main items on the subject. The paper devoting most attention to women's oppression was the *Morning Star*, though with only three per cent of its main items on sexism it can hardly be said to have given the issue much more priority than its political rivals, who devoted a ludicrous one per cent of their main coverage to this issue.

These results are so stark that they cannot be brushed aside as a freak of my selection. They indicate the other side of the coin of economism: the virtual neglect of oppression outside the workplace, by the state or in the home. What this tends to mean in practice is concentration on white male trade unionists' actions, by force of the fact that blacks and women are grossly under-represented in the British trade unions' officialdom. The 'other' workers' movement to which we referred in chapter 1 and elsewhere, in which women and imigrant workers play an

191

important part, is also downstaged by this focus on official trade union politics.

Let us examine some illustrations of what tends to happen in these three papers on the rare occasions they do discuss racial or sexual oppression.

Two items on racist attacks on Pakistanis appeared in the *Morning Star* in April 1970. Some Pakistanis were interviewed and quoted. One item linked the casual tolerance of racism in everyday conversation and jokes to this extreme violence (two had been killed). It also urged support for black organisations. The other item quoted the general secretary of the National Council for Civil Liberties, attacking the 'horrifying' level of police attacks on black people.

The next items in the sample were in April 1976. There was coverage of some counter-demonstrators at a 'Stop Immigration' rally. In another item, the Home Secretary was reported as being urged to set up an official enquiry into a clash between racist demonstrators and their anti-racist opponents in Bradford. Also, a march against the National Front was covered.

With the exception of the first item, which was a model of analysis of racism, the problem of racism was presented as something curiously external. It appeared to be something that fascists and policemen suffer from, but that lots of 'decent people' protest against. The basic slogan of the Communist Party against racism during the seventies was 'One Race—the Human Race'; and on the masthead of the *Morning Star* it would sometimes carry the slogan 'Clear Out Racism!'

The political implications of this treatment were that racism, although evil and a threat, is something the vast majority of humans, decent humans, will easily recognise as such, and will be ready to pick up their brooms and sweep away for good. The pervasiveness of racism, including within the organised left, was given little recognition. This was the politics of humanistic marxism and the popular front in action.

In the case of the *Socialist Worker* sample, there were rather more items on racism, though eight of them were concentrated in a

192

single issue of the paper, which heralded a huge London demonstration against the National Front. (The Socialist Workers' Party had helped to organise this demonstration through the Anti-Nazi League, an anti-racist campaign organisation which it had set up.)

The aspects of racism dealt with in *Socialist Worker* concerned the inhuman effects of immigration laws on Cypriots (two items), the super-exploited conditions of Asian seamen (two items), the violence of the police against young blacks in a London clash (one item), and the National Front (nine items). In these, the workerism of the paper was usually well to the fore.

We can see this in one of the items on Cypriot immigrants, in which a member of the Cypriot family himself said (in language suspiciously marked with SWP jargon): '. . . we cannot resist this obscene treatment on our own. We need the public protest and industrial muscle of dockworkers, transport workers, miners and engineers . . .'

However, the main drift of the *Socialist Worker* treatment of racism was concerned with fascism and the National Front. It explicitly and relentlessly linked the NF with the Nazis in an attempt to discredit them, and to make people see beyond the NF's political propaganda about race to its frightening political programme for the country as a whole. It did so in a way which was, yet again, economistic to the core:

> [In a severe economic crisis the ruling class's only hope] lies in the total regimentation of the workers. The trade unions have to be hamstrung or even broken. The Labour parties have to be dissolved. The workers have to be *commanded* through every part of their lives.

Hence fascism, swept in by an economic crisis. But why did the hyper-inflation of 1923 not bring fascism to power in Germany? Can the rise of fascism be reduced in any meaningful political sense to economic crisis?

But if it can, then 'it could happen' as the *Socialist Worker* said, in England, given the economic crisis of capitalism in the seventies.

193

They showed how blissfully simple it is: (In Italy) 'the bosses . . . *promoted* Benito Mussolini'. (In Germany) 'they started to subsidise and to support Adolf Hitler, a *crackpot* ex-corporal'. (My emphases.) If the capitalist economy cracks up, as it inevitably must, then presumably it follows that a crackpot can come to power . . .

There are problems with this presentation which go beyond its economism, workerism and oversimplification of historical fascism. It presents the main danger to the working class as coming from the potential growth of the National Front rather than the present growth of the strong state. It also relies on fear to get its message across. Thus the presentation made much of Pastor Niemoeller's famous poem in which he describes how the Nazis picked off their opponents one by one, until 'when they came for me there was no one left'.

But what does it say about the *Socialist Worker*'s own understanding of the British working class that it cannot confront the widespread and tenacious racism within that class and its organisation, *including* factory-floor trade unionism? What happens if a worker, instead of being afraid, decides to join the winning white side? Surely, the strength of racism within the British working class is given powerful testimony by this silence about it. It is the main basis of the NF's appeal. All *Socialist Worker* could do was to skip over racism, and point to the horrors ahead. For 'its' working class to be strongly influenced by racism, was hard to fit with its workerism.

Workers, fascist violence, manipulation by the powerful, these were all present. But the fabric of everyday racism, its penetration of the deepest processes of individuals, its colouring of the workers' movement, were nowhere to be found. Perhaps its stress on arousing fear reflects the fear of the NF among many British leftists, since for the first time in the experience of many of them – coming as they do from a fairly sheltered and comfortable childhood – they can smell an oppression directly threatening themselves.

In an interesting article, Thom has suggested that the

194

language used by the *Socialist Worker* against the NF parallels in a curious way the language the NF itself used about its enemies. 'Vermin', 'sewer', 'rats', 'poison', 'germs', 'filth', 'stinking', were all frequently used terms to describe the NF and its views. Thom develops the implications of this in terms of an analysis of the Unconscious which cannot be discussed here, but his survey does at the very least suggest that anti-fascist and anti-racist communication by the British left somehow remains within the assumptions and style of its fascist opponents, keeping the images but reversing the target. This implies a kind of political paralysis in the face of white racism in Britain, which has very disturbing implications for the future.

The Militant carried eight items on racism. Six were in fact about the NF, rather paralleling the *Socialist Worker*'s greater interest in the fascism component than the racism component. As one article said in 1974:

> What the National Front represents—an *attempt to whip up* support for a 'strong government' against 'rowdy pickets' and other 'subversives' behind a *smokescreen* of racial diversions between British workers. (My emphases.)

The words emphasised underline the casual and superficial nature of racism in the working class as defined by their writer.

On another occasion the nature of racism was similarly defined:

> If we *allow* black and white workers to be divided, then *in no time* we will be at each other's throats, while our bosses look on and laugh all the way to the bank. THIS is the argument against racialism . . . (My emphases.)

Economism rules OK: the fact racism condones super-exploitation, police brutality, teachers' neglect, social workers' contempt, and massive discrimination, is as nothing to the fact that employers can laugh all the way to the bank. The absurd unreality of saying that blacks and whites must not be allowed to be divided when they plainly are, is overridden in the statement by the

195

mysterious potential for sudden, violent conflict: 'in no time we will be at each other's throats'.

On another occasion, a meeting on racism was held in Reading, organised by the Labour Party Young Socialists (a main area of *Militant* support). The speaker's view was quoted that racialism breeds in 'slums and grime', and must have its 'material base taken away from the fascists and the Tories by the elimination of poverty'. The report of the meeting concluded that the 'enthusiasm of the meeting, the number of West Indian people who came along . . . were signs that the fight against racialism and for socialism is now really being taken up.' Earlier, the numbers at the meeting had been said to be – over thirty!

The *Militant*'s economistic and workerist position on racism is very close to *Socialist Worker*'s. The effects of racism on blacks appear to be of less importance to either than the effects of the NF on leftists. The *Morning Star*'s handling of racism was wider, though its handling of anti-racist strategy was extremely weak.

In the *Morning Star*'s coverage of sexism, links with economic issues were once again well to the fore. Equal pay, equal training opportunity at work, opposition by Labour Party women to Conservative housing policy, greater participation by women in trade unions and in 'the industrial struggle', were the staple diet of a slender ration of items.

Other themes were the superiority of eastern European countries in their provision for women: the right of women to choose abortion in the German Democratic Republic, the achievement of the first woman astronaut in the USSR. Just from time to time other dimensions appeared, such as the recognition in one article that school curricula are often saturated with sexism, and so of the influence of sexism from the earliest years.

Socialist Worker covered sexism three times, as such, together with an article on a particular cut in state spending – in nursery school provision – with direct implications for women with young children. Its determined economism once again governed its interpretation of women's struggle.

For instance, the biggest item was a front page spread on
196

women's unemployment, shortly before a major London march to defend existing rights to abortion, organised by the National Abortion Campaign (a broadly based women's campaign). At the time, in the experience of many socialist feminists the International Socialists, now SWP, were heavily engaged in trying to dominate NAC policy and push it into their own box. Their box was to stress the 'hard' issues for women – e.g. unemployment. Abortion itself was consigned to an inside page. Even there its defence was described as 'a battle that only trade unionists can win'.

The workerism of the paper was also in evidence on the front page, with its reluctant admission of working class sexism: 'The government wants to forget us (i.e. women workers). So do many of the trade-union leaders – and even some men workers.' In an item on threatened nursery closures, nurses' redundancy was defined as the issue, to which the solution was a curious mix of women's moral fibre and trade-union muscle – each in its place:

> We'll have to fight to save the jobs of nursery nurses . . . the teacher training colleges will have to join the fight. So will the members of the local government union (NALGO) and the teachers (NUT). Mothers and children can't fight on their own, but their guts and determination can lead the fight.

What was good though was one article which described the oppression by social security officials of a single mother whose marriage had broken up. It was written by the woman herself whose experiences they were, and was excellent.

The *Militant* addressed itself twice to these questions in my selection. Or perhaps once, since the second item was about some strikers who happened to be women.

The main item concerned the Conference of Labour Party Women. The writer, a participant as usual in this paper, described her reluctance in going to a women-only conference, which was initially increased by the strongly reformist nature of the conference resolutions.

However, the conference turned out to be very militant, so

197

not a full disaster. Equal pay was insisted on immediately; and the Labour Party leader was widely felt to have insulted the women present by not talking about the EEC. This is no doubt true, since the EEC had been a hot issue in the conference debates, but what is apparent from the whole account is that it was an insult because the conference was just as good as a men's conference. It was just as good because it addressed itself to real, men's issues for debate – like the EEC. As the writer summed it up:

> While the workers [i.e. male and female] are fighting and bickering among themselves, the employers can heave a sigh of relief as they jealously guard their profits . . . [the trade unions must] draw women into the movement . . . [what about the reverse?] . . . nurseries, contraception, abortion, communal domestic facilities, full pay at maternity, are essential in this fight against *prices, wages and oppression.* [My emphasis.]

Profits, prices, wages, the trade unions. (And oppression.)

The sexism of the marginal, almost non-existent coverage of sexism is balanced by the resolute economism of all three papers (with the two exceptions listed above).

Conclusions

One factor sustaining the entrenched economism, and workerism, and humanistic marxism, of these three socialist media, is that they are marginal to the various struggles of the British working class. A living, *two-way* relationship would be more likely to produce a newspaper that relaxed its bulldog grip on economic issues, and instead voiced the variety of working class concerns.

For even when these papers are contrasted with bourgeois newspapers in respect of the opportunities offered to workers to speak in them, there is still an important barrier in most cases to self-expression. The *Morning Star* tends to open its columns to leading authorities in or close to the Communist Party, such as senior trade-union officials or university professors. The *Socialist Worker* and *The Militant* – the latter written almost exclusively by

198

its members – tend only to have the faithful open their mouths. The Cypriot immigrant talking about the 'industrial muscle' of the organised working class, the woman *Militant* member talking about trade unions having to draw women into the movement, are examples. But they cannot be organs of proletarian socialist democracy if only their letters columns are open to the general members of the working class.

In the end, then, on certain decisively important issues – the massive priority given to economic struggles, the boxed-up treatment of racism and sexism, the range of people involved in producing the papers – these three socialist media in Britain are still confined inside a flattened-out version of marxism (not to say a sect – like, insulated existence). While they do not assist capitalism to be stable, they certainly do not subvert it in any major way. And this is *not* because of their small circulation. The Italian Communist Party's *L'Unità* or the French CP's *L'Humanité* have huge circulations compared to the *Morning Star*, but they still do not meet the four criteria of socialist mass communication set out earlier. There is no formal guarantee, neither circulation, nor vividness of language, nor even the openness of a paper to the oppressed to write its pages themselves, which of itself is sufficient to ensure effective socialist communication.

For mass communication for liberation also has to have a *content* related to the full experience of oppression of the working class, including the divisions and oppressions within it. To define politics in terms of wages and the gyrations of the established British labour movement, was the albatross of these three socialist newspapers. Despite their differences from each other, they did not often succeed in breaking out of these straitjackets. To that extent, the problems of socialist transformation included the problems of organised socialist politics, not merely of capitalist hegemony.

199

9. Socialist Media II: Italy

I have consciously set out in this work to produce a spur to the creation of new mass communication, avoiding the traps of established socialist media as well as capitalist media. For this reason I shall conclude the book with an introduction to the most advanced use of media by the socialist movement in a capitalist society, the Italian experience of free radio. (I intend to expand this account substantially in a future publication which will assess experience of media under popular socialist control in Italy, Portugal and elsewhere.)

In order to grasp the significance of free radio in Italy, we first need a basic map of Italian political development since the second world war, and the place of established media within it. Afterwards we will focus on some specific instances of socialist radio stations in action.

The political background to socialist radio in Italy

From 1922 to 1944, Italian politics effectively meant Mussolini's fascism, which naturally enough governed mass media development. Any notion of the media as a critical 'fourth estate' was out of the question. Perhaps the turning point of 1944, in the light of the ensuing thirty-five years, rather than the defeat of Mussolini and the expulsion of the Nazis (which would have taken place anyway), was the call from Togliatti (general secretary of the Italian Communist Party) to the large and armed resistance movement to lay down its weapons and collaborate with the Allied troops. Thus a strongly socialist mass resistance movement was disarmed by its Communist leadership, and only four years later the Communist Party (PCI) was manoeuvred out of a share in Italian central government. From 1948 onwards the Christian Democratic Party (CD) was firmly in the saddle. Broadcasting was controlled by them as single-mindedly as it had previously been controlled by the fascists.

However, this is only one dimension of political power in Italy since the war. Although manoeuvred out of central government, the PCI has had a steadily growing share in urban government. In many of the industrial centres of northern and central Italy (Bologna being the classic case for thirty years), there was a permanent PCI majority on the city council. Over time, firm links came to be forged between these PCI city administrators and major employers. The effective exchange of advantages between these parties was on the one hand a coherent economic plan for the area (worked out by capital, unions and the PCI town hall); and on the other hand, a workforce disciplined by its local trade-union establishment. Thus the famous 'historic compromise' of the Communists with the Christian Democrats in the seventies at national level, where the PCI chose to act as unofficial second party in central government with CD, was first hammered out in local practice. This 'compromise' also has its roots in the PCI's parliamentary practice, where it has supported no less than three-quarters of CD legislation since the war. This has come to be the economic core of the so-called 'eurocommunist' strategy, a 'communism with a human face' which accepts the necessity for parliament and open elections as instruments of open and accountable government, far removed from the political structures of eastern Europe.

However, just as in chapter 1 we saw that a major problem with keynesian concordats can be the gulf that opens up between labour leaders and their base, so in Italy the Communist Party and its trade union officials have had increasing difficulty in maintaining their hold on certain sectors. Critics within it, such as Tronti, and outside it, such as Negri, have strenuously attacked its strategy. The result of these developments has been the growing alienation, especially of the younger left, from the PCI. This alienation has expressed itself forcefully since 1968 with the growth of a large socialist movement outside and against the PCI. There has been no movement quite comparable in size and energy elsewhere in Europe. It has been based to a large extent on the unemployed, on students (a much more fluid category in Italy than in Britain), on feminists, on younger workers, on gays. Until the very end of the seventies, the traditional working class stayed largely aloof from it, encouraged in this stance by the hostility of the PCI leadership toward 'the movement'.

The political self-expression of this movement, while never a socialist nirvana, has been varying and imaginative. It has organised alternative unions to the established ones. It has thrown up a mass of political groups and grouplets, some recognisable in their dogmatic sectarianism, others experimenting in more open marxism and forms of political organisation. There have been movements of self-reduction in prices, not only in supermarkets but also of bus-fares and home electricity tariffs. There have been major insurrectionary upsurges, such as those in Bologna – yes, Communist-controlled Bologna – and Rome in 1977. The movement has often used irony and the humour of the absurd to attack its targets. There has been flood of pamphlets, papers, songs, poetry, books, magazines, journals – and, not least, radio stations.

As we noted above, until 1968 the Christian Democrats controlled broadcasting completely. In that year, however, as a result of the entry of the Socialist Party into the coalition government, there began a process of what might be called 'competitive colonisation' of RAI (*Radio Audizioni Italia*, the formal equivalent of the BBC). To start with this was not particularly effective in denting the CD stranglehold, despite the appointment of top personnel for the first time from other parties. Nonetheless, it marked the first crack in the broadcasting monolith.

The impact of this monolith has been described by Macali in graphic terms:

> . . . for thirty years it has been the trusty mouthpiece for the ideas of the Christian Democrats and the bosses . . . For thirty years the

202

opinions, the wishes, the threats, even the internal rifts of CD have been the only yardstick to measure governments, heads of state, unions, singers, popular movements, laws and decrees, news of the day, inflation, civil wars, foreign statesmen, sports events, popes, student struggles, Sanremo festival, battles for civil rights and every other happening. For years, millions of Italians have had the sole freedom to decide whether to listen to channel one on radio (CD) or channel two (CD), almost always produced in Rome far from their own towns, and equally far from the problems, language, customs, needs of local town and country communities in different regions of Italy.

This stifling uniformity in broadcasting was offensive to the big political parties, who were determined to have their slice of air-time. Hence their competitive colonisation of RAI. In partial response, a campaign developed to abolish RAI's broadcasting monopoly by introducing a parallel commercial network, as in Britain. Any astute CD supporter could see that commercial broadcasting would sooner or later become controlled by an oligopoly of big firms. Further considerations were that the regionalisation of authority within RAI was being seriously discussed, which would have meant Communist domination in certain regions. Commercial broadcasting stations would mean a pro-regime station in every area.

The result of this campaign was a long series of parliamentary blockages between the various political parties over how and whether to reform RAI. One government coalition actually collapsed on this issue. At the same time there was a consistent series of strikes and stoppages by RAI's own staff to back reform. Sometimes newspaper workers came out as well in their support.

While these various clashes were taking place, there was also a sharp increase in illegal broadcasting by stations based outside Italy, such as Radio Monte Carlo, who were adding to the number of their relay transmitters inside Italy. It should also be recalled that numerous experiments with cablevision were taking place in the early seventies. Finally, to complete the picture, a number of independent radio and TV stations began broadcasting over 1974 to 1976 without official permission. Most were closed down quite quickly by Escopost, the Post Office police unit, but nonetheless there was a great deal of division and uncertainty among magistrates and judges as to their correct judicial reaction to these breaches in the law.

It was in this political atmosphere, in which virtually the only point of agreement for the majority was their view that broadcasting had to change in some way, that the Constitutional Court produced its now famous Verdict 202 in July 1976, declaring the RAI monopoly of local broadcasting unconstitutional.

There followed a heady period of mass experimentation with radio and – much less so – with TV (because of its higher costs). As an indication of the broadcasting explosion, there were, in June 1978, an estimated 2,275 radio stations and 503 TV stations, spread fairly evenly through the population centres of the country. Italy was leading even the USA in the number of TV and radio stations per head of the population. On an average day in 1977, over a quarter of radio listeners were tuned to the independents rather than RAI or the foreign stations. In a 1977 survey of 266 radio stations, a quarter broadcast round the clock and a further half between 14 and 19 hours a day. The listeners, according to this survey, seem to have been mostly from the younger section of the population.

In terms of content, the dominant feature of the TV stations was their showing of films, in some cases pornographic. The radio stations mostly transmitted music. Many stations went on the air for a period ranging from days to months, and then closed down. Finance for the successful ones came from advertising, with an obvious cumulative tendency to make the successful more so, and the unsuccessful fail altogether. A large proportion of TV stations were owned by newspaper magnates.

A small percentage of the radio stations which went on the air were socialist in inspiration. Trasatti has categorised the radio stations as follows: 'tendency' radios (i.e. movement radios); party radios (e.g. the PCI's Radio Blue); escapist radios (non-stop music etc.); feminist radios; TV stations' adjunct-radios; specific function radios (e.g. Radio Sicilia for Sicilian migrants in Rome); mini-radios (three or four young people, a transmitter and a pile of records); community radios, by which Trasatti means local Catholic stations, normally CD in outlook. Clearly then, movement (obviously including feminist) radio stations are only a fraction of the whole, even though they did form a national Federation of Democratic Radio Stations (F.R.E.D. in Italian) with over eighty member stations.

Radio stations of the movement

How has the movement used radio in Italy? The first recognition must be its variety of uses, though at the same time it should not be forgotten that even in these stations music usually forms about 60 per cent of output. The types of music vary though, from very slickly presented jazz through to 'spontaneous working-class music' . . .

Perhaps the most famous of all the stations was Radio Alice in Bologna, described by Gamaleri as a 'guerrilla electronic tom-tom' because of its dramatic role in the insurrection in Bologna in 1977, when it relayed information from phone-kiosks to groups of demonstrators about police movements and positions in the fighting, until the police arrived, smashed the doors in and closed it down.

It was also famous however for the radio communication philosophy of its leading figure, Franco Berardi (Bifo'), and the A/Oblique Collective which organised its running. Radio Alice probably combined the roles of 'creative stimulus' and 'practical semi-ghetto'. Creative stimulus, in that Alice insistently raised the question for the movement in general of the *imaginative* in communication, moving beyond the factual=rational bias and repetitive formulas of many socialist communicators. Practical semi-ghetto, in that its own output was often only understandable to university students familiar with some very complex perspectives, and in its initial tendencies to sneer at and write off the factory workers who had difficulty in relating at all to the movement. Radio Alice was influential certainly, but not representative, and we must move on to other examples.

There is a crop of far left stations which effectively treat radio as if it were the equivalent of a political party newspaper. That is to say, the waveband is seen as an extra outlet for the revolutionary truth as defined by the party or group in question. Radio Onda Rossa (Red Wave) in Rome opens its broadcasts 'Hello comrades'. In the early days, quite a number of people experienced something of a lift on hearing the Internationale broadcast by their own radio station.

In some cases however, arguments about whether the station should follow this model have been so bitter that the station has actually closed down. A case is Radio Trento in the north of Italy, which broadcast for seven months from December 1976 to June 1977. One particular political group, Avanguardia Operaia, (Workers' Vanguard), insisted that the radio must have an identifiable political line. The internal clashes on this issue forced its closure altogether.

Another instance of violent rows on this question, once again involving Avanguardia Operaia, was in Radio Canale 96 (Waveband 96) in Milan. Macali, who resigned as producer over the insistence of AO that Waveband 96 should be a party station, instanced the way in which former leading AO cadres who had been expelled by it, were regarded as absolutely unacceptable to speak on the station by AO members of the radio collective. Macali also cited the attitude of some AO members toward a gay group who organised one slot on the station's output, that they didn't want any more of this 'arse-radio stuff'.

These cases are cited, not to belabour Avanguardia Operaia, but to illustrate a particular definition within the movement of the proper use of radio. It is the kind of far left definition most immediately recognisable to readers of the British socialist press. The existence of this wing of opinion within the movement has to be acknowledged, but at the same time it must be realised that it is only one wing.

Elsewhere there are different examples of radio use. Radio

Popolare (People's Radio) in Milan follows quite an open policy towards the established left in the PCI and other official formations, and also makes strenuous efforts to ensure that the language it uses is clear and free from stereotyped formulas. One Sicilian radio station offers a different picture again, being quite unable to enjoy the freedom of attacking public figures. One of its collective was foolhardy enough to attack a leading Mafia member by name, and was murdered a few days later. In a moment we will focus on yet another model, Radio Città Futura (City of the Future) in Rome, which has already been referred to at the beginning of the chapter on sexism.

There is one general point though which must first be made about all movement radio stations, namely the link they discovered between the transmitter and the telephone. There is a definite difference between revolutionary telephone-transmitter use, and the radio phone-ins of bourgeois local broadcasting. For one thing, the bourgeois stations generally have a delay-device to put people's voices on the air some seconds after they have actually spoken. Ostensibly this is so that anyone who suddenly lets fly with a string of obscenities can be cut off, but it enables quite effective censorship, as does the practice of checking out first what the person wishes to say. Furthermore, bourgeois phone-ins are cast very often in the form of interviews by the linkperson. Thus, as a member of the A/Oblique Collective once put it, they become like a crossword where the person who phones in is faced with something resembling numbered blank squares which have to be filled in with the single correct answer. Verbally skilled and experienced linkpersons are very adept at unnerving or dismissing telephoners who express dissonant views. Finally, the bourgeois stations are completely open to organised telephoning by fascist groups, like readers' letters pages of some local newspapers. In Britain the NF and similar bodies have utilised this to some effect.

By contrast, from a revolutionary radio perspective, the telephone means that a studio is not essential for public debate on radio. It means immediacy, the most dramatic case being that of

Radio Alice in the Bologna insurrection, but there being plenty of other less dramatic uses. Radio Mantova (Mantua) at one time used to ring up leading politicians and try to get them to answer questions on the air. People can read their poetry over the air, sing songs, sometimes speak from their workplaces. Radio fulfils Brecht's vision of a 'colossal canal-system'.

Of course, there are problems. Fascists ring up and threaten to blow up the transmitter. Some people can't be stopped from talking, and comrades don't want to be accused of censorship by a later caller. Some ring up and ask the linkperson for their – meaning the radio station's – view on a matter. If the radio collective does not see the station in this way (see below on Radio Città Futura), i.e. as the personal property of its activists, then this can place the linkperson in a dilemma.

Let us turn now to a particular case-study which represents an absorbing advance in socialist communication practice, to study some of the organisational detail and conflicts and problems of Italian socialist radio.

The case of Radio Città Futura

RCF was begun in February 1976 (i.e. *before* Verdict 202) in the flat of a comrade which was situated in a part of Rome especially suited to transmission to the whole city. When the experiment was clearly successful after a few days, she moved out and stayed for some weeks in a hotel at RCF's expense until she found a new flat. Their first transmitter was a 600-watt affair cannibalised from various sources by a comrade with technical training. Two years later they moved to a working-class stronghold in Rome.

In discussing RCF we will focus on the following questions. First, RCF's specific 'philosophy' as a radio station. Second, its form of organisation and finance. Third, the part played by feminist broadcasts in its organisation. Fourth, the place of imaginative material in its output. Fifth, some lessons of experience in running a radio station. Sixth, the question of the language

208

used on RCF. Seventh, the relation between RCF and RAI, the state broadcasting organisation.

RCF's broadcasting philosophy differentiates it from many other stations, though Controradio (Counter-radio) in Florence has a very similar broadcasting perspective. In essence its philosophy is founded on the recognition that radio offers peculiar possibilities not provided by a newspaper. Instead of simply pushing out a party line, or of producing counter-information – which is valuable, but still places the journalists at the centre of the process with the right to have their views dominant – radio enables people to confront each other. Among the oppressed, this means the chance of breaking down the insulated compartments that we have seen capitalist media keeping us in earlier. Radio means the possibility of slowly and painstakingly confronting our contradictions, for ourselves, gradually dissolving the filters through which we see each other – which capitalist media feed us as our daily bread. In this sense, radio can be a resource, not a tool.

It does not mean the people most closely involved in running the station somehow disguise their own political perspectives, that they pretend a version of bourgeois journalistic 'neutrality'. It does mean that they do not claim the authority of the station for their own views, but rather offer the station as a means of growth in the political integration and maturity of all the oppressed. In political terms, the difference between the RCF activists and, say, the Rome Autonomists (an ultra-left group), was that RCF comrades did not consider the oppressed had achieved the necessary self-consciousness and self-organisation to confront the state immediately and head-on in revolutionary action. They felt, in the political terms in currency, that the 'social subject' was no longer just the working class, but also that this 'subject' was not yet 'complete' – indeed, that RCF had a major role to play in enabling its maturation.

In the words of an RCF position document dated 29 April 1979, the RCF Collective was committed to struggling for 'the democratisation of information' and 'the highest socialisation of the power-centre that we are seeking to develop in this station'.

209

The following excerpts from their 4-point programme help to concretise what this meant:

1. To combat, on the terrain of daily information and culture, the operation of the dominant class through the major media . . .

2. . . . to give voice to the issues raised in social struggles that aim not merely to transform the economic relations of production, but which also set themselves intermediate aims such as direct intervention against established power in the territory: in the fields of culture, the urban setting, patterns of leisure activity, the neighbourhood, education, etc.

3. To provide a reference point in the information field for those mass movements (women, students, unemployed) which do not possess their own means of communication . . . this means to link up the voices of these new forces, without any filtering process, with the overall mesh of social forces at work in the society.

4. To produce information laterally, based on a type of mass relation to the city and national social life, which involves the people themselves, as transforming their role from ordinary passive consumers into *active subjects* in the work of the radio-station . . .

Later on in the same document, they defined what they meant by the radio station's necessary autonomy. The station, they argued, must not be the 'transmission belt' for any particular political line, nor a clique of radio experts, nor a new political party formation. The station's autonomy therefore:

signifies information activity from the viewpoint of the class, based on the necessity to give utterance and space to *its* expressions, *its* growth, and all *its* crises, to *its* leading elements . . . This linkage does not exist simply in the mind, but is worked out through continuing relations with all the city's mass organisms and movements of struggle. These relations are not simply technical, practical or service relations, since we are inside, not outside, these struggles.

This position, it is important to recognise, was not uncontested inside RCF. Activists of the political groups of the sixties, such as Il Manifesto (a left splinter from the PCI), had a clearer view of the rightfulness of consistent political leadership of the masses, and wanted to use the station for that purpose. This was an

210

intermittent battle inside RCF, not least because its origins were partly with political groupings of this type.

The organisation and financing of RCF were as follows. The station was constructed into a series of commissions. There was the Information Commission, which was responsible for the news, broadcast daily at 2 p.m., 7.30 p.m., midnight and 7 a.m. (the recorded midnight news). There was the Press Reading Commission, commenting on the main stories in the day's papers as Rome's office workers and sub-professional workers were on their way into work (there are very few industrial workers left in Rome). There was the Open Space Commission which broadcast certain days from 11 to 1, and which would cover particular issues in depth, for instance H-Block in Long Kesh concentration camp in Northern Ireland. There was also the International Commission, which organised a weekly 2-hour programme on international politics.

The Music Commission, rather weak in the early days, originally saw itself simply as being there to produce 'fillers'. Later on it became one of the politically most dynamic features of RCF. The Cultural Commission was responsible for discussion of books, plays, media. People could ring in during its slots and talk critically about books they had read. The Cinema Commission did similar work on films, and also produced a 'What's On' guide to Rome cinemas.

There was also a series of slots during the week for feminist broadcasts from Radio Donna (Radio Woman) which we will discuss in more detail below.

The three remaining Commissions were the Administration Commission, whose remit included finance; the Technical Commission, which is self-explanatory; and the Programming Commission, which has equally self-evident tasks.

Anyone was free to join any of these commissions. A general distinction was usually drawn, however, between radio workers and *autogestiti*, the latter being mainly concerned to use a slot allocated to them for their own purposes, but not to help organise the station itself. Anyone, including listeners, was free to attend the

211

Assembly, which met every Thursday, and was the formal democratic point of integration and authority for the station. In practice, Assembly meetings were often poorly attended. The rather wearisome and repetitive nature of their business was probably the main cause.

As regarded financing, RCF was effectively dependent on subscriptions, fund-raising efforts, and voluntary commitment from activists to run the station. The attempt to organise an advertising agency for far left radio stations never recovered from the collapse of the F.R.E.D in autumn 1978 on this and other issues (the Autonomists and many tiny stations in the south were either hostile to, or unconcerned with, advertising). Thus income from this source was practically nil. It meant the radio station ran on half a shoestring. (One consequence was that it was often difficult to get volunteer radio workers to carry out their commitments on time.)

The part played by feminists in the station is of particular interest, given Italy's powerful cultural tradition of male supremacy. This was a division among the oppressed much more sharply defined than in Britain say. In fact, the large-scale women's movement in Italy and RCF itself both emerged into being at about the same time. At the outset, the Italian women's movement was strongly separatist, so that Radio Donna for instance would not accept telephone calls at that stage from any male. They also insisted on being made fully au fait with all the technical details of broadcasting, so as to be completely independent thereafter in organising their own broadcasts. They were usually allocated slots from 10 to 11 a.m. and 6.30 to 7.30 p.m. In the first site, Radio Conna used one of the two rooms purely for itself, RCF occupying the other one.

One of the most advanced aspects of Radio Donna was the Housewives' Collective, whose experience at the hands of fascist terrorists was described earlier on. This collective was composed of middle-aged housewives, a category of women normally outside the contemporary women's movement. They came into RCF/ Radio Donna through personal connections in the first instance (the mother of one of the women activists in RCF was the first

212

link), but rapidly spread in influence and developed numerous new connections. Some of the women involved actually had to conceal their activity from their own husbands. But still, they were there, and contributing.

Within the Radio Donna slots, were various women's collectives who produced regular programmes. Instances were the Pomponazzi Collective, a leading separatist women's group, and other collectives such as Women and Politics, Women and Medicine, Women and Law, the Actresses' Collective. In fact, in the period leading up to the fascist attack, feminist involvement in Radio Donna had slackened off considerably, following the launching of *Quotidiano Donna* (Woman Daily) in spring 1978.

After the attack there were some sharp clashes between the RCF activists and some feminists, especially the Pomponazzi Collective. The latter accused RCF, which had organised a massive demonstration about the attack, of making capital for itself out of the Housewives' Collective. They argued the attack was on women, not RCF. They also argued the RCF subscription fund should be spent on looking after the injured women, there being no national health service in Italy. In the event, the Housewives' Collective insisted they did not want subscription-fund money to be diverted to them, and the final decision was to make available a certain amount of it mostly to provide nursing and help for the worst-injured woman.

The role of imaginative material in RCF broadcasts was an important one. A classic case was their mock announcement that there had been a leftist coup, and that leftwing MPs were standing in the turrets of tanks that were rolling down the main streets of Rome! This caused such a stir that there was a sharp clash inside RCF on the issue. Another time they put on a mock broadcast of a boy who claimed to be a test-tube baby, and desperately embarrassed about the fact! Many of the phone-calls this time as well took the broadcast seriously. (They called the boy 'Salvatore' – Saviour – a standard boy's name in Italy, but nonetheless with overtones of Christ!) As an education in not believing broadcasts, these were interesting experiments.

213

There were other instances however. RCF was completely tolerant of a young woman who used to ring regularly, but whose real identity no-one knew. She described herself as 'Giada' (jade), spoke with a high-pitched, childish voice, and aroused very strong reactions among listeners for and against herself. Radio Onda Rossa used simply to tell her to shut up. There was constant speculation that she might be in a psychiatric hospital or confined to a flat. Her comments were usually disconnected and even fantastic at first reaction, but always on reflection presented an inner logic in her linkage of matters normally dissociated from each other. This stimulus to people's imagination and thought was seen by the RCF activists as a good aspect of their work in radio.

A different example comes from their use of spontaneous events. While they were planning the march after the fascist attack, two police sergeants came to try to persuade them to call it off. They invited them into the studio room, saying it would be a quiet place to talk, and then gradually turned the microphones up. Listeners started phoning in asking what was happening, as they heard the policemen argue that the Autonomists would cause violence on the march, and the RCF activists insisting they would not condemn anyone in the movement.

A little later on, a police superintendent turned up on the same mission, but expressing himself more suavely. Him they talked to in the courtyard at the foot of the inner well inside the block of flats where they had their station. While he was talking, they dangled a microphone from an upstairs window to pick up his words, and then one of them went down with a pocket tape-recorder held behind his back in order to record what he said. When he noticed the tape-recorder his suave manner vanished in an almost incoherent outburst of rage – which was broadcast through the dangling microphone there and then to the rest of Rome!

Lastly, RCF developed a Saturday night programme composed of songs, both rehearsed and spontaneously phoned in. People would ring in to read their or other people's poems. Once as part of this fairly intimate programme, they put on a record of

214

Chopin, and had a call from an old Polish woman living in Rome, to say how the record had vividly brought back to her her youth in Poland, the lake near her home, the boats on it. Sometimes people would phone in some words for a song, and the studio group from the Music Commission would immediately put them to music.

On the important subject of gains in broadcasting experience, it is clear that the excitement of the first months was bound to wear off in time. The RCF activists became increasingly aware of the value of experience, but the need to disentangle experience from the ideology of professionalism which derives some of its plausibility from it. In their view, the Commissions would function partly as memory-banks of the broadcasting experience gained, with whom new workers or collaborators could be asked first to discuss their project in order not to repeat past mistakes needlessly. As one of the RCF comrades put it, the station needed to develop a grid for effective programme-making, without turning the grid into a grille excluding people from making programmes. But it was clear that good intentions alone might not be adequate to radio communication.

On a different subject, there was a debate about the problem of comrades turning up late for work in the station, or of not turning up at all. The old-style political activists immediately set to to create an elected 12-person secretariat to produce organised reliability. It had two or three meetings, no impact, and collapsed. The lesson was clear, that while people are committed to a project it will run, but there is no way in volunteer work to whip people into line if they don't want to be.

The language used by RCF and many other stations continued to be stereotyped in many ways. RCF asked a sociologist comrade to comment on their language style, and his assessment was blistering in its indictment of their tendency to produce formula expressions and jargon. From time to time they publicly ridiculed their own phrase-mongering on the air, but at the same time there were only rarely listeners' complaints about it. Given the existence of the movement, its base in Italian society, political jargon was less alienating than in a different context.

215

The relationship of RCF to RAI is instructive. The RAI third channel which began in 1979, a minority channel set up as window-dressing for RAI's normal operation, came to model itself on the radicalism and even a little on the spontaneity of the independent socialist stations. Some of the older style politicos even preferred this channel to RCF. Certainly, some people once active in movement radio later moved over to work for this channel for a living. Clearly, if the third channel were successful in diverting talent and energy from the movement radio stations, they might largely collapse for want of support, leaving RAI free to do with the third channel what it wished. This aspect of the question underlines what is too easily forgotten, how revolutionary broadcasting never took place in a media vacuum. There was a constant if gradual tendency to modernise RAI, with its own appeal to those less than fully committed to RCF's own broadcasting philosophy.

Lastly, a two-pronged attack on RCF's operation must be mentioned. On the one hand, there was perpetual interference by the police and the courts. Many of the RCF activists had been in prison for short periods because of their radio involvement. One comrade had between thirty and forty charges hanging over him over an 18-month period. Two or three times the police announced their intention of closing RCF down. They recorded all its broadcasts in case they could pin 'incitement to insurrection' on them. By purest accident, the very morning of the kidnapping of the Prime Minister, Moro, by the Red Brigades in 1977 (Moro being the principal CD architect of the 'historic compromise' with the PCI), the comrade doing the comments on the press happened to deliver himself of the view that there would need to be some new development that day to cement the 'historic compromise'. He was soon dragged in by the police for questioning.

The other attack came from within, from some of those who had put up money to help the station get off the ground in the first place. They belonged to small political parties to the left of the PCI, but still operating with some of its arrogance. They were opposed to the vision of radio-use set out in the RCF document quoted above, preferring a more formal, 'transmission-belt' station. Because their views had been for some time in a perpetual minority in assembly meetings and in the Commissions, they had reluctantly gone along with the majority view. In September 1979, a major meeting was held at which these people hardly turned up. Yet a few days later, they occupied the station and physically forced out the members of the RCF collective.

At once a core of the collective set to work discussing how to set up another station. The story was not over therefore. The dismaying aspect of this clash of political views was that the old guard – the 'zombies' as RCF members tended to describe them – were more successful and bolder in their attack than the police. It is a reminder that revolutionary radio in Italy is no utopia.

Conclusions

The experience of using radio within the Italian movement suggests then that there are no easy solutions to entrenched problems, whether of funding, police harassment, political splits, or relations between men and women. Secondly, however, it indicates how some of Brecht's glimpses of the possibilities existing in radio may be realised, consolidated, and vastly extended. The scope offered by radio for internal, lateral communication, independent of capital and the capitalist state – though never insulated from their pressures – is immense. The studies of capitalist and socialist media in the body of this book showed one thing above all, the endemic segregation of the oppressed from each other, especially of the most combative groups of the oppressed from their own specific constituencies and the rest of the class. Radio opens up a unique and not impossibly costly form of encounter and experience between the various segments of the oppressed, in order to integrate their understandings of their oppressions into a mature self-awareness of the *full* dimensions of class struggle. This encounter will never be easy, but it is irreplaceable in the struggle for the socialist transformation of social relations.

Siliato has argued that the Italian far left's embrace of radio is a serious form of self-delusion. He points to the international trend toward the use of satellites in broadcasting, and the parallel (but in his view complementary) wave of experiments in cablevision and local participatory broadcasting in the imperialist countries, especially Canada. He concludes that community broadcasting is simply an element in the more general strategy of mystification by 'participation' in the most localised decision-making, with the result that local symptoms of national or international forces become identified as locally caused, diffusing people's energy to resist on to purely local targets – and so defusing it. Meanwhile the basic decisions about mass international broadcasting via satellite are increasingly being made by the electronics transnationals such as ITT.

Siliato has undoubtedly drawn attention to extremely important trends in mass communication and their interrelation with each other. He seems to have overlooked the specific difference however, between say, the Italian and Canadian cases. Italy has a mass movement of the far left, which is able to seize this sudden opportunity offered by Verdict 202. In Canada there are a number of officially sponsored and *provided* local broadcasting outlets, open in principle to any and every interest group, almost however reactionary its perspective. There is all the difference in the world between a radio station open to the expression of one or many perspectives on liberation from among the oppressed, and a radio station open to everyone, even fascists. The latter case also suffers from an inbuilt anxiety even among radical staff at being publicly labelled as too hospitable to revolutionary perspectives. Lastly, Siliato has missed the crucial question, raised by the Radio Città Futura document, of the *form of organisation* of these radio stations.

By the criteria set out at the beginning of the previous chapter, it is fair to say that the use of radio by the Italian revolutionary movement has been a high-water mark in socialist mass communication.

General Conclusions

The logic of this book leads first to the recognition that a mass-based politics has to be centrally concerned with the media. Stripping away every apparently spontaneous – but actually media-communicated – assumption about capitalist work, racism, and sexism, is a major task.

Second, it means that strategies for reforming existing media, for making them more democratically accountable, are worthwhile but utterly insufficient to defeat these oppressions. Media for internal communication among the oppressed are a priority. In Europe in the 1970s, British socialists may have recorded rather a low-water mark in this respect, but important new experience was gained in Italy through the revolutionary movement's seizure of the airwaves. Patchy, experimental and crisis-ridden as this action was, it still represented that self-determination by the oppressed which stands as the benchmark of our authentic progress.

In the tight conditions of the eighties, defensive rather than offensive movements are much more likely to be the order of the day. The failures of the organised left have their share of responsibility for this retrenchment, as well as – and perhaps as part of – the power of capitalist hegemony. Understanding these forces has been the aim of this book, as a preparation for sharper and more effective combat against oppression. For the realities of class exploitation, imperialism, racism, sexism, ageism are such that either we move forward – or capitalist society moves us backwards. The alternative – 'socialism or barbarism' – is disagreeable in its starkness to those at home in the heyday of keynesian capitalism; but it persists. In Walter Benjamin's distilled expression of this alternative (from his sixth thesis on the philosophy of history):

> In every era the attempt must be made anew to wrest tradition away from a conformism that is about to overpower it . . . [for] *even the dead* will not be safe from the enemy if he wins. And this enemy has not ceased to be victorious.

Sources and Further Reading

I have arranged these in the order in which they are cited, or in which they contribute to the argument. Within each subsection, however, the books are cited alphabetically by author.

An asterisk * indicates a book or article which has been especially helpful or which represents an excellent development of the argument.

Place of publication of books is London unless otherwise indicated (or Harmondsworth in the case of Penguin titles).

1. Class Struggle in Work, *pp. 6–31*

*H. Beynon, *Working for Ford*, Penguin 1977

*P. Carpignano, 'US class composition in the sixties', *Zerowork* vol.1 1975

S. Castles and G. Kosack, *Immigrant Workers and Class Structure in Western Europe*, Oxford University Press 1973

*D. Demac and P. Mattera, 'Developing and underdeveloping New York', *Zerowork* vol.2 1977

P. Kinnersly, *The Hazards of Work*, Pluto Press 1977

*R. Kriegler, *Working for the Company*, Sydney: OUP (Australia) 1980

M. Mellish, *The Docks After Devlin*, Heinemann Educational Books 1972

T. Nichols and P. Armstrong, *Workers Divided*, Fontana Books 1976

The Little Red Blue Book – fighting the layoffs at Ford's Red Notes pamphlet 1978 (2A St Paul's Road, London N1)

J. O'Connor, *The Fiscal Crisis of the State*, New York: St Martins Press 1973

B. Ramirez, 'The working class struggle against the crisis: self-reduction of prices in Italy', in *Zerowork* vol.1 1975

M. Tronti, *Ouvriers et Capital*, Paris: Christian Bourgois 1978

Workers' Struggles and the Development of Ford in Britain, Red Notes pamphlet 1, 1976

The wage, *pp. 8–14*

H. Braverman, *Labor and Monopoly Capital*, Monthly Review Press 1974

J. Harrison, *Marxist Economics for Socialists*, Pluto Press 1978

K. Marx, *Capital I*, Penguin 1976

*K. Stone, 'The origin of job-structures in the steel industry', *Radical America* vol.7, no.6 1973

Workers' resistance, *pp. 14–18*

T. Clarke and L. Clements (eds), *Trade Unions under Capitalism*, Fontana Books 1977

J. Dromey and G. Taylor, *Grunwick: The Workers' Story*, Lawrence & Wishart 1978

M. Haraszti, *A Worker in a Worker's State*, Penguin 1977

T. Lane and K. Roberts, *Strike at Pilkington's*, Fontana Books 1971

*J. Pomlet, 'The toolmaker', in R. Fraser (ed) *Work 2*: Penguin 1969

*K.-H. Roth, *Die 'Andere' Arbeiterbewegung*, München: Trikont Verlag, 2nd ed. 1977

Technology and the decomposition of the working class, *pp. 18–23*

H. Beynon, *Working for Ford*, Penguin 1977

*S. Bologna, 'An Overview', in *Italy 1977–78 – Living with an Earthquake*, London: Red Notes pamphlet 1978, 2a St Paul's Rd, London N1

H. Braverman, *Labor and Monopoly Capital*, Monthly Review Press, 1974

Counter-Information Services, *The New Technology*, 1979

C. Palloix, 'The labour process: from Fordism to neo-Fordism', in *The Labour Process and Class Strategies*, CSE pamphlet 1, Stage One 1978

The keynesian state, *pp. 23–31*

S. de Brunhoff, *The State, Capital and Economic Policy*, Pluto Press 1978

CSE, *Struggle Over the State*, CSE Books 1980

*T. Negri, 'Théorie capitaliste de l'État en 1929', in his *La Classe Ouvrière Contre l'État*, Paris: Christian Bourgois 1978

L. Panitch, *Social Democracy and Industrial Militancy*, Cambridge University Press 1976

D. Thomson and R. Larson, *Where Were You Brother? An Account of Trade Union Imperialism*, War on Want, 467 Caledonian Road, London N7, 1978

D. Winch, *Economics and Policy*, Fontana Books 1976

2. The Media and Class Struggle in Work, *pp. 32–49*

J. Downing, 'Class and "race" in the British news media', 1971. This paper was quite widely circulated in 1971 and later, after being read to the International Working Convention on Racism in the Political Economy of Britain, held that year 13-16 December at South Bank Polytechnic, London; and to the working group on mass communication of the British Sociological Association. Because of the problems of placing it in or out of socialist journals at that time, I never troubled to rewrite and publish it. It did however precede and inform much in later work on the media and industrial or racial conflict. Anyone who wants a copy should write to me c/o Social Sciences School Office (*media paper*), Thames Polytechnic, London SE18, enclosing a stamped, addressed A4 envelope, and postage to cover 90 gms weight. It also contains a discussion of my methodology, and an appendix with extensive samples of my material in it. Material on workers' voices in TV news, and the basis for chapter 8, was first in a paper that Ash Corea and I read to the conference on Popular Alternatives to Media, Tarragona/Barcelona, 22–28 May 1978

*O. Negt and A. Kluge, *Öffentlachkeit und Erfahrung*, Frankfurt/Main: Suhrkamp Verlag 1973

G. Wallraff, *Wallraff: The Undesirable Journalist*, Pluto Press 1978

The mysterious origins of senseless strikes, *pp. 33–35*

P. Ambrose and B. Colenutt, *The Property Machine*, ch.4: Penguin 1976

Glasgow University Media Group, *Bad News*, Routledge & Kegan Paul, 1977

P. Hartmann, 'Industrial relations and the news media', *Industrial Relations Journal* vol. 6 1975

P. Hartmann, 'News and public perceptions of industrial relations', in *Media Culture and Society* vol.1 1979

D. Morley, 'Industrial conflict and the mass media', *Sociological Review* vol.24 1976

J. Young & J. Crutchley, 'May the first 1973 – a day of predictable madness', in P. Beharrell and G. Philo (eds), *Trade Unions and the Media*, Macmillan 1977

The focus on the impact, *pp. 35–37*

Apart from the studies above, R. Miliband, *The State in Capitalist Society*, Quartet Books 1976, has many references to the ideology of the 'national interest'.

Journalists' political interventions in strike accounts, *pp. 41–43*

G. Philo and others, 'One-dimensional news – television and the control of explanation', in P. Beharrell and G. Philo (eds) *Trade Unions and the Media*, Macmillan 1977

*P. Schlesinger, *Putting 'Reality' Together*, Constable 1977

J. Tunstall, *Journalists At Work*, Constable 1971, has some material on industrial correspondents

3. Racism in Modern Britain, *pp. 50-80*
The genesis and development of racist ideology, *pp. 50-56*

C. Bolt, *Victorian Attitudes to Race*, Routledge & Kegan Paul 1971

*A. Dummett, *A Portrait of English Racism*, Penguin 1973

*J. S. Haller, *Outcasts From Evolution*, New York: McGraw-Hill 1975

C. L. R. James, *The Black Jacobins*, New York: Vintage Books 1963

*W. D. Jordan, *White Over Black*, Chapel Hill: University of North Carolina Press 1968

Malcolm X, *By Any Means Necessary*, New York: Pathfinder Press 1970

The era of metropolitan labour migrants, *pp. 57-74*

*J. Berger, *A Seventh Man*: Penguin 1975

S. Castles and G. Kosack, *Immigrant Workers and Class Structure in Western Europe*, Oxford University Press 1973

C. Demuth, *'Sus': a report on section 4 of the Vagrancy Act 1824*, Runnymede Trust 1978

J. Downing, 'The community relations industry: harmony without justice', *Race Today* 4.10 1972

J. Downing, *Racial Oppression in Britain*, War on Want, 467 Caledonian Road, London N7, 1980

*I. Katznelson, *Black Men, White Cities*, Oxford University Press 1973

R. Moore and T. Wallace, *Slamming the Door*, Oxford: Martin Robertson 1975

D. Smith, *Racial Disadvantage in Britain*, Penguin 1977

Unit for Manpower Studies, *The Role of Immigrants in the Labour Market*, Department of Employment 1976

A. Ward, 'European capitalism's reserve army', and 'European migratory labour', in *Monthly Review*, vol.27 1975

Responses, *pp. 74-79*

M. Billig, *Fascists*, European Monographs in Social Psychology 15, 1978

*T. Cottle, *Black Testimony*, Wildwood House 1978

P. Foot, *The Rise of Enoch Powell*, Penguin 1970

E. Greer, 'Racism and US Steel', *Radical America*, vol.10 1976

R. May and R. Cohen, 'The interaction between race and colonialism: a case study of the Liverpool race riots of 1919', *Race and Class* vol.16 1974

*R. Moore, *Racism and Black Resistance in Britain*, Pluto Press 1975

T. Nairn, 'Enoch Powell: the new Right', in his *The Break-Up of Britain*, New Left Books 1978

E. Rudwick, *Race Riot at East St Louis*, New York: Meridian Books 1966

A. Spear, *Black Chicago*, Chicago University Press 1967

*A. Wilson, *Finding A Voice: Asian Women Speak*, Virago 1978

4. The Media and Racism, *pp. 81–100*

'A party-political broadcast? the Kennedy-Webster interview', *Searchlight* vol.32 1978

Campaign Against Racism in the Media, *In Black and White*, CARM 1977

C. Critcher and others, 'Race in the West Midlands provincial press', in *Ethnicity and the Media*, Paris: UNESCO 1977

J. Downing, 'The (balanced) white view', in C. Husband (ed), *White Media, Black Britain*, Arrow Books, Hutchinson 1975

*P. Hartmann and C. Husband, *Racism and the Mass Media*, Davis-Poynter 1973

P. Hartmann and others, 'Race as News', in J. Halloran (ed), *Race as News*, Paris: UNESCO 1974

C. Husband, 'Social identity and the language of race relations', in H. Giles and B. Saint-Jacques (eds), *Language and Ethnic Interaction*, Oxford: Pergamon Press 1979

L. Kushnick, 'Black power and the media', *Race Today* 1.12, 1970

White racism? Yes, it does exist, *pp. 85–90*

E. Butterworth, 'The smallpox outbreak and the British press', *Race* vol.7 1966

S. Chibnall, *Law-and-Order News*, Tavistock 1977

P. Foot, *Immigration and Race in British Politics*, Penguin 1965

*C. Husband, 'Introduction', in his *White Media, Black Britain*

Blacks in entertainment media, *pp. 97–98*

P. Boulanger, *Le Cinéma Colonial*, Paris: Editions Seghers 1975

*C. Husband, 'The mass media and the function of humour in a racist society', in A. J. Chapman and H. C. Frost (eds), *It's a Funny Thing, Humour: International Conference on Humour and Laughter*, Oxford: Pergamon Press 1977

D. Leab, *From Sambo to Superspade*, Secker & Warburg 1975

From 'immigrant' to 'mugger', *pp. 98–99*

F. Fanon, 'The necessity of violence', in his *The Wretched of the Earth*, Penguin 1967

S. Hall and others, *Policing the Crisis*, Macmillan 1978, chs. 1–4

W. D. Wood and J. Downing, *Vicious Circle*, SPCK 1968, chs. 2–3

5. A Dissection of Sexism, *pp. 101–124*

*S. Brownmiller, *Against Our Will*, Penguin 1978

*B. Ehrenreich and D. English, *For Her Own Good*, Pluto Press 1979

W. Thönnessen, *The Emancipation of Women: Germany 1863–1933*, Pluto Press 1973

Women's Position in Advanced Capitalism, *pp. 103–112*

D. Barker and S. Allen (eds.), *Dependence and Exploitation in Work and Marriage*, Longman 1976 (essays by Gardiner, Davidoff, Hope et al)

D. Barker and S. Allen (eds), *Sexual Divisions in Society*, Tavistock 1976 (essays by Land, McIntyre, Shaw)

V. Beechey, 'Some notes on female wage labour in capitalist production', *Capital and Class* vol.3 1977

J. Chetwynd and O. Hartnett (eds), *The Sex Role System*, Routledge & Kegan Paul 1978 (essays by Land, Hartnett, Lobban)

C. Miller and K. Swift, *Words and Women*, Penguin 1979
*S. Rowbotham, *Women, Resistance and Revolution*, Penguin 1975

Rationales for Women's Oppression, *pp. 112–119*

A. Clark, *The Working Life of Women in the Seventeenth Century*, Cass (reprint) 1968

C. Dreifus (ed), *Seizing Our Bodies*, New York: Vintage Books 1978 (essays by Seaman, Arditti)

L. Gordon, 'The politics of birth control 1920–40', in J. Ehrenreich (ed), *The Cultural Crisis of Modern Medicine*, New York: Monthly Review Press 1978

C. Hymowitz and M. Weissmann, *A History of Women in America*, New York: Bantam Books 1978

S. Lewenhak, *Women and Trade Unions*, Benn 1977

J. Mitchell and A. Oakley (eds), *The Rights and Wrongs of Women*, Penguin 1977 (essays by Alexander, Marks, Blackstone)

M. Springer (ed), *What Manner of Woman*, Oxford: Blackwell 1978

The Dialectic of Class and Sex, *pp. 119–122*

M. Barrett and M. McIntosh, 'Christine Delphy: towards a materialist feminism?' in *Feminist Review* vol.1 1979

*B. Berch, *Industrialisation and Working Women in the Nineteenth Century*, Connecticut: Arnot Press 1980

*C. Broyelle, *Women's Liberation in China*, Brighton: Harvester Press 1978

M. Dalla Costa and S. James, *The Power of Women and the Subversion of the Community*, Bristol: Falling Wall Press 1973

C. Delphy, *The Main Enemy*, Women's Research and Resources Centre 1978

Z. Eisenstein (ed), *Capitalist Patriarchy and the Case for Socialist Feminism*, New York: Monthly Review Press 1979 (essays by Gordon, Dubois, Ryan)

H. Hartmann, 'The unhappy marriage of marxism and feminism', *Capital and Class*, vol.8 1979

A. Kuhn and A. M. Wolpe (eds), *Feminism and Materialism*,

228

Routledge & Kegan Paul 1978 (essays by Beechey, McIntosh, Wolpe)

I. Pinchbeck, *Women Workers and the Industrial Revolution*, Cass (reprint) 1969

H. Scott, *Women and Socialism*, Allison & Busby 1978

The Media and Sexism, *pp. 125–142*

M. Marzolf, *Up From the Footnote*, New York: Seabury Press 1977

M. Morris, 'Newspapers and the new feminists', *Journalism Quarterly*, vol.50 1973

M. Morris, 'The public definition of a social movement', *Sociology and Social Research* vol.57 1973

C. and B. Smart, 'Accounting for rape', in C. and B. Smart (eds) *Women, Sexuality and Social Control*, Routledge & Kegan Paul 1978

*R. Smith, 'Sex and occupational role on Fleet Street', in D. Barker and S. Allen (eds) *Dependence and Exploitation in Work and Marriage*, Longman 1976

G. Tuchman and others (eds) *Hearth and Home*, New York: OUP(NY) 1978 (essays by Tuchman, Ferguson, Phillips, Lopate, Lemon)

Entertainment media and women, *pp. 128–136*

*G. Frankl, *The Failure of the Sexual Revolution*, Mentor Books 1975

M. Haskell, *From Reverence to Rape*, New York: Harper & Row 1974

M. Lang and R. Simon, 'The roles and statuses of women on children and family TV programmes', *Journalism Quarterly* vol.51 1974

J. Mellen, *Big Bad Wolves*, Elm Tree Books 1977

H. Northcott and others, 'Trends in TV portrayal of blacks and women', *Journalism Quarterly* vol.52 1975

G. Pollock, 'What's wrong with images of women?', *Screen Education* vol.24 1977

J. Spence, 'Class, gender, women', *Screen Education* vol.25 1978

229

Women in advertising, *pp. 136–141*

J. Dispenza, *Advertising the American Woman*, Dayton, Ohio: Pflaum Publishing Co. 1975

J. Downing, 'But that's history!', in L. Donnelly (ed) *Justice First*, Sheed & Ward 1969

S. Ewen, *Captains of Consciousness*, New York: McGraw-Hill 1976

E. Goffman, *Gender Advertisements*, Macmillan 1979

*B. Lavoisier, *Mon Corps, Ton Corps, Leur Corps: Le Corps de la Femme Dans la Publicité*, Paris: Éditions Seghers 1978

R. Lindner, *Das Gefühl von Freiheit und Abenteuer*, Frankfurt/Main: Campus Verlag 1977

J. Williamson, *Decoding Advertisements*, Marion Boyars 1978

M. Wolfgang, *Patterns in Criminal Homicide*, Philadelphia: University of Pennsylvania Press 1958

7. Capitalist Media, *pp. 143–179*
The birth of mass media, *pp. 143–147*

*J. Habermass, *Strukurwandel of Öffentlichkeit*, Neuwied: Luchterhand 1969

P. Hollis, *The Pauper Press*, Oxford University Press 1970

A. J. Lee, *The Origins of the Popular Press in England 1855–1914*, Croom Helm 1976

R. Williams, *Television: Technology and Cultural Form*, Fontana Books 1974

Gramsci's theory of 'hegemony', *pp. 147–155*

A. Gramsci, *Prison Notebooks*, Lawrence & Wishart 1971

J. Klapper, *The Effects of Mass Communication*, New York: Free Press 1960

R. Miliband *The State in Capitalist Society*, Quartet 1976, chs. 7–8

J. M. Poitte, *La Pensée Politique de Gramsci*, Paris, Éditions Anthropos 1970

H. Portelli, *Gramsci et la Question Réligieuse*, Paris: Éditions Anthropos 1974

N. Poulantzas, *Fascism and Dictatorship*, New Left Books 1975 (section 5)

The concept of hegemony and theories of the media, *pp. 156–160*

*A. Mattelart, *Multinational Systems and the Control of Culture*, Brighton: Harvester Press 1979

A. Mattelart & S. Siegelaub (eds), *Communication and Class Struggle*, vol.1 New York: International General, PO Box 350, NY 10013, 1979

C. Wright Mills, *The Power Elite*, New York: OUP(NY) 1958

G. Murdock & P. Golding, 'For a political economy of mass communication', *Socialist Register* 1973, Merlin Press 1973

O. Negt & A. Kluge, *Öffentlichkeit und Erfahrung*, Frankfurt/Main: Suhrkamp Verlag 1973

H. Schiller, *Mass Communication and American Empire*, New York: Kelley 1969

H. Schiller, *The Mind Managers*, Boston: Beacon Press 1974

P. Schlesinger, *Putting 'Reality' Together*, Constable 1977

The specific roles of media in capitalist hegemony, *pp. 160–172*

P. Golding & S. Middleton, 'Making claims', *Media, Culture and Society* vol.1 1979

*J. Halloran and others, *Demonstrations and Communication*: Penguin 1970

K. Lang & G. E. Lang, *Politics and Television*, New York: Quadrangle Books 1968

*D. Prokop, *Massenkultur and Spontaneität*, Frankfurt/Main: Suhrkamp Verlag 1974

I. D. Stone, *The Hidden History of the Korean War*, New York: Monthly Review Press 1969

Capitalist media: their production control, *pp. 173–178*

W. Breed, 'Social control in the newsroom', *Social Forces* vol.33 1955

M. Cantor, *The Hollywood TV Producer*, New York: Basic Books 1971

P. Elliott, *The Making of a Television Series*, Constable 1972

E. J. Epstein, *News From Nowhere*, New York: Vintage Books 1973

*C. Heller, *Broadcasting and Accountability*, British Film Institute Television Monograph 7, 1978

A. McBarnet, 'Disciplining the journalist', in *Media, Culture and Society* vol.1 1979

R. McKay & B. Barr, *The Story of the Scottish Daily News*, Edinburgh: Canongate Press 1976

*A. Mattelart, Mass Média, Idéologies et Mouvements Révolutionnaires, Chili 1970–73, Paris: Éditions Anthropos 1974

M. Mayer, *Madison Avenue USA*: Penguin 1958

P. Schlesinger, *Putting 'Reality' Together*, Constable 1977

J. Tunstall, *The Westminster Lobby Correspondents*, Routledge & Kegan Paul 1970

8. Socialist Media I: Britain, *pp. 180–199*

B. Brecht, 'Radiothéorie 1927 bis 1932', *Gesammelte Werke* vol.18, Frankfurt/Main: Suhrkamp Verlag 1967

S. Hood, 'Brecht on Radio', *Screen* Vol.20 Nos 3/4, Winter 1979/80, pp. 16–23

V. Lenin, *What Is To Be Done?*, Selected Works vol.1, Collected Works vol.5, Lawrence & Wishart n.d.

Mao, *Selected Works of Mao Tse-Tung*, vol.5 (1978), Peking: Foreign Languages Press

G. Williams, *Proletarian Order*, Pluto Press 1975

Three socialist newspapers in Britain, *pp. 187–198*

L. Colletti, 'Bernstein and the Marxism of the Second International', in his *From Rousseau to Lenin*, New Left Books 1972

A. Magaline, *Lutte de Classe et Dévalorisation du Capital*, Paris: Maspéro 1975 (Part I)

Redaktionskollektiv, 'Theorie des staatsmonopolistischen Kapitalismus', *Probleme des Klassenkampfs* vol.1, 1971

D. Thom, 'Anti-racism – infections of language', *Wedge* vol.3 1978

9. Socialist Media II: Italy, *pp. 200–218*
The political background to socialist radio in Italy, *pp. 200–205*

F. Cavazza, 'Italy: from Party occupation to Party partition', in
   A. Smith (ed), *Television and Political Life*, Macmillan 1979
D. Fano & C. Sardone, 'The fiscal crisis of the state: notes on the
   Italian case', *Capital and Class* vol.7 1979
M. Morris, 'Eurocommunism vs. semiological delinquency',
   Language, Sexuality and Subversion, Sydney: Working Papers in
   Cultural Studies, Australia, 1978
T. Negri, *Working Class Autonomy and the Crisis*, CSE/Red Notes
   1979
Semiotext(e) III.3 (1980), New York: 'Italy: Autonomia – post-
   political writings', 522 Philosophy Hall, Columbia University,
   New York 10027

Radio stations of the movement, *pp. 205–218*

Collectif A/Traverso, *Radio Alice, Radio Libre*, Paris: J.-P.
   Delarge 1977 'Free radio in Italy', *Wedge* vol.1 1977
G. Gamaleri (ed), *Un Posto nell'Etere*, Rome: Edizioni Paoline
   1978 (Gamaleri, Zaccaria, Trasatti, Cascino)
P. Hutter (ed), *Piccole Antenne Crescono*, Rome: Savelli 1978
G. Macali, *Meglio Tardi Che RAI*, Rome: Savelli 1977
F. Siliato, *L'Antenna dei padroni*, Milan: Mazzotta 1977

General Conclusions, *pp. 219–220*

W. Benjamin, 'Theses on the philosophy of history', in his
   Illuminations, Fontana Books 1973

Index

Radio Alice, 205–6, 208
Radio Audizioni Italia (RAI), 202–4, 216
Radio Città Futura, 101, 208–17
Radio Donna, 212–13.
Rape, 126–7
Lord Reith, 153–4
Religion: and fascism, 154; and racism, 51; and sexism, 113–14
Rousseau, J.-J., 115

Science: and racism, 55–6; and women's oppression, 116–19
St. Paul, 114
Salazar, A., 174
Sandys, D., 68
Scottish Daily News, 176
Sex Discrimination Act, 111
Sexism, 101–24: and class, 119–22, 197; images of, 112–13, 133–4, 138; and language, 109; and male supremacy, 123–4; and media, 125–42; and socialist papers, 191, 196–8; *see also* Patriarchy, Women
Sexuality: and advertising, 167; and pornography, 135–6; women's, 113–14, 117–19
Slavery, 9, 16, 51–4
Social darwinism, 55–6, 75
Socialist Worker, 187–99 *passim*
Southern Africa, 82, 90–1, 93–4, 168
Soviet Union and Soviet-type societies: 16, 49, 123; Russian revolution, 147–8, 180–1
State: and labour, 23–31; and media, 39–41, 49; and sexism, 109–12; shift of power in, 157–8; *see also* Hegemony, Keynes and keynesianism, Police
Steel industry, US, 12–13
Stone, I. F., 168
Strikes, 18, 29–30; *see also* Media, Working class
Surplus value, 8–11; absolute, 10; and migrant workers, 57; relative, 11, 20, 21
SWAPO, 93

Taft-Hartley Act, 25–6
Taylorism, 21–2
Technology: of media, 166; and working class, 18–23
Television: *see* Media
Third World, 90–1, 93, 157, 169
Trade unions, 14: craft, 17–18; leaders and media, 43–5; racism of, 62; and women, 120
Tristan, F., 115
TUC, 26

USA: black–white relations, 91–2; blacks in media, 97–8; entertainment and sexism, 128–31; expansion, 54; government secrecy, 157–8; labour discipline, 25–6; media and women, 126; press, 97; women workers, 106; *see also* New York, Steel industry

Wage and wages, 6–14, 24, 27–8
Walker, P. G., 67
Wallraff, G., 32
Weber, M., 155
West Indians, 61–2, 65–6, 78–9; *see also* Blacks, Immigrants, Race and racism
Wollstonecraft, M., 115
Women: in advertising, 136–41; and domestic labour, 103–4, 121; in media, 125–6; resistance of, 109–10, 123–4; *see also* Family, Sexism, Women's liberation movement
Women's liberation movement, 121–2; and media, 126, 212–13; *see also* Radio Donna, Sexism, Women
Woodcock, G., 26
Work: and class struggle, 6–31; hazards of, 7; *see also* Labour and labour power, Surplus value, Technology, Women
Working class: consciousness of, 150–2, 188: and media, 159–60, 161–3, 179, 209; de-composition of, 18–23; resistance of, 14–18, 19–20, 28, 29–30; *see also* Hegemony, Racism, Sexism, Trade Unions, Work

237